Cultural Orphans in America

University Press of Mississippi—*Jackson*

CULTURAL ORPHANS IN AMERICA

Diana Loercher Pazicky

Copyright © 1998 by University Press of Mississippi

All rights reserved

Manufactured in the United States of America

"Print-on-Demand Edition"

The paper in this book meets the guidelines for permanence and durability of the Committee on Production Guidelines for Book Longevity of the Council on Library Resources.

Library of Congress Cataloging-in-Publication Data
Pazicky, Diana Loercher.
Cultural orphans in America / Diana Loercher Pazicky.
p.   cm.
Includes bibliographical references.
ISBN: 978-1-60473-192-7
1. American literature — History and criticism.   2. Literature and society — United States.   3. Orphans in literature.   I. Title.
PS173.O75P39   1998
810.9'35206945 — dc21
98-15894
CIP

British Library Cataloging-in-Publication data available

To my mother and the memory of my father

Contents

Introduction XI

CHAPTER 1 The Puritans as Orphans 1

CHAPTER 2 The Puritans as Aggressors 25

CHAPTER 3 The Revolution 51

CHAPTER 4 Tales of Captivity and Adoption 86

CHAPTER 5 The Rise of the Republic 118

CHAPTER 6 Sentimental Strategies in "Orphan Tales" 149

CHAPTER 7 The Negro as Ultimate Orphan 178

Notes 203

Bibliography 211

Index 225

Cultural Orphans in America

> Orphans only live more intensely than others what is the fundamental human experience.
> ANDRÉ HAYNAL

Introduction

This book is about orphans, real and imaginary, in early America and what their actual treatment and textual representation signify about cultural values. This book is also about how the past is the present, how the legacy of early America—of the Puritans, the revolutionaries, the Founding Fathers, and the leaders of the new republic—has shaped the "family values" that are a social and political touchstone in our culture today.

Images of orphanhood have pervaded the American imagination ever since the colonial period. The orphan appears in varying degrees of intensity—sometimes as palpable presence, other times as mere shadow—in every manner of text: fictional and nonfictional, religious and secular, poetical and polemical. But whatever shape the orphan assumes, the figure signals identity formation, not only individual but cultural.

In retrospect, I think I found orphans because I was looking for them. I am not an orphan, but I have always been fascinated by orphanhood as an existential predicament. Orphanhood, the loss of parents who represent the moorings of a child's identity, is the ultimate metaphor for identity issues. If a child never knew his or her parents, the loss entails personal history as well. Even when the parents are known the child is faced with the challenge of forging a new identity, a project complicated by the circumstances under which the loss occurred.

From a psychoanalytic point of view, Oedipus is the original orphan and the prototype of the orphan in search of a Self. Sigmund Freud considered Sophocles' tragedy *Oedipus Rex* to be the *ur*-narrative of our culture because it postulates the nature of identity as relational. One of Freud's most provocative hypotheses, which he outlines in "Three Essays on the Theory of Sexuality," is that the infant's initial perception of union with the mother gradually shifts to an awareness of difference, and inherent in that awareness is a profound sense of loss of the earliest love object. This sets in motion the desire to replace that object through substitution. It is through identification with the father, the rival, that symbolic repossession becomes possible.

Building on Freudian theory, French psychoanalyst Jacques Lacan perceived the irony that the loss of the undifferentiated Other, the mother, entails the discovery of the differentiated Self. The awareness of the Self as separate and autonomous is implicated in a sense of loss and desire for reunion with the mother. As Lacan elaborates in his seminal essay "The Mirror Stage as Formative of the Function of the I," the resolution to the problem of fragmentation is identification with the father, the rival, who has the power to repossess the mother at will. Thus, fundamental to the Oedipus complex is the child's dependence on the father as an object of identification and a source of recognition, and this dependence transfers to the social Other.

The psychoanalytic implication of the Oedipus myth is that we are all born into a condition of separation and loss and are doomed to define ourselves only in relation to others. In short, identity does not exist in a vacuum or as an essence; it is mediated. This is exemplified by Oedipus's psychological journey. First he thinks he knows who he is and tries to define himself through his actions. Then he discovers, from others, that he is someone else. In other words, he depends on others to reveal his identity. Part of the irony is that as a result of this knowledge, he changes.

The appeal of orphans to the literary imagination is that they incarnate this aspect of the human condition. Their quest for an identity hinges upon an understanding of the Self not as an essence formed in the past but as a dynamic, interactive process that takes place in the present and projects into the future. Another of Freud's theories is that groups, and even nations, behave like individuals. Following this logic, one can infer that a group or nation, like an individual, can experience a sense of orphanhood and that its process of collective identity formation is also relational in nature.

The purpose of this study is not to suggest that the orphan trope is a unique or "exceptional" feature of the American literary tradition.[1] Its ubiquity in the nineteenth-century British novel alone is enough to discredit such a notion. Nevertheless, I am proposing that the nature of American historical development left its own distinctive imprint upon the orphan trope. For example, the fact that orphan imagery tended to erupt at times of challenge and crisis supports its grounding in specific historical events and its connection to identity issues.

During the course of my research, it gradually became clear to me that orphan imagery is inseparable from familial imagery, and that the metaphorical meaning of orphanhood depends on the larger symbolic context of the family, specifically the relationship between parents and children. In American history, the family is the paradigmatic institution that defines cultural values. Of course, the imposition of familial (particularly patriarchal) imagery onto the relationship between government and citizens, like that between deities and humans, is a cross-cultural phenomenon, but the nature and sequence of events in American history reinforced this predisposition and placed a national inflection on the imagery. The family as an institution provides the stage on which the struggle for American identity is played out, and on that stage the orphan is a primary, though not the only, character.

Orphan imagery appears as a response to the social upheaval and internal tensions generated by three major episodes in American history: the Great Migration, the Revolution, and the rise of the republic. During these periods, the orphan trope signifies the threat to the identity of the dominant culture, which eventually became the white Anglo-Saxon Protestant middle class, whose interests and values are represented in the texts.[2] Those who considered themselves the natural or adopted "children" of that "family" came to fear orphanhood and needed scapegoats onto whom their identification with orphanhood could be displaced.[3] The targets of such displacement were groups of marginalized racial, religious, and ethnic outsiders—Negroes, Indians, and immigrants—who represented difference. By becoming cultural "orphans," they enabled the "children" to protect their identity within the family of the colony or the republic.[4]

For example, during the colonial period, the trauma of separation from England, a composite parental figure in the form of the mother country and the father king, created doubt among the Puritans about their mission in the New

World and their status as God's adopted "children," his chosen and his elect, and fostered an identification with political and spiritual orphanhood. There was a direct historical precedent for viewing the relationship between England and America as familial. The family was of supreme importance to the English Puritans as a hierarchical model for social and political institutions and as the repository of religious values. Moreover, the Puritans regarded their children as the future of the faith and emigrated partly on their behalf.

The child-centeredness of the Puritans reflected both their typological identification as God's children and their situational identification with wicked children who had symbolically rejected their parents. The combination of hardships, homesickness, and guilt that beset the Puritans after "coming hither" exacerbated their conflict and doubt about their elite identity and gave rise to the terrifying suspicion that instead of being God's children, they were spiritual as well as political orphans. Thus, the irony of the Great Migration, which was supposed to represent the apotheosis of Puritanism, is that it compromised the covenant by inspiring a thinly disguised identification with orphanhood. I attempt to show how this implicit identification is embedded in the poetry of Anne Bradstreet, the writings of Puritan leaders and ministers, and the conversion narratives of ordinary citizens.

In reaction to this internal crisis of confidence, the Puritans tried to protect their identity, to solve the problem of an unstable "self," by appropriating the identity of their English oppressors and excluding dissenters, heretics, and heathen, just as they had been excluded in England. Foremost among these pariahs were the Indians, whose heathenness represented the ultimate religious difference and whose land represented the ultimate opportunity to create a new familial identity. Thus, the Puritans attempted to preserve their spiritual identity as God's children through strategies of scapegoating that shifted the burden of orphanhood onto Indians and religious dissenters. The dissenters were often poor as well, and the practice of religious exclusion gradually overlapped with social and economic discrimination, as laws against admitting impoverished outsiders into the community provided the Puritans with an additional pretext for excluding undesirables.

The Revolution recapitulated the original separation between England and America in more violent form, and a sense of familial identity was once again obtained by displacing orphanhood onto scapegoats. Not surprisingly, there was a revival of familial rhetoric during this period, as is evident in both loyalist and Revolutionary texts. The parent/child imagery employed by Thomas Paine and his fellow revolutionaries suggests that their attitude toward orphanhood was more positive than that of the Puritans. As the young nation shifted its filial allegiance from the parent country to the Founding Fathers, orphanhood seemed to represent an opportunity for self-creation rather than a loss of identity.

But there was also a dark side. The American Revolution, with its symbolic overthrow of British rule, also entailed a gradual identification with the oppressor that shaped government policy following the Revolution and culminated in the 1790s with the Alien and Sedition Acts. Sons inevitably became like the father; as the ideal of a fraternal community gave way to internal conflict and competition, the need again arose for common enemies. The Federalists and even well-intentioned "republicans" like Thomas Jefferson predicated citizenship on the elitist criterion of owning property and allowed religious and racial prejudice to dictate who would number among the adopted children of the republic and who would constitute its orphans. In short, the notion of adoption, which was a religious concept for the Puritans, became politicized during this period to signify citizenship in the new republic rather than membership in the church.

The discussion of the Revolutionary period also encompasses the dispossession of the Indians and describes how the motive behind it became blatantly economic, shifting from revulsion at heathenism to desire for land. In seizing Indian lands, the government not only served expansionist interests but appropriated the Indians' identity as native or indigenous. Furthermore, as the writings of Benjamin Franklin and St. John de Crèvecoeur intimate, the Indians, with their cultural, racial, and religious differences, also served as a model for the scapegoating of immigrants, and by the end of the century oppression of the Indians was inseparable from xenophobia, as well as from racism. As scapegoats, Indians and immigrants in particular served the purpose of unifying the "natural aristocracy" of white Anglo-Saxon Protestant landholders, and became cultural orphans in relation to the children of the new republic.

The orphanhood of the protagonists in two early nineteenth-century novels, Charles Brockden Brown's *Edgar Huntly* and James Fenimore Cooper's *The Prairie*, dramatizes these social tensions. Edgar Huntly was literally orphaned in childhood, and Natty Bumppo is described as a metaphorical orphan. Both protagonists appear to be alienated from the dominant culture, but the novels ultimately reveal their complicity with its values. The key issue in the novels is that the identity of both protagonists is intertwined with that of the Indians (and in Edgar's case, also with that of the immigrant, Clithero) and ultimately depends on the overcoming of that identification by displacing their orphanhood onto the Indians. The vision these two novels endorse is one of cultural separatism, whereas *Hobomok* and *Hope Leslie,* two novels by women, take a relatively (but not totally) permissive view of both biological and cultural miscegenation and, by extension, a more inclusive view of the American "family."

During the rise of the republic, the orphan trope becomes an expression of class conflict, specifically of the hostility of the burgeoning middle class to the lower class and the poor. In the nineteenth-century sentimental novel, the female orphan protagonist serves as an allegorical figure who represents the anxiety of the white Anglo-Saxon Protestant middle class about maintaining its status in the wake of social upheaval. Economic instability, industrialization, urban riots, pauperism, racial conflict, and immigration were among the factors that created tensions within the middle class during the Jacksonian period and allied its interests primarily with those of the upper class. Also torn by internal competition and class antagonism, the middle class blamed the clamorous, corrupt, and burdensome poor for their troubles.

This profound aversion was at odds with the Christian call to virtue and benevolence sounded by the Cult of True Womanhood and resulted in a displacement of middle-class hostility to the poor that took the form of nativism, the scapegoating of those who represented ethnic, religious, and racial difference. The treatment of actual orphans during this period exemplified not only overt hostility toward these groups but covert hostility toward the poor and resulted in their cultural orphanhood.

The "orphan tale," which represents the dominant plot formula in women's sentimental fiction during the 1850s, enacts a middle-class fantasy of loss and recovery in fictional form. For example, whereas the orphan protagonists who populate the novels of this period appear to be members of the impoverished lower class, they actually represent the prevailing social order, the middle class, to which they are restored at the end. Thus, the sentimentalized orphan figure epitomizes the middle class's concern with maintaining its power, status, influence, and values, as defined by the institution of the family, which forms the backbone of the republic. By not portraying immigrants, Negroes, Catholics, and Indians as protagonists, the novels mimic the culture that ostracizes these "orphans" from the middle class and uses them as scapegoats for its internal conflicts.

Introduction

These allegories of social redemption share with children's literature of the period a tone of moral didacticism, and in both genres the authors' posture of sympathy for the poor is both a manifestation of Christian benevolence and a sentimental subterfuge that distracts readers from the need for social reform. The fact that sentimental novels were written by middle-class women who had fallen on hard times and were read by a middle-class audience is an indication of their true ideological perspective. To illustrate these points, I focus on four best selling sentimental novels of the early 1850s: Susan Warner's *The Wide, Wide World*, Maria Cummins's *The Lamplighter*, Ann Stephens's *The Old Homestead*, and Elizabeth Oakes Smith's *The Newsboy*. Although the first four feature a female orphan protagonist and the last a feminized male, I argue that class is a more important issue in these novels than gender and that class issues are, in fact, displaced onto gender.

This study ends with an exploration of the relationship between race and class and maintains that in both Frederick Douglass's autobiographies and Harriet Beecher Stowe's depiction of Topsy in *Uncle Tom's Cabin*, the orphanhood of slaves, many of whom were separated from their families at birth, represents a loss of humanity as well as identity and is the result of the inextricable relationship between capitalism and racism. It is apparent from these texts that just as capitalism is an underlying force driving slavery, the middle class is also responsible for perpetuating the cultural orphanhood of emancipated slaves by keeping them oppressed legally and economically. The contrast between Topsy and Vara in Jane Elizabeth Hornblower's *Vara; or, Child of Adoption* illustrates these dynamics. The two young women, one white and one black, both become missionaries, but for very different reasons that confirm the elite status of the former and the denigrated status of the latter.

In the sentimental novels I discuss, the orphan's task of creating a Self is inseparable from class issues. As these novels imply, class, like gender and race, is not only a social construct but a hereditary condition that determines identity. The restrictive lines drawn around the middle class in these novels are uncannily similar to the boundaries the Puritans drew around their community three centuries earlier to protect it from outsiders, and in this respect the middle-class orphan in the sentimental novel represents the culmination of an effort to preserve identity through strategies of socioeconomic oppression.

What most outsiders—criminals, vagabonds, rogues, dissenters, heretics, and immigrants—shared in colonial days was their poverty, and the effect of ostracism was to keep them poor by preventing them from participating in the economic life of the community. But it should also be remembered that poverty in itself was not only a *means* but a *reason* for exclusion from the community and the "family," and with this provision the Puritans established a precedent of hostility to the poor that persists to the present. In keeping with their protocapitalist concerns, the Founding Fathers mingled economics with expansionism by restricting citizenship, or membership in the family, to those who owned property and by pushing the borders of the republic deeper and deeper into Indian territory. In the nineteenth century, the socioeconomic issue underlying the racial, religious, and ethnic prejudices of nativism became too obvious to ignore and indicated that an ulterior motive behind the scapegoating of outsiders was the desire to conceal hostility toward the lower classes, particularly the poor, who threatened class stability. The result was that the figurative orphanhood of those who represented cultural differences was inextricably linked to the literal orphanhood of many poor people, and together they protected the familial identity of the privileged classes as dominant. By desentimentalizing the nineteenth-century orphan, I try to expose this figure as a literary device that masks these policies of socioeconomic exclusion and reinscribes the spectral presence that haunted the Puritan and the post-Revolutionary imagination.

It is also a presence that haunts American society today. Except where they prove irresistible, I have deliberately avoided suggesting parallels between the early history and representation of orphanhood and the current scene, to avoid distracting the reader with such interpolations or offending the reader with polemical interpretations. Suffice it to say here that current government policies, such as welfare reform, immigration restriction, affirmative action revision, and cutbacks on aid to Native Americans reflect exclusionary attitudes that are obvious "family" legacies from earlier periods in American history and are similarly based on economic considerations, specifically hostility to the poor. Moreover, the eruption of hate crimes, such as the burning of black churches and synagogues, and the resurgence of right-wing groups, such as the Ku Klux Klan, the neo-Nazis, and the skinheads, fall squarely within the nativist tradition and are extreme versions of xenophobic and racist social attitudes that have persisted since the nineteenth century, despite all the liberal rhetoric and legislation of the twentieth. Finally, the religious Right, in turning the family into an icon and "family values" into dogma, has recapitulated the conflation of the family with the Christian tradition while managing to ignore not only the multiplicity of alternative family configurations that exist today but the cultural pluralism that defines the nation. In short, orphanhood remains an ideological reality as well as a fact of contemporary life.

In summary, I have situated the orphan trope in history in order to suggest an interpretation of orphanhood that extends beyond the quest for individual identity to a broader cultural context. My underlying assumption is that literary imagery is equivalent to the dream life of a culture, expressing in symbolic form ideological conflicts buried in the unconscious. As Cathy Davidson writes in her preface to *Revolution and the Word*, "One of the larger fictions of history, as Foucault reminds us, is that one individual, an author writes a book.... authors and books exist within historical moments, as junctures of ideas, controversies, and tensions in a society" (ix). Rather than subscribe to the extreme version of this theory, which denies the role of individual creativity and the simple fact that authors, not cultures, write books, I want only to emphasize that symbiosis exists between authors as creators of culture and cultures as creators of authors.

In connecting orphan imagery to the quest for identity in early America, I have tried to shed light on the kinds of changes that threatened the cohesion of the dominant culture and created the need for scapegoats on whom orphanhood could be displaced. In a broader sense, I have also tried to make clear, through the American example, the degree to which social identity is relative, constituted by hierarchy and imbalances of power. Finally, I hope I have provided an historical and cultural framework for understanding that the "family values" so highly touted in our culture today originated in, and perpetuate, policies of social inclusion and exclusion, as current policies toward immigrants, African Americans, Native Americans, and the poor attest. These policies illustrate that the fundamental exclusionary dynamics of the "family" still exist; that in spite of progressive and because of reactionary legislation, the identity of its "children" is still influenced by race, class, and ethnicity; and that symbolic orphanhood continues to be as much a social reality today as actual orphanhood.

Just as books take on a life of their own, they often depend for that life on others than the author. This is a book that would not have come into being without the help and support of family, friends, and colleagues. I would like most particularly to thank the following members of the faculty at Temple University: Miles Orvell, who blended critical acumen, an Olympian view, and high standards of scholarship with good humor and common sense; Carolyn

Karcher for her ideological perspective, moral support, and incisive editing; and Alan Singer for helping me apply aspects of psychoanalytic theory to the material.

I am also indebted to John Canup of Texas A & M University for his perceptive criticism and suggestions and his referral to William Gilmore-Lehne of Richard Stockton College of New Jersey, who was enormously helpful and forthcoming in recommending primary sources. Special thanks to Seetha A-Srinivasan, Associate Director and Editor-in-Chief of the University Press of Mississippi, for sensitively and astutely guiding me through the revision process; Production Editor Anne Stascavage for her scrupulous editorial assistance; Phil Lapsansky, Chief of Reference of the Library Company of Philadelphia, who was ever willing to share his encyclopedic knowledge; and Judith A. Hunter for giving me permission to quote from her paper. Finally, words cannot express the thanks I owe to my husband and my son for their steadfast patience, encouragement, and support.

CHAPTER ONE

The Puritans as Orphans

> A family is a little commonwealth, and
> a commonwealth is a great family.
> —JOHN WINTHROP

The most important secular institution in Puritan culture was the family. The family was not only the primary source of stability and security but a model for social and political institutions that incorporated its patriarchal and hierarchical structure. The family model also influenced the nature of interaction with other groups and cultures. Despite the earlier belief that the Puritan family was an extended unit that embraced a range of generations and relatives, more recent scholarship points to its nuclear nature. As John Demos asserts in *A Little Commonwealth*, "It is now apparent... that small and essentially nuclear families were standard from the very beginning of American history, and probably from a still earlier time in the history of Western Europe" (62).

Endemic to the nuclear structure of the Puritan family were the dynamics of inclusion and exclusion through which one family distinguished its identity from that of others by strict criteria of kinship. The primary characteristic of the family that the Puritans imported to the New World was the insularity of both individual families and the collective family of Puritan culture. John Winthrop, the first governor of the Massachusetts Bay colony, wrote in "A Defense of an Order of Court" (1637), in which he justified the exclusion of heretics, "A family is a little commonwealth, and a commonwealth is a great family. Now as a family is not bound to entertain all comers, no not every good man (otherwise than by way of hospitality) no more is a commonwealth" (166).[1] In generations to come, the family that served as the definitive principle of the commonwealth became the controlling metaphor for the republic.

The importance of the family as an institution derived from the Puritans' belief in typology, the recapitulation of the Old Testament in the New. What was unique about the Puritans and what distinguished them from other groups of immigrants who voyaged to the New World was their typological belief in their "chosenness." The Puritans believed that they were the New Testament version of the Israelites fleeing out of Egypt into the promised land of Canaan, and that they would fulfill God's special purpose in the New World by creating a model society, "a city upon a hill," as Winthrop terms it in "A Model of Christian Charity."

The most inspirational and influential lay sermon in American history, Winthrop delivered it onboard the *Arbella* just before the Puritans' arrival in Massachusetts Bay in 1630 (Mitchell, 295). Throughout his speech, Winthrop not only compares the Puritans to the Israelites but uses familial imagery to describe the relationship between the Puritans and God as well as to each other within the community. For example, he refers to the Puritans as "brethren" united in the body of Christ and distinguishes the Puritans from God's other children as "elect" on the basis of their resemblance to Him: "he [the Lord] loves his elect because they are like himself, he beholds them in his beloved son: so a mother loves her child, because she thoroughly conceives a resemblance of herself in it" (290).

Winthrop also sexualizes the relationship between God and the Puritans, as if the Puritan community represents God's wife: "In regard of the more near bond of marriage between him and us, wherein he hath taken us to be his after a most strict and peculiar manner which will make him the more jealous of our love and obedience, so he tells the people of Israel, 'You only have I known of all the families of the earth'" (293). By extension, the individual members of the community are the seed, the children of the union. Winthrop closes with this exhortation:

> *Therefore let us choose life,*
> *that we, and our seed,*
> *may live, by obeying his*
> *voice, and cleaving to him,*
> *for he is our life, and*
> *our prosperity.* (295)

Other colonists — French, Dutch, Spanish, and even English — were lured to the New World by a mixture of financial and religious motives, but none were compelled by this unique sense of mission, this special covenant with God. As an institution, the family was the emblem of that covenant, and the familial imagery that permeates Puritan discourse describes the peculiarly intimate relationship between God and his "children." It was a relationship that reinforced the patriarchal world view embedded in Christianity whereby Christians viewed God as a divine "father" to whom they owed unqualified obedience and allegiance, in return for which he disciplined and cared for his children. But the Puritans placed a unique imprint on this construct by viewing themselves not simply as God's generic children, like other Christians, but as God's specially adopted children, his chosen, a bias that shaped the self-mythologizing nature of American ideology.

This identification was the basis of the Puritan mission and the essence of the colonial experience, and it deeply colored the Puritans' attitude toward their own children. The focus of the tight, nuclear family structure was on the children. One of the primary motives behind the migration of Puritan families was the welfare of the next generation. Migration represented for the Puritans both the salvation of their children's souls and the preservation of the faith. As Increase Mather put it in 1685, "It was for your sakes especially, that your Fathers ventured their lives upon the rude waves of the vast Ocean. Was it not with respect unto Posterity that our Fathers came into this Wilderness, that they might train up a Generation for Christ?" (quoted in Bremner, *Children and Youth in America*, 3).

Immigration and demographic patterns in New England suggest a conscious effort to perpetuate Puritanism through the institution of the family. The reason the Puritans emigrated in families (in contrast with colonists in the Middle Atlantic states who consisted primarily of individuals) was out of concern for their children. The "Planter's Plea" of 1630 justifies the formation of the colony on the basis of the holy mandate to perpetuate the family: "so long as there shall be use of marriage, the warrant of deducing colonies will continue" (White, 3). Once they arrived, the Puritans made a concerted effort to marry young and propagate quickly. The combination of marital stability and low mortality resulted in large New England families and significant population growth that strengthened the Puritan community and the sense of mission (Beales, 16–17). Even the names of the children, such as Seaborn, Oceanus, Waitstill, Relieve, and Believe, evoked the millennial nature of the migration experience and the role of children in bringing the covenant to fruition (Illick, 324).

In short, Puritan parents regarded their children not only as a spiritual responsibility but as a spiritual investment in the future, a means of perpetuating their faith and ideology. As Winthrop states in "A Model of Christian Charity," the Puritans viewed their children as seeds, as carriers of the true word of God, and the agricultural imagery of planting and transplanting the Puritans use derives from this fundamental concept (Canup). Puritan minister William Stoughton, in his celebrated sermon "New Englands True Interest; Not to Lie" (delivered in 1668) was to declare later in the century, "God sifted a whole nation that he might send choice grain over into this wilderness" (19).

Based on their belief in the spiritual connection between parents and children, the Puritans even construed election as hereditary, a genealogical affair. According to Edmund S. Morgan in *The Puritan Family*, "The argument was simple: comparatively few people were saved anyhow and those who are almost always belong to the same families. Given two generations, the persons who are saved in the second generation will almost invariably be the children of those who were saved in the first. The children of the saints in one generation will be the saints of the next" (182). In other words, the Puritans used their identity as God's children to impute a connection between kinship and election that embraced their own children.

But this elite spiritual identity was complicated by an undercurrent of anxiety in the Puritan imagination. After all, not everyone, not even every Puritan, was a member of the elect. To be a child of the covenant, the child must be born to those who are members of the church and baptized, but even then the child would not necessarily be saved. Thomas Shepard, in "The Church Membership of Children, and their Right to Baptism," raises the specter of spiritual orphanhood in his exegesis of the "double seed," which distinguishes between the external seed, church members, and the internal seed, the elect, in terms of adoption. Although both are God's "adopted" children, the children of internal adoption have the distinct advantage of "saving grace," which means that the children of external adoption occupy a precarious spiritual limbo verging on orphanhood (1). Election was, in short, an unfathomable mystery that predicated salvation on an inscrutable metaphysic of belonging and not belonging, of spiritual adoption and spiritual orphanhood.

Max Weber, in his seminal analysis *The Protestant Ethic and the Spirit of Capitalism*, describes the Puritan deity as an incomprehensible, transcendental free being of Kafkaesque capriciousness who has arbitrarily decided who is saved and who is damned and is thus unmoved by human action. The result of the "extreme inhumanity" of this doctrine is an irrational cosmos that is characterized by "a feeling of unprecedented inner loneliness of the single individual. In what was for the man of the age of the Reformation the most important thing in life, his eternal salvation, he was forced to follow a path alone to meet a destiny which had been decreed for him from eternity. No one could help him ... not priest, sacraments, or church" (104).

Adding to the Puritans' *Angst* about their relationship with God was their complete powerlessness over their own salvation. Since human action had no effect on determining who was saved and who wasn't, the Puritans were placed in a paradoxical and even absurdist position in relation to their own behavior. One would think, since it didn't matter what they did, that they would have few or no standards of human conduct and would sin freely. Yet precisely the opposite occurred. With regard to predestination, the challenge was to *prove* that they were chosen rather than to earn salvation.

The Puritans were obsessively concerned with convincing themselves and others that they were among the elect, and they took refuge not only in their faith, embodied by the church, but in the security of the family headed by the father, who functioned as both a powerful symbol and a source of stability in the Puritan imagination. David Leverenz, in his psychoanalytic study of Puritanism, explains that "securing the father's authority, both local and cosmic, was central to the Puritan mission" (46). The father's role as God's intermediary helped alleviate the spiritual loneliness and isolation that devolved from the theory of predestination.

Not surprisingly, the Puritans also applied the patriarchal template to their political and social experience. For example, they regarded the King as their "father," in keeping with the British tradition of equating fatherhood and the monarchy, which harks back to Sir Robert Filmer (ca. 1588–1653). Filmer, in comparing the duties of fathers and kings in *Patriarcha* (1680), wrote, "We find them to be all one, without any difference at all but only in the latitude of extent of them. As the Father over one family, so the King as Father over many families, extends his care to preserve, feed, clothe, instruct and defend the whole Commonwealth."[2] Sir Thomas Hobbes drew the same connection in *Leviathan* (Bremner, 27). In short, the patriarchal relationship between God and his children extended to the King and his subjects (including the colonists) and also served as a model for the relationship between the governors and the governed within the colony.

Within the context of the family, the father as God's surrogate held a position of supreme social and political authority. But although they occupied a lower station, mothers were not entirely devoid of parental power, as the Puritan minister John Cotton indicated in his interpretation of the fifth commandment, "Spiritual Milk for Babes in either England Drawn out of the Breasts of both Testaments of their Souls." Not only does the title illustrate the conflation of physical and spiritual sources of nourishment; it underscores the importance of maternal as well as paternal authority in the Puritan world view.

Given the overriding importance of family as a model for all forms of social and political interaction, it is hardly surprising that separatism was such an emotionally charged issue for the Puritans. Unlike the Pilgrims, the Puritans did not regard themselves as radicals who wanted to break with the Church of England, and Winthrop tried to avoid all forms of separatism that would be destructive to the Puritan mission. Rather, they viewed their role as one of reform rather than rejection, and it was for this reason that the Great Migration, the *separation* from England, created in them such feelings of discomfort and even guilt, feelings that are manifest in early accounts of the crossing.

Seeing themselves metaphorically as children separated from their "mother," who variously represented England and the Anglican church, and their "father," who variously represented God and the king, the American Puritans strove to mitigate the trauma and assuage their guilt by rationalizing that as God's children, they were joining a spiritually superior family. For example, Thomas Hooker effused, "We are alive as a child taken out of one family and translated into another, even so we are taken out of the household of Satan, and inserted into the family of God; yea into the mystical body of *Christ*" (Leverenz 119).

But underlying this fantasy of ascension was the Puritans' uncomfortable suspicion that by abandoning their "father" and "mother," they had turned themselves into orphans. The physical hell of the crossing reinforced the psychological trauma of the separation. The perils of the crossing were so severe that as they became known, many Englishmen decided to stay home. Accounts of the early voyages include a list of hardships nightmarish enough to deter even the most determined. Pirates, storms, leaks, disease, accidents, overcrowding, filth, foul food and fetid water, abusive sailors, and high mortality were typical of the harrowing conditions.

Yet the accounts of the voyage by the Puritans, who led their followers from England primarily for religious reasons, are surprisingly restrained. For example, when the *Arbella* undertook its two-month crossing in 1630 to "plant" the Massachusetts Bay colony, its passengers were afflicted by cramped and squalid living conditions, disease (especially scurvy), seasickness, pirate attacks, hunger, and thirst. But Winthrop glosses over the difficulties of the voyage. "A Model of Christian Charity" is patently a pep talk, a desperate effort on Winthrop's part to rally the flagging spirits of the frightened and exhausted Puritans by reminding them they are God's chosen people and exhorting them to build the "city upon a hill." His only allusion to the hardships of the voyage is a shipwreck metaphor near the end of the sermon (presumably the most terrifying image he could conjure up), which he uses to threaten the Puritans with God's retribution if they fail to keep his covenant: "Now the only way to avoid this shipwreck, and to provide for our posterity, is to follow the counsel of Micah, to do justly, to love mercy, to walk humbly with our God" (294).

In his journal, where Winthrop meticulously records in diary form the events of the voyage, his tone might also be described as one of forced optimism. Whenever disaster impends or a crisis occurs on board ship, Winthrop maintains a stiff upper lip and casts the reaction of the Puritans in the most positive light. For example, of being threatened with attack by eight enemy ships, he wrote in his journal: "it was much to see how cheerful and comfortable all the company appeared; not a woman or child that showed fear, though all did apprehend the danger to have been great... but our trust was in the Lord of Hosts, and the courage of our captain, and his care and diligence did much encourage us" (I:28).

Most of his accounts of illness and seasickness also end happily, such as the following description of a gale, which focuses not on the passengers' misery but on their recovery: "Monday, 12.] The more large to the N. a stiff gale, with fair weather. In the afternoon less wind, and our people began to grow well again. Our children and others, that were sick, and lay groaning in the cabins we fetched out, and... they soon grew well and merry" (I:31). Similar in tone is Winthrop's assessment of the voyage as a whole, which he describes in a letter to his wife, the first letter from New England, as "a long and troublesome passage, but the Lord made it safe and easy to us: and though we have met with many and great troubles... yet he hath pleased to uphold us, and to give us hope of a happy issue" (Twichell 159–160).

Ursula Brumm characterizes the reticence of Winthrop and the Puritan ministers about the hardships of the crossing as part of a general and official "conspiracy of silence," the purpose of which was to downplay the negative (32). Denial was the Puritans' major defense against the ambivalence about their mission that was to haunt them throughout the colonial period. The sources of the ambivalence are complex and express themselves in the Puritans' conflicting identification as "adopted" children who belong to God's family and orphans who are prohibited from joining it.

The first identification is obvious, and most critics have interpreted the metaphorical significance of the crossing in glowingly positive terms because of the typological construction the Puritans placed on their emigration. For example, Sacvan Bercovitch invokes the New England colonists' vision of the "baptismal efficacy of the ocean-crossing" and Cotton Mather's later interpretation of the "ocean crossing as a spiritual rebirth" (113, 115). But while he is correct in pointing out the birth imagery embedded in Puritan accounts of the crossing, Bercovitch fails to acknowledge the profound sense of loss that also pervades these texts. The ocean crossing constituted both an individual and a collective trauma for the Puritans. In fact, the frequent association of the crossing with the imagery of birth, baptism, and rebirth seems to be as deeply rooted in the pain of separation as in the religious signification imposed upon it.

The birth trauma for the Puritans was not simply crossing the Atlantic and being born into an unknown New World (and presumably a new identity) but leaving the Old World, which represented the security of parents (however stern and rejecting). Donald Wharton describes the Atlantic as "the first American frontier" and keenly observes that although the sea was the "umbilical" that linked the colonies to Europe,

> the link was a fragile one, and perhaps more than it connected men to their European homeland, it threw them upon their own resources, isolating them from the security and guidance of former practice. By its mere vastness alone—a voyage of six weeks was uncommonly swift—the ocean forced modification of European precedent and rule. (*Trough*, 4)

Wharton's metaphor of the umbilical could hardly be more apt because the Puritans interpreted what John Cotton called their "voluntary exile" as a metaphorical separation of a child from its mother (Simmons, "Way of Congregational Churches Cleared," 22). A striking example of an early Puritan text in which such imagery describes the relationship between Old and New England is "The Company's Humble Request" (1630), in which Winthrop and his company rather desperately beseech "the rest of their brethren, in and of the Church of England, for the obtaining of their prayers, and the removal of suspicions, and misconstructions of their intentions" by using the poignant metaphor of a mother and child:

> we desire you would be pleased to take notice of the principals and body of our company, as those who esteem it our honor to call the Church of England, from whence we rise, our dear mother; and cannot part from our native country, where she specially resideth, without much sadness of heart and many tears in ours eyes, ever acknowledging that such hope and part as we have obtained in the common salvation, we have received in her bosom and sucked it from her breasts. (296)

In the same year, Cotton uses the same metaphor in "God's Promise to His Plantations" to exhort the Puritans to be "not unmindful of our Jerusalem at home": "forget not the womb that bare you and the breast that gave you suck. Even ducklings hatched under an hen, though they take the water, yet will still have recourse to the wing that hatched them: how much more should chickens of the same feather, and yolk?" (14). In contrast, Captain John Smith, who voyaged to New England for purely commercial reasons, also avails himself of maternal imagery but without a hint of guilt because he feels he is of service to his "mother": "What so truly suits with honor and honesty, as the discovering of things unknown? erecting towns, peopling countries, informing the ignorant, reforming things unjust, teaching virtue; and gain to our native mother country a kingdom to attend her" (Pearce, 11).

The Puritans' departure from England entailed a symbolic separation not only from the mother but from their father and, by extension, a more dreaded separation from God. Because the father represented the deity, the focus on him was unusually intense, and the result was a variation on the Freudian postulate of separation anxiety in which the fear of being separated from the mother was superseded by fear of separation from the father. Because sin was associated with the mother and salvation with the father who saved her and the rest of the family, the loneliness and self-loathing of the Puritans who felt themselves to be in a state of sin entailed a sense of separation from both human and divine patriarchs (Leverenz 149). In other words, the Puritans feared they were not only political but spiritual orphans.

Obviously the Puritan experience does not conform to the classic definition of orphanhood, the loss of parents, but the emotions of grief and desolation with which they reacted to separation from their metaphorical parents are characteristic of orphanhood. Moreover, there is evidence that the Puritans regarded orphanhood with a peculiar dread. For example, attachment to a family was so important to the Puritans that they defined orphanhood very broadly not only as homelessness but singleness and required all single adults as well as children that belonged to the community to live in families in order to receive the benefit of the family's spiritual influence. It is also significant that the Puritans made an effort to control parents and even inspected families to make sure that parents were raising their children properly. In cases where the parents were not deemed fit, the court could remove the children from the family. But instead of becoming orphans, these children were placed in other families. Because of their sense of community, the Puritans felt obligated to each other's children and were also accustomed to taking them in through the practice of binding out.

Given this context, the mere suspicion of collective orphanhood was a pressing social issue that impinged upon the Puritans' sense of communal identity. The voluntary nature of the political orphanhood the migration experience entailed inevitably elicited intense feelings of alienation and guilt. Rather than losing their parents, the Puritans rejected them through an act of rebellion and therefore share a great deal in common with the runaway. But these feelings were complicated by the unfitness of the parent from whom they were running away. Just as there is a burden of guilt on the children who abandon their parents, there is also a burden of guilt on parents who deserve abandonment. Thus, the voluntary separation from their political "parents" predisposed the Puritans to a complex identification with orphanhood that assumed spiritual dimensions.

Riddled with doubt, anxiety, and guilt about leaving England, the Puritans wandered through the wilderness like children trying to convince themselves that they were not lost. They carried with them across the Atlantic not only their convictions but their doubts, doubts that stemmed from their guilt over betraying England. They also felt guilty about leaving their brethren behind. At first glance, this guilt would seem unwarranted. As Kai Erikson points out, the Puritans did not intend to abandon England or replace it with a world of their own but rather to establish a model society that would inspire reform. In other words, the Puritans saw themselves as still tied to Europe through the obligation to set an example for it to follow (v–vi).

But their state of mind was more confused than these lofty goals suggest. First, the Puritans felt guilty about abandoning England to the moral corruption that the Anglicans and Catholics represented, as illustrated by the defensive tone of Winthrop's "Reasons to Be Considered for Justifying the Undertaking of the Intended Plantation in New England and for Encouraging Such Whose Hearts God Shall Move to Join with Them in It" (1629), which he casts in the form of a debate reflecting the irresolution in his own mind. Protesting too much, Winthrop justifies the flight as a "service to the church to carry the gospel into those parts of the world" and depicts the New World as a "refuge for many whom He means to save out of the general calamity" of England, where "it is almost impossible for a good and upright man to maintain his charge" and "the foundations of learning and religion are so corrupted" that children are threatened (71–72).

Second, Winthrop acknowledges an economic motive, which underscores the fact that the Great Migration was not just a religious but a commercial venture: "This land grows weary of her inhabitants, so as man who is the most precious of all creatures is here more vile and base than the earth we tread upon, and of less price among us than a horse or a sheep; masters are forced by authority to entertain servants, parents to maintain their children, all towns complaining of the burden of their poor" ("Reasons...," 71). In fact, the earliest English settlements in New England were trading missions, not religious missions, and the backers who secured the royal charter for the Massachusetts Bay colony were entrepreneurs who sent John Endecott to Salem with a group of fishermen, planters, traders and two ministers. Both the Pilgrims and the Puritans had to receive a patent or commercial backing in order to emigrate and were thus not without commercial obligation, as well as commercial incentive, to succeed economically. It was only gradually, as religious oppression of the Puritans increased in England, that New England came to be seen not only as a site of economic opportunity but as a potential religious refuge. Economic conditions in England, such as depression in the cloth trade and bad harvests in East Anglia, played a role in driving the emigrants to the New World, and Puritan emigrants included yeomen, artisans, and servants who were hoping not incidentally to better their economic lot.

As confidence in the Puritan mission waned, the economic motive for the migration became less of a "reason" than a source of embarrassment and even guilt. David Cressy points out that because religious apologists wrote Puritan history and were trying to manipulate attitudes, they created a distorted picture that left out the complex social and economic motives behind the migration (106). Furthermore, the self-recrimination prompted by the establishment of Cromwell's Commonwealth, when it appeared that if the emigrants had only bided their time they could have assisted in the Civil Wars and gained the freedom to worship, put even greater pressure on Puritan leaders such as Winthrop to play up the religious purpose of the Great Migration and play down economic motives. Winthrop was even hypocritical enough to declare in 1646 that "while the inhabitants of other plantations had 'come chiefly for matter of profit,' the people he had led to Massachusetts Bay 'came to a bide here, to plant the gospel and people the country'" (M. Jones, 12).

Winthrop's guilty conscience over abandoning England is typical of that of the early Puritans, and it fostered a need to deny their mixed motives. Precisely because of the covenant, the Puritans were reluctant to state explicitly, and perhaps even to acknowledge, their fear of spiritual orphanhood. The Pilgrims, who were true Separatists from the Church of England, were drawn to a similar identification, but they expressed their feelings of desolation more openly.[3] Consider, for example, the following lament in Robert Cushman's "Reasons and Considerations Touching the Lawfulness of Removing out of England into the Parts of America" (1622), in which he tries to rationalize the homelessness of the Pilgrims by arguing that we are all spiritually homeless on this earth because our true home is in heaven:

> But now we are all in all places strangers and pilgrims, travellers and sojourners, most properly, having no dwelling but in this earthern tabernacle; our dwelling is but a wandering, and our abiding but as a fleeting, and in a word our home is nowhere, but in the heavens in that house not made with hands, whose maker and builder is God, and to which all ascend that love the coming of our Lord Jesus. (42–43)

While the Puritans could identify with this sense of homelessness, they could not readily admit to it because it contradicted their belief in the covenant.

Another example of the contrast is William Bradford's history, *Of Plymouth Plantation*, which, while also defensive at times, is generally far more candid about the troubles and disappointments of Plymouth plantation than Winthrop's account of the early Massachusetts Bay colony. The pivotal difference between the Massachusetts Bay settlement and the other colonies was the sense of mission, "the city upon the hill," and it is this difference that explains why Winthrop was so anxious to gloss over misfortune.[4] For example, Bradford indulges in a lengthy, doleful peroration on the "wild and savage hue" of Cape Cod, the like of which is never to be found in Winthrop's *Journal*. In a typical passage Bradford laments,

> Being thus passed the great ocean, and a sea of troubles before in their preparation... they now had no friends to welcome them nor inns to entertain or refresh their weatherbeaten bodies; no houses or much less town to repair to, to seek for succour.... what could they see but a hideous and desolate wilderness, full of wild beasts and wild men—and what multitudes there might be of them they knew not. (69–70)

Perry Miller considers Bradford's "great hymn... about the land" the prototype of subsequent immigrant accounts and catches its underlying mood of despair: "it vibrates with the sorrow and exultation of suffering, the sheer endurance, the pain and the anguish, with the somberness of death faced unflinchingly" (4). A different perspective is that of psychotherapist Eileen Simpson (who also happens to be an orphan). She comments that the opening pages "read like a fairy tale about the ordeal of children without parents in search of a home" (221). The fairy tale to which she alludes is "Hansel and Gretel," in which the children are rejected and abandoned by their parents and left to survive in the unfamiliar environment of the forest. Child psychologist Bruno Bettelheim has interpreted "Hansel and Gretel" as a story "about the debilitating consequences of trying to deal with life's problems by means of regression and denial, which reduce one's ability to solve problems." The regression and denial manifest themselves in Hansel's repeated efforts to return home, which reduce "his initiative and ability to think clearly" (160).

Many of the Puritans in the Massachusetts Bay colony reacted like Hansels, children who feared orphanhood and wanted to go home to their parents. Some were successful: as many as one in six Puritans, several thousand in all, returned to England during the 1630s and 1640s, and during the time of the Civil War in England reverse migration exceeded immigration for reasons ranging from simple homesickness to culture shock (Cressy, 192–193, 201). Naturally the defections of these "Hansels" were embarrassing to the colony's leaders, particularly to Winthrop, who had already endured the humiliation of losing two hundred members of his original fleet in 1630 practically upon their arrival. Thomas Dudley, the outspoken deputy governor who sailed with Winthrop on the *Arbella*, surmised that they left not just because they feared famine but because they disliked the oppressive government (Cressy, 195). The response of Puritan leaders to any form of religious deviance, notably the Antinomians in 1636 and later the Quakers, was repressive because of the perceived threat dissenters posed to the community. Some Puritans found this repression alienating and all too familiar, and as the government became more and more authoritarian, the Puritans experienced a crisis in confidence, which was in part responsible for the wave of reverse migration (Delbanco, 205–206).

Edward Johnson, author of *Wonder-Working Providence of Sion's Savior in New England* (c. 1650), wrestled uncomfortably with the tension created by the persistent longing for the mother country. He blamed isolation and homesickness, exacerbated by distance, for the colonists' misery: "and that which added to their present distracted thoughts, the ditch between England and their now place of abode was so wide, that they could not leap over it with a lope-staff" (quoted in Cressy, 194–195). Homesickness was so widespread among the early colonists that even such eminences as ministers Thomas Shepard, Richard Mather, and John Davenport admitted to it. Shepard, in his autobiography written in the 1640s, could not forget lamenting the loss of his native country, even a decade later. According to his son Increase, Richard Mather once had serious thoughts of returning to England, and John Davenport confided to Winthrop that he wanted to go home (Cressy, 206–208).

Not surprisingly, Winthrop tried to ignore these defections, but in 1645 when an increasing number of Harvard men were heading back to England, he rationalized that England needed ministers and the graduates needed employment. This feeble excuse is in keeping with Winthrop's evasive account of the hardships not only of the voyage but of the early settlement. Unlike Bradford and Dudley, Winthrop, as governor of the colony, was loath to complain about the difficulties and disappointments that were such a large part of the early Puritan experience and clearly felt an official obligation to keep the faith by continuing to profess it.

Winthrop's journal, which purports to be a scrupulous record of events in the colony, is actually a model of public relations, at least when it comes to unpleasant events. As in his account of the voyage, Winthrop shows a genius for damage control that is a reaction to the Puritans' sense of orphanhood. By far the most dramatic instance of Winthrop's understated response to adversity is the following laconic entry in his journal in 1630, shortly after their arrival: "Friday, 2.] The *Talbot* arrived here. She had lost fourteen passengers. My son, Henry Winthrop, was drowned at Salem" (1:151). While Winthrop is somewhat more expressive of his grief in his letter to his wife, the offhand nature of this entry seems an extreme instance of self-restraint in service of the covenant.

In his journal Winthrop fleetingly reports the various calamities that befell the colonists, such as fires, starvation, drownings, and Indian attacks, and by focusing on the trees he manages to avoid looking at the forest. Moreover, he has a way of burying painful details in the paratactic style of his account whereby deaths from pestilence and the fishing reports, for example, are given equal attention: "Much sickness at Plymouth, and above twenty died of pestilent fevers. Mr. Graves returned, and carried a freight of fish from hence and Plymouth" (1:105). And here is Winthrop straining to look on the bright side: "There was great scarcity of corn, by reason of the spoil our hogs had made at harvest... yet people lived well with fish and the fruit of their gardens" (1:103).

In a similar vein, Winthrop frequently invokes God's Providence to interpret tragedy as evidence of support or punishment. For example, he takes grim satisfaction in the judgment he sees being passed on the colony's undesirables, such as the two servants who drowned while gathering oysters: "it was an evident judgment of God upon them, for they were wicked persons." He is especially judgmental toward the colony's malcontents and defectors: "It hath been always observed here, that such as fell into discontent, and lingered after their former conditions in England, fell into the scurvy and died.... Of those that went back on the ship this summer, for fear of death of famine, etc., many died by the way and after they were landed, and others fell very sick and low, etc." (1:58).

The discrepancy between the representation and the reality of the migration experience manifest in Winthrop's discourse exists in other Puritan texts as well. Admittedly, ministers and other politicians generally used metaphorical references to the crossing in a positive, almost promotional manner. For example, Thomas Shepard typically transformed the experience into proof of God's Providence ("The Lord hath brought you by a strong hand and blessed you, and he hath when you cried to him saved you from sins, from storms"), and Thomas Hooker identified error with "a ship that is foundered in the midst of a main ocean without the sight of succour or hope of relief" (quoted in Cressy, 175–176). It is important not to forget, however, the propagandistic intent of these texts, the "conspiracy of silence" to which Brumm alludes, and the admissions by these same authors in other writings of their doubts, fears, and longing for "home."

What the migration represented to ordinary Puritans is the subject of a significant scholarly dispute. Sacvan Bercovitch asserts that the major difference between English Puritan and American Puritan autobiographies is that in the latter "migration to America displaces conversion as the crucial event." He insists that a pattern of "inversion" exists in all the accounts of the ocean crossing, both by the leaders and by the laity, whereby the intent is "not primarily to show God's favor to the saint, and not to recount oceanic marvels... but, combining the spiritual and naturalistic levels, to extol the enterprise in general." Maintaining that the inversion is "most pronounced" in the autobiographies, Bercovitch cites Thomas Shepard's equation of "new life with New World and... baptism with the Atlantic as a greater Red Sea" as "a staple of early colonial biography" (117–118).

But Patricia Caldwell, in her study of conversion narratives, disputes Bercovitch's assertion by countering that the autobiographies of ordinary people send a quite different message from Shepard's: "the greater number of conversion stories... evince a different and unexpected kind of 'inversion,' namely, that the failure of New England, of 'state and country alike,' to meet the spiritual expectations of the individual who is trying to articulate his experiences devolves back upon that person and presses him into a doubtful limbo of semiconversion or even nonconversion." Thus, while Caldwell agrees with Bercovitch that the migration experience, signaled by the incantatory "Hither I came," is the "spiritual pivot in the narrative," she does not agree that this reference to the migration was a joyful one and argues instead that the professions of faith of those seeking to join the church in New England were permeated with conflict and doubt (133–134).

It is apparent from a close reading of extant conversion narratives that many of the emigrants were weighed down by regret at coming to the New World and by a thinly disguised disillusionment with the Puritan enterprise. For the Massachusetts Bay Puritans who "came hither," the circumstances of the migration encouraged an identification with spiritual as well as political orphanhood. Many emigrants who undertook the voyage to New England were already displaced and uprooted, and the arduous crossing, combined with adverse conditions in the colony, compounded their sense of alienation and confusion. To convince themselves that they had made the right decision in coming to this country, they rationalized that they were chosen for the experience and led by Divine Providence (Handlin, 7–8, 10–11).

As in Winthrop's narrative of the crossing, a determination to deny the sometimes overwhelmingly negative effect of their experiences in the New World pervades many of these texts. Consider, for example, Richard Cutter's account in *Thomas Shepard's* Confessions: "And so I came to this place and coming by sea and having a hard voyage my heart was dead and senseless and I found my heart as stubborn as before" (Selement and Woolley, 179). But even if the emigrants admit to disappointment initially, they attempt to keep the faith by invoking the migration experience as the key event in their conversion. Apparently the implications of disappointment were so dangerous that reservations had to be suppressed and negative experiences transformed, however implausibly, into manifestations of the Divine Plan or consequences of human sinfulness.

Take, for example, the hollow protestations of Edward Collins, a public official and deacon in the Cambridge church, who tries to blame his obvious disappointment in the colonial experience on his ingratitude for "several providences" that befell him after his arrival: "Yet after this his frame was quickly lost by distractions and thoughts and cares which deadened my spirits which God seasonably took care to cure by a heavy hand of God. And then I saw and was convinced of my unthankfulness and discontent and so by a servant of His I was brought upon my knees. And I blessed God that He would not let me lie still but to show me my unthankfulness" (Selement and Woolley, 84). The peculiar shift in pronouns in the first sentence from the third person reinforces the impression of a divided self.

One of the most dramatic examples of barely concealed conflict is the confession of Nicholas Wyeth, who left England in a mood of confidence and self-righteousness to escape religious persecution, only to lose his son on the voyage and his wife shortly after his arrival. The result was a crisis of faith: "The Lord's hand hath been much out against me and is so still. He gave me a child after my own heart and God hath taken it from me and 'tis so just for I have gone formally and coldly since I came here. Though I have enjoyed much in public yet I have been very unfruitful and unchristianlike" (Selement and Woolley, 185). In the remainder of his confession, Wyeth obviously feels himself pressed to contrive an explanation of his own sinfulness and comes dangerously close to questioning whether he deserves the suffering God has inflicted upon him.

Another revealing conversion narrative is Elizabeth Cutter's, which clearly conflates her actual and spiritual orphanhood. Cutter lost her father when she was very young, and her mother placed her with a family. Her narrative is a chronicle of loss—of parents, of husband, of friends—a kind of orphan's lament in which the search for a "father" (God) is the paramount concern: "But when come [to New England] I had lost all and no comfort.... So I saw I was a Christless creature and hence in all ordinances was persuaded nothing did belong to me. Durst not seek nor call God Father nor think Christ shed his blood for me" (Selement and Woolley, 145). At the close of her confession, she numbers herself among the "lost and broken hearted" whom Christ saves and brings to the "Father."

Thus, the sense of loss, separation, and alienation—a disturbing undercurrent in the discourse even of those who professed the greatest loyalty to the Puritan enterprise—finds expression in the ambivalent, depressed, and resentful discourse of the ordinary people who are struggling to convince themselves that their "transplantation" to this inimical New World is cause for rejoicing rather than mourning. The inherent tensions suggest a subversive Janus vision of the migration experience, a simultaneous facing forward and backward, that is at odds with millennial and typological interpretations of the New World. In short, the discrepancy in these texts between the representation of Puritan identity as stable and the reality of Puritan identity as unstable creates a gap, and it is this gap that the orphan inhabits.

The tension between certainty and doubt, between representation and reality, between God's children and God's orphans, finds particularly eloquent expression in Anne Bradstreet's poetry. To bridge the gap, Bradstreet internalizes the migration experience and the trauma of political, cultural, and spiritual orphanhood it represents and uses it as a metaphor to express her grief over personal losses, her ambivalent attitude toward England, and her troubled spiritual journey toward God, the supreme father from whom she fears she is estranged.

Bradstreet came to the New World at the age of eighteen on board the *Arbella*. Having withstood the hardships of the voyage, the colonists proceeded to the plantation at Salem where conditions were so primitive that they quickly transplanted themselves to Charlestown. Dudley, who happened to be Anne's father as well as Winthrop's deputy governor, described in a letter to the countess of Lincoln in 1631 (written after their first summer, fall, and winter in the New World) the sickness, suffering, hunger, and mortality that beset the settlers and rebuked those who had portrayed New England in misleadingly glowing terms to lure their compatriots across the Atlantic: "In a word, we yet enjoy little to be envied but endure much to be pitied in the sickness and mortality of our people.... I do the more willingly use this open and plain dealing lest other men should fall short of their expectations when they come hither" (quoted in Cressy, 16).

Bradstreet left no explicit testimony of her own reaction to the first months in the New World beyond the often quoted statement in her letter "To My Dear Children," written many years later: "I... came to this country, where I found a new world and new manners, at which my heart rose. But after I was convinced it was the way of God, I submitted to it and joined to the church of Boston" (Hensley, 241). But Bradstreet's biographer Elizabeth Wade White notes the longing expressed by both Bradstreet and her father for the manners, "the amenities of gracious behavior," to which they were accustomed in England and speculates that "it must have been disheartening to see the formality of everyday communication, the respect for individual privacy, the quick concern for a troubled neighbor, and the dignity of innate self-possession, too often falter and fail under the weight of outrageous circumstance" (116).

Not surprisingly, most of Bradstreet's early poetry, often designated her "public" poetry (1630–1642) to distinguish it from the personal writings of the later years (from the mid-1640s on), is derivative of European traditions, particularly conventions of Renaissance epic and elegiac poetry and also the encyclopedic poetry of creation by Guillaume Du Bartas, the leading French Calvinist poet. The "Quaternions," for example, her major early work, consists of four poems on the humors, the elements, the ages of man, and the monarchies. What is noticeably absent from this impersonal poetry are references to the migration, New England, and Puritanism. Adrienne Rich perceptively surmises that Bradstreet "appears to have written by way of escaping the conditions of her experience, rather than as an expression of what she felt and knew," as if poetry provided her with an opportunity for cultural regression (xiv).

But one of her last "public" poems, "A Dialogue between Old England and New; Concerning Their Present Troubles, Anno 1642," is a key poem in Bradstreet's oeuvre because, in using mother/daughter imagery to depict the intense relationship between the colony and the Crown in dramatic form, it not only marks the transition from her public to her private poetry but suggests a solution to the dilemma of political orphanhood. The poem consists of a dialogue between Old England and New England about the circumstances leading up to the outbreak of the English Civil War, waged by the Puritans against the Anglican and Catholic sympathizers of Charles I, who claimed to rule by divine right. The mother/daughter personification suggests that a close tie between them persists, and the emotional rhetoric of the poem reinforces that impression. For example, New England, when trying to ascertain the cause of Old England's troubles, proffers sympathy and declaims: "Your humble child entreats you, show your grief, / Though arms, nor purse she hath for your relief, / Such is her poverty, yet shall be found / A suppliant for your help, as she is bound" (Hensley, 180–181). Further evidence of the intimate nature of the relationship is that the "daughter," upon hearing the recitation of the sins of the "mother," partakes of the mother's guilt: "My guilty hands, in part, hold up with you, / A sharer in our punishment's my due" (183).

Yet the most interesting aspect of the poem is the inversion of the hierarchical relationship between mother and daughter. Old England, not New England, is the country in distress and calls upon New England for help in an almost plaintive fashion: "If any pity in thy heart remain, / Or any childlike love thou dost retain, / For my relief, do what good there lies in thee, / And recompense that good I've done to thee" (185). In a classic case of role reversal, it is New England, the daughter, who has the final word, advising her distraught parent, while reassuringly prophesying a happy outcome to the conflict.

The familiar parental metaphor around which this poem is structured implies, by extension, that the Puritan colony in New England is like a child separated from its mother. But the poem suggests that the geographical separation has had little effect on the emotional closeness. The major change in the relationship pertains less to distance than to power. New England develops strength and authority as she matures, whereas Old England declines into the confusion and weakness of old age.

While the poem is ostensibly about "real" events, the elaborate mother/daughter conceit creates an atmosphere of false intimacy that suggests a very different relationship. The poem is a typical orphan's fantasy in which the loss of the mother is denied, the closeness between the mother and child remains undiminished, and the daughter becomes the powerful person in the relationship while the all-powerful parent is reduced to a state of childlike dependency. Looked at as a poem about the denial of loss and the appropriation of identity, "Dialogue" expresses, and attempts to resolve, the tensions created by political orphanhood.

A far more troubled relationship is that between Bradstreet and her spiritual "father." Bradstreet finds her own personal voice as a poet during her late period, and she uses it to articulate the issues of separation and loss that are so troubling to her. During the colonial period the death of children and grandchildren was common, and the Bradstreet family was not spared these painful losses. The standard response was to use religion to rationalize the loss and assuage the grief. But the problem for Bradstreet was that her faith failed to sustain her, just as it had in the migration experience, and she was left to mourn her orphanhood from God, as well as the loss of her loved ones.

Her elegies for her grandchildren exude unresolved tension between her anger at God's will and her attempt to accept it, as is evident in "In Memory of My Dear Grandchild Anne Bradstreet...," who died at three:

> With troubled heart and trembling hand I write,
> The heavens have changed to sorrow my delight.
> How often with disappointment have I met,
> When I on fading things my hopes have set....
> Mean time my throbbing heart's cheered up with this:
> Thou with thy Savior art in endless bliss. *(Norton, 112)*

Her memorial for her infant grandson Simon Bradstreet ("On My Dear Grandchild Simon Bradstreet...") goes even further, verging on the sarcastic and even the irreverent:

> No sooner came, but gone, and fall'n asleep.
> Acquaintance short, yet parting caused us weep;
> Three flowers, two scarcely blown, the last i' th' bud,
> Cropped by th' Almighty's hand; yet is He good.
> With dreadful awe before Him let's be mute,
> Such was His will, but why let's not dispute,
> With humble hearts and mouths put in the dust,
> Let's say he's merciful as well as just. *(Norton, 112)*

Yet another loss, almost as painful and certainly as ironic, is that of her house in a fire, the home in the New World to which she had finally become attached: "And when I could no longer look, / I blest His name that gave and took, / That laid my goods now in the dust" ("Here Follow Some Verses upon the Burning of Our House...," *Norton*, 114).

Much of the power in Bradstreet's personal poetry derives from her conflation of experiences of loss. She transforms the migration experience into a source of imagery, using metaphors of voyages and journeys to express the emotional and religious tension created by her personal losses. It is as if the separation trauma is recapitulated in her present life, so it is quite logical that she invoke the imagery of the migration to express her anxiety and grief about separation not only from home and family members but from God because of her intense earthly attachments. The irony of this imagery is, of course, unmistakable. Leaving England, separating from one's physical home, has become a metaphor not only for a spiritual pilgrimage to God, as was the Puritans' intent, but for spiritual orphanhood.

Bradstreet's prose writings "To My Dear Children" and "Meditations Divine and Moral" provide the most explicit testimony of this conflict. In the former, which she writes in anticipation of her own death to help her children draw closer to God, she describes her trials upon coming to New England and then condones rather than complains of her chastisement: "Among all my experiences of God's gracious dealings with me, I have constantly observed this, that He hath never suffered me long to sit loose from Him, but one affliction or other hath made me look *home* and search what was amiss" (Hensley, 241–242; italics mine). Clearly Bradstreet is trying to hold herself up as an example for her children, who also may presumably experience doubt some day, of one whose faith was tested by adversity, in the form of her migration to the New World, and who discovered that the true meaning of "home" is spiritual, not spatial or geographical.

She later confirms this, in the context of describing herself with unflinching honesty as a bad child, or a spiritual orphan: "I have been with God like an untoward child, that no longer than the rod has been on my back (or at least in sight) but I have been apt to forget Him and myself too. Before I was afflicted, I went astray, but now I keep Thy statutes." Bradstreet then goes on to locate her sense of home with God, her spiritual father: "yea, oft have I thought were I in hell itself and could there find the love of God toward me, it would be a heaven. And could I have been in heaven without the love of God, it would have been a hell to me, for in truth it is the absence and presence of God that makes heaven or hell" (Hensley, 243).

The touching candor of this confession of her "sinkings and droopings" locates the problem of faith squarely within her own spirit. This is what she means by looking "home" and by finding heaven or hell not outside but within, in her perception of the presence or absence of God's grace. Elsewhere, in the "Meditations," she compares man to a tenant in a house of clay, and God to the landlord of "an everlasting habitation" (Hensley, 289). In short, Bradstreet is blaming herself for the disappointment of the Great Migration. She is trying to convince herself that God is either within or above because she has not found her "father" alive and well and living in New England.

In the "Meditations" Bradstreet uses a nautical metaphor to describe the Christian pilgrimage as a voyage from one world to the next. There she compares the pilgrim to a ship:

> He that is to sail into a far country, although the ship, cabin, and provision be all convenient and comfortable for him, yet he hath no desire to make that his place of residence, but longs to put in at that port where his business lies. A Christian is sailing through this world unto his heavenly country, and here he hath many conveniences and comforts, but he must beware of desiring to make this the place of his abode, lest he meet with such tossings that may cause him to long for shore before he sees land. We must, therefore, be here as strangers and pilgrims that we

may plainly declare that we seek a city above and wait all the days of our appointed time till our change shall come. (Hensley, 283)

Here Bradstreet seems finally to have arrived at a transcendent metaphorical synthesis of migration with spiritual pilgrimage and renunciation of this world.

Yet her last known poem, "As a Weary Pilgrim," revives her old conflict by describing in graphic terms the trials of the wilderness experience, as if they were not simply a metaphor for her spiritual trials but also their *cause*:

> All cares and fears he bids farewell
>   And means in safety now to dwell.
> A pilgrim I, on earth perplexed
>   With sins, with cares and sorrows vext,
> By age and pains brought to decay,
>   And my clay house mold'ring away.
> Oh, how I long to be at rest
>   And soar on high among the blest. (Hensley, 294)

In the rest of the poem she dwells on her past and present miseries and deliberately ignores the affections and pleasures that wedded her to the earth, as if to convince herself that she is at last ready to be transplanted to heaven. Supplanting her husband with Christ, she ends the poem with this summons, which sounds a note more of resignation than exultation: "Then come, dear Bridegroom, come away" (295). And yet, reading Bradstreet and knowing her deep love for her husband, it is hard to believe that the "Bridegroom" she addresses is not also her earthly one whom she so deeply misses.

For Bradstreet, it was a long, difficult, circuitous pilgrimage to God, that distant, elusive father, not a direct migration, and her oeuvre suggests that baldly to equate, as Bercovitch does, the experience of the crossing with a typological interpretation is to overlook its unresolved and often unacknowledged complexity. Bradstreet's translation of the migration into metaphorical language is pervaded with tension between the desire to express doubt and the need to deny it. It can thus be interpreted as the first of many attempts throughout the American tradition to master that complexity and come to terms with the disillusionment that lay on the other side of the promise.

It can also be read as a reaction to the repressed identification with orphanhood that troubled the Puritans. The fundamental facts of the Puritan migration experience were real separation from their native land and imaginary separation from God, both of which generated feelings of political and spiritual orphanhood. Bradstreet's poetry vividly illustrates the way in which the trauma of the Great Migration embedded itself in her unconscious, erupted in her poetic images, and undermined her faith. Anne Bradstreet did not consciously see herself as an orphan, nor did the other emigrants who came to this country. But by virtue of the circumstances that brought them to the New World, the means of their passage, and the nature of the New World itself, they led a precarious double life as God's children and his orphans.

It is little wonder that the Puritans became inordinately concerned with convincing themselves that they belonged in the New World. The fact that they expended so much rhetoric on denial as a defense, on persuading themselves and others that they did the right thing in emigrating, reflects their lack of certainty about their identity as God's chosen people. The Puritans felt like orphans, but they could not admit it because it contradicted their self-proclaimed identity as God's children. This conflict put them under tremendous pressure to cling even more tenaciously to their convictions and combat any and all threats to their collective identity, not only by repressing dangerous thoughts but by oppressing dangerous outsiders.

CHAPTER TWO

The Puritans as Aggressors

> Consider a time of separation must come wherein the Lord
> Jesus will divide and separate the holy from the unholy, as a
> shepherd separates the sheep from the goats.
> — PETER BULKELEY

In terms of their social attitudes, the Puritans were marked by nothing so much as their insularity, their antagonistic, exclusionary policy toward those whom they viewed as different. While this policy devolved logically from aspects of Puritan tradition and history, the colonial experience had the effect of calcifying the hermetic social order and encouraging hostile attitudes toward outsiders.

The Puritans' deep-seated, underlying insecurity about their mission in the New World, and hence about their identity, put them in the awkward position of having to dispel their sense of orphanhood by whatever means were at their disposal. One tactic, obviously, was to protest too much. Another was to reject any intruders who, through their differences, could further undermine that already shaky edifice. This led to the scapegoating of Indians and religious dissenters onto whom they could displace their orphanhood and thereby reaffirm their identity as God's children.

Certainly the migration experience itself contributed to the Puritans' predisposition to insularity. For evangelicals in particular, migration represented not only uprootedness but isolation. Their sense of separation from all that was familiar created both anxiety and apprehensiveness about corrupting influences. The result was that the Puritans enhanced the sense of separateness that derived from the migration by acting it out within their own families and the community, from which they excluded anyone whose influence they feared (Greven, 25–27).

A common denominator among all types of Puritan families was exclusion of the unregenerate because of the bad influence they might exert on the children of the presumed elect. As the bedrock of society, the family adopted a policy toward membership similar to that of the church. The church existed primarily to serve its own members rather than to convert outsiders. While the Puritans made a token effort to convert the unregenerate, they concentrated their attention on those who had proven to the church members that they were already converted. An exception was the children of the saints who, though they could not yet prove their conversion, were considered members by virtue of spiritual heredity. (They were, however, required to prove conversion when they reached adulthood.) As Edmund S. Morgan summarizes, "The church was thus turned into an exclusive society for the saints and their children. Instead of an agency for bringing Christ to fallen man it became the means of perpetuating the gospel among a hereditary religious aristocracy" (173–174).

The church's policy on adoption had a determining influence on Puritan attitudes toward membership in the family. Adoption into the church was predicated on God's saving grace and required *proof* of divine conversion rather than conversion by church members, along the lines of Thomas Shepard's distinction between external and internal adoption. The circular reasoning implied that the only people who could prove conversion were the regenerate and ensured that adoption into the church was restricted to insiders rather than outsiders. In keeping with the policy of exclusivity, children of members were automatically considered members until they became old enough to prove their conversion. Because of the hereditary nature of membership, which privileged Puritan children above all other candidates, it followed logically that the children of the *non-elect* (i.e., outsiders) would be unadoptable, excluded from membership not only in the church but also in the family.

The Puritans' attitude toward orphans within their own community served as a model for the scapegoating and exclusion of outsiders. In keeping with their near idolatry of their own children and their exclusion of "unregenerate" nonfamily and even family members from their families, the Puritans were disinclined to admit to their homes, and even into the community, orphans who might be the carriers of noxious influences. London teemed with homeless, destitute children, specifically orphans, who stood out as a particularly troublesome problem. So-called "spirits," commissioned agents of merchants or shipowners, lured and sometimes kidnapped children to become servants in the colonies. Children were eagerly sought after in the mid-Atlantic colonies as a source of population and cheap labor, and Virginia was particularly hospitable to orphans (A. Smith, 149).

In contrast, the Puritans came to America primarily in families. A high proportion of the population consisted of *their own* children, and the existing evidence suggests the Puritans wanted to keep it that way. For example, there was a serious labor shortage in New England. The London-based Council of New England solicited orphans and poor children, and the anonymous pamphlet "New England's First Fruits" (1643), a promotional tract for the colony intended to help raise funds to establish a school of higher education (which was to become Harvard College), petitioned "the well-minded [in England] to clothe and transport over poor children boys and girls, which may be a great mercy to their bodies and souls, and a help to us, they being superabundant here, and we wanting hands to carry on our trades, manufacture and husbandry there" (42). But despite these solicitations, few orphans were ever admitted.

Winthrop barely mentions orphans in his journal, except to note the arrival of twenty in 1643, one of whom was subsequently abused so badly by his master that he died in 1644. Winthrop writes sympathetically, "the boy had the scurvy, and was withal very noisome, and otherwise ill disposed. His master used him with continual rigor and unmerciful correction" (2:187–188). Puritan legislation condoned severe punishment for their own children, and one can only imagine how much harder they must have been on children who were not members of the community. One is tempted to infer that the child's status as an outsider justified, to the master at least, treatment as an outlaw. In a 1633 letter from Edward Howes in London to John Winthrop Jr. in Massachusetts recommending a young Irish orphan as a servant, the overriding concern with conformity is apparent: "At his first coming over he would not go to church nor come to prayers; but after we got him up to prayers and then on the Lords Day to catechize, and afterwards very willingly he hath been at church four or five times. He as yet makes conscience of Fridays fast from flesh; and doth not love to hear the Romish religion spoken against, but I hope with Gods grace he will become a good convert" (Bremner, *Children and Youth in America*, 19–20).

In keeping with their policy that all single persons had to become attached to a family, Puritans took emigrant orphans into their families, but only as indentured servants, and tried to both regulate their conduct and influence them spiritually. But although they lived with a family, these orphans were not in any sense adopted (Bremner, 104). The Puritans' reluctance to adopt emigrant orphans stemmed from fear of their influence upon Puritan children, so naturally they tried to keep them as socially removed as possible. The treatment of these orphans contrasts vividly with that of the Puritans' own children, who were frequently "bound out" to other Puritan families as apprentices and treated like members of the family.

There has been much speculation about how to interpret the puzzling custom of "binding out," a Puritan form of adoption whereby children old enough to work were often placed with other Puritan families as apprentices, taught a trade, and raised like members of the family. Among the explanations for binding out are educational and occupational advantages, fear that too much parental affection would spoil the children, and family variables, such as the number, gender, and age of children. It is unclear how widespread the custom was, and it may have been a legacy of the British upper class that bound children to their class origins (Beales, 34). What it does illustrate is the intimate relationship between the family and the group, insofar as the Puritan community functioned like an extended family in which the members were related through conversion. By virtue of this transcendent spiritualized blood tie, any converted family could raise any converted child and protect that child from the corrupting influences of orphans and outsiders.

In short, the Puritans took care of the dependent children of their own communities by accepting them into their families, though class distinctions continued to play a role. For example, because of the high number of widows and orphans as a result of epidemics, losses at sea, and work accidents, a lower-class population of individuals irregularly attached to families gradually proliferated (Bremner, 64–65). Thus, although the Puritans theoretically welcomed all orphans from their community into their own families, in practice they favored the orphans of the well-born.

In keeping with the Puritan concept of community as an aggregate of nuclear families related through spiritual and social ties of kinship, the community incorporated the family's insular, elitist attitudes and hierarchical structure. In this regard, aspects of the Puritan religious and historical tradition in Old England are just as relevant to an understanding of the attitudes that evolved in New England as is the migration. For example, in keeping with the principles set forth by the French philosopher Petrus Ramus during the sixteenth century, the Puritans described the structure of reality in terms of "relatives" — relationships between "negative contraries," or exact opposites, and affirmative contraries, or opposites that shared a causative connection, such as buyer and seller. The Puritans applied this relational concept, or Ramist logic, to the divinely ordained social order and believed that God had arranged human society in dual subordinate relationships (or relatives), following the model of creatures to man (Morgan, 23). In other words, it was divinely ordained that servants be subordinate to masters, wives to husbands, children to parents, subjects to rulers, and so forth, and the Puritans used the principle of *hierarchical differentiation* to create order within their society. As Morgan puts it: "The Puritans indeed honored every kind of superiority among men as part of the divine order: old men were superior to young, educated to uneducated, rich to poor, craftsmen to common laborers, highborn to lowborn, clever to stupid" — insiders to outsiders (25).

The experience of migration, which entailed separation from culture, country, and civilization and required settlement in the alien, anarchic environment of the New World, threatened to subvert the sense of hierarchy on which the Puritan social order depended so heavily. It is no coincidence that Winthrop's major point in "A Model of Christian Charity" is that the social order is divinely ordained, and he exhorted the Puritans to reinscribe it on their community in the New World: "God Almighty in his most holy and wise providence hath so disposed of the condition of mankind, as in all times some must be rich some poor, some high and eminent in power and dignity; others mean and in subjection" (Mitchell, 282).

Puritan exclusionism in the New World also derived from the nature of Protestantism itself, which was predicated on a spirit of negation rather than affirmation, a sharp distinction between insiders and outsiders that established a historical precedent for the familial dichotomy between God's children and orphans in the New World. The essence of the Reformation was one of protest against the established church, but the Puritan movement in England was imbued not only with antagonism toward and rivalry with the Church of England but also with intolerance toward those other sects that differed in their religious beliefs. Foremost of these sects was the Familists, also known as the Family of Love, and the rivalry between these two groups had lasting effects that reverberated in the New World.

The Familists were an Anabaptist sect that traced its origins to the Dutch mystic Henrik Niclaes and appeared in England during the sixteenth century.

What is significant about the Familists is that they shared with the Puritans a typological belief in their own chosenness, an identification with the people of Israel, and the reification of the family as the prototype for their faith. The Familists, who believed that they were the fulfillment of all scriptural prophecies and agents of divine judgment, modeled the structure of their sect after the family, with the elders representing the "fathers" of the family holding authority over their "children," the future of the faith. They also shared the Puritans' sense of elitism, the belief that they were God's special children, and while they emphasized love within their own community, they were, again like the Puritans, hostile to the outside world. Eerily reminiscent of David Koresh and other leaders of religious utopias, "Niclaes urged his followers to love and tolerate even their enemies, [but] he also advised them that all those existing beyond the Family were utterly without spiritual worth," states historian Christopher Marsh (26).[1] In a comment that could apply equally well to the Koresh compound or Winthrop's "city upon the hill," Marsh adds in reference to Niclaes's seminal work, *Terra pacis*: "Niclaes portrayed the Family of Love quite deliberately, as a besieged city of godliness, cut off almost completely from a hateful outside world" (196–197).

It was precisely the profound similarities that made the differences matter so much. Unlike the Puritans, the Familists disavowed grace and believed that a person could be saved by faith alone. In other words, they maintained that a man could improve morally, perfect himself, and contribute to his own salvation. Equally as heretical to the Puritans, the Familists minimized the importance of scripture and emphasized instead the spirit of God, which could enter a godly individual and transform him into one of the elders by rendering him "godded with God."

The Puritans were outraged by these heresies and the challenge they posed to their own grandiose self-image as God's family. While aspects of the sects' theology differed, the similarities were so pronounced that King James I confused them. But in the revision of the introduction of *Basilicon Doron* written in 1603 to prepare his son Henry for the monarchy, he tried to qualify an earlier general indictment of Puritanism by specifically attacking only its most extreme branch, which he equated with the Family of Love: "First, then as to the name of Puritans, I am not ignorant that the style thereof doth properly belong only to that vile sect among the Anabaptists, called the Family of Love; because they think themselves only pure, and in a manner without sin, the only true Church, and only worthy to be participant of the Sacraments, and all the rest of the world to be but abomination in the sight of God. Of this special sect I principally mean, when I speak of Puritans" (6).

King James was using the Familists as a scapegoat, as if they were his real target all along, and in so doing he was simply following a precedent established under the reign of Elizabeth. During the 1570s and 1580s Elizabeth's attitude toward radical Protestant groups seemed to be "hardening," and the Puritans sought to deflect attention away from themselves by attacking the Familists (Marsh, 115–116). There was such a degree of antagonism between the two sects that the Puritans gradually channeled their energies away from anti-Catholic legislation and attempted to pass a law in 1580 that would suppress the Family of Love (130).

While the Familists did not directly influence Puritan dogma, the sense of elitism, the intensity of rivalry, and the social expression of the rivalry in familial terms laid the groundwork for Puritan intolerance in the New World. In general, the legacy of this troubled relationship was that outsiders who differed religiously from the core community were treated with the kind of intolerance that drove the Puritans out of England in the first place.

With the self subsumed to the group and personal loyalty to group loyalty, the "little commonwealth" under patriarchal authority should have constituted an impregnable ideological and spiritual fortress. But it was not strong enough to withstand the impact of the migration and the "identity crisis," to borrow Erik Erikson's term, generated by that traumatic separation. In short, the best way for the Puritans to deal with the crisis that threatened their identity was through policies of exclusion. The exclusion of outsiders that was so much a part of the Puritan ethos, the belief in their election and their chosenness, became a survival strategy for preserving their identity as God's children. Thus, the need for the Other, for outsiders, for those who represented difference, was inseparable from identity formation in the New World because outsiders united the Puritans against a common enemy. In other words, more important than the threat of external difference was its unifying function in the face of internal doubt and dissension. In using religious outsiders as scapegoats and excluding them from the community, the Puritans displaced their sense of orphanhood onto them and reaffirmed themselves as God's children.

Insight into scapegoating, as the Puritans' response to orphanhood, is afforded by those aspects of psychoanalytic theory that describe the process of identity formation in terms of the antagonistic but mutually dependent relationship between the Self and the Other.[2] To put it simply, we are all orphans, insofar as each of us undergoes the primal experience of separation from the mother and loss of our original identity. If one accepts this premise, then it follows that we live in a state of ontological anxiety, unsure that we truly exist and engaged in a struggle to prove it. This insecurity stems from the primal separation from the mother and our subsequent awareness of our separation from others, of whom the father is the prototype. Hence, the double bind: we depend on others to recognize our existence, but others also pose a threat to that existence by underscoring its contingency. The result of this mortal dependency is the aggressiveness of the Self toward the Other. In practical terms, this requires the displacement of hostile and destructive impulses away from those who represent the father figure onto "others" outside our immediate family or community.

A relevant application of this process to group behavior is Freud's theory of the "narcissism of minor differences," which he sets forth in *Civilization and Its Discontents* (1930) to describe how in European culture aggression is diverted from members of the community and displaced onto outsiders:

> It is always possible to bind together a considerable number of people in love, so long as there are people left over to receive the manifestations of their aggressiveness. I once discussed the phenomenon that it is precisely communities with adjoining territories, and related to each other in other ways as well, who are engaged in constant feuds and in ridiculing each other.... I gave this phenomenon the name of "*the narcissism of minor differences*," a name which does not do much to explain it. We can now see that it is a convenient and relatively harmless satisfaction of the inclination to aggression, by means of which cohesion between the members of the community is made easier. (751–752; italics mine)

This passage is important because it establishes a crucial link between identity formation and aggression. In other words, the formation and preservation of a group are inseparable from the process of differentiating that group from other groups and displacing onto outsiders the hostility its members would otherwise feel toward each other.

The usefulness of psychoanalytic theory for understanding the relationship between identity formation and aggression in the Puritan experience is most apparent in the writings of the French scholar René Girard, who developed the concept of the scapegoat out of the opposition between the Self and the Other. Girard explains in *The Scapegoat* that while identity formation in both individuals and groups depends on the process of differentiation, the dynamics intensify when there is an actual crisis, such as the Great Migration, that threatens identity. In his analysis of collective persecutions, Girard describes the conditions that lead to scapegoating as an external crisis, such as an epidemic, drought, flood, famine, etcetera, or an internal crisis, such as political disturbances or religious conflict.

By weakening social institutions, hierarchy, and functions, the crisis threatens to break down the entire social order, which depends on cultural distinctions in order to survive. The result is that "rather than blame themselves people inevitably blame society as a whole, which costs them nothing, or other people who seem particularly harmful for easily identifiable reasons. The suspects are accused of a particular category of crimes" (16). These suspects, who become victims of persecution, are scapegoats, in Girard's sense of the term, that satisfy society's need for action and "appetite for violence. Those who make up the crowd are always potential persecutors, for they dream of purging the community of the impure elements that corrupt it, the traitors who undermine it," whereas those who are chosen to become scapegoats represent extreme forms of difference: "Ethnic and religious minorities tend to polarize the majorities against themselves.... The further one is from normal social status of whatever kind, the greater the risk of persecution. This is easy to see in relation to the bottom of the social ladder" (17–18).

According to Girard, the paradox of external differences is that even though they threaten a culture by eroding its internal differences, they also keep it stable. A culture *needs* the external differences embodied in other cultures to preserve its identity, particularly in times of crisis. Thus, difference is both abhorred and desired, to the extent that "religious, ethnic, or national minorities are never actually reproached for their difference, but for not being as different as expected, and in the end for not differing at all." Hence, the irony: as much as unstable cultures or cultures in crisis are threatened by the external differences that render internal differences insignificant, they also depend on them in order to survive (21–22). Viewed from this perspective, the need for scapegoats renders efforts to acculturate outsiders dubious at best.

Girard gives the following definition of the scapegoat: "Scapegoat indicates both the innocence of the victims, the collective polarization in opposition to them, and the collective end result of that polarization," which is violence (39). The relevance of this definition to the Puritan experience is that it explains why the crisis of orphanhood, or feared loss of identity as God's children, created the need for scapegoats. The Puritans blamed outsiders—those who represented religious differences—for the inner turmoil and conflict caused by the Great

Migration and either wreaked violence upon them, as in the case of the Quakers and the Indians, or ostracized them. They thereby reinforced their own sense of identity by displacing not only their hostility but their orphanhood onto others.

Kai Erikson's explanation of how the Puritans used deviance to bind the community more closely together is basically a sociological version of Girard's theory. Suggesting that social organization would be impossible without episodes of deviant behavior, Erikson writes: "The deviant act, then, creates a sense of mutuality among the people of a community by supplying a focus for group feeling. Like a war, a flood, or some other emergency, deviance makes people more alert to the interests they share in common and draws attention to those values which constitute the 'collective conscience' of the community" (4). Moreover, the Puritans were accustomed to basing their sense of identity on their minority experience as a spiritual "outgroup," and as immigrants in a land where they were finally free to practice their religion without opposition, they were in the ironic position of needing new enemies who represented varieties of difference to preserve their identity (Delbanco, 13–15).

Certainly the most "different" of the different peoples were the Indians and the Negroes. As Winthrop Jordan asserts in *White Over Black*, "the two more primitive peoples rapidly came to serve as two fixed points from which English settlers could triangulate their own position in America; the separate meanings of Indian and Negro helped define the meaning of living in America" (90). The question is what made the Indians and the Negroes "special candidates for degradation" (91). A primary factor was their heathenness. According to Jordan, "From the first, then, vis-à-vis the Negro the concept embedded in the term *Christian* seems to have conveyed much of the idea and feeling of *we* as against *they*. To be Christian was to be civilized rather than barbarous, English rather than African, white rather than black" (94).

The perception of "blackness" as emblematic of heathenness had its roots in English tradition and was part of the legacy the Puritans brought with them to the New World. Typology also influenced Puritan attitudes. After all, the Canaanites whom the Israelites drove out of the Promised Land were Ham's descendants, cursed because of sexual offenses. This predisposed the Puritans to think that as God's chosen they were carrying out his will by driving out the heathen in the New World (Jordan, 36).

To the New England Puritans, the Indians were the most obvious manifestation of "the heathen." As the embodiment of the wilderness, they epitomized the absence of civilization and Christianity. The Puritans felt a deep dread of Indian influence and were racist in their attitudes toward them, associating them not only with the darkness of Satan but with the blackness of the Negro. Thus, the Indians rather than the Negroes became the major target of persecution in New England.

Although trade brought Negroes to New England and there is evidence of a brief period of Negro slavery in the seventeenth century, slavery offended the English concept of liberty, and Puritans were uncomfortable with the practice. Moreover, given their fear and loathing of Negroes, whom English tradition variously equated with beasts, sexuality, and the devil, they were hardly inclined to welcome them into the colony. In 1641 the Puritans enacted a law stipulating "that there shall never be any bondslavery, villenage or captivity amongst us, unless it be lawful captives taken in just wars, as willing sell themselves or are sold to us" (*Colonial Laws*, 10). In other words, the Puritans regarded slavery as a punishment only captives (i.e., Indians) deserved. But the attempts made to enslave the "savages" were largely unsuccessful because of their cultural resistance to any form of captivity, and Jordan draws an interesting distinction between the Indians as "independent nations" and the Negroes as "governable subnations" (90).

A symbol of the continent and a victim of American imperialism, the Indian occupies a unique position in American history as the prototype of the scapegoat, for it was "the Indian" whom the colonists first encountered as a cultural Other when they came to the New World. Evidence that the Puritans came to regard the Indians as a monolithic Other is the fact that they lumped together in a single stereotype more than 2,000 cultures and societies and a multiplicity of customs and beliefs to form a single potent counterimage. Robert Berkhofer summarizes this prototypical dichotomy between "we" and "they": "As with images of other races and minorities, the essence of the White image of the Indian had been the definition of Native Americans in fact and fancy as a separate and single other. Whether evaluated as noble or ignoble, whether seen as exotic or degraded, the Indian as an image was always alien to the White" (xv).

Obviously "the heathen" had little hope of ever numbering themselves among God's children and were destined to become and remain his orphans.[3] As the inhabitants of the New World, the Indians represented not only the farthest outpost of heresy but also sexuality, violence, and evil personified; in short, the repressed, sinful nature of the Puritans. As Richard Drinnon puts it, "Indian-hating identified the dark *others* that white settlers were not and must not under any circumstances become, and it helped them wrest a continent and more from the hands of these native caretakers over the lands" (xvii–xviii). In these alien surroundings where the social controls that upheld civilization were no longer secure, the Puritans feared their own propensity for sin and evil. The colonists regarded the Indians as products of the soil, as if they were organisms growing naturally in the wilderness; and they feared they could become such organisms themselves through a biological process of "'savage' contamination" (Canup, 4–5). In order to survive as a culture, the Puritans tried to master the threats the New World posed by scapegoating the Indians and trying to inculcate in them the values of Christian civilization. This entailed a twofold task of conversion: conversion of the wilderness into property and conversion of the heathen into Christians.

Economic factors also shaped Puritan policy toward the Indians. After all, settlers came here to acquire land and achieve economic independence as well as to obtain religious freedom, and Winthrop's vision of the "city upon the hill" was a proto-capitalist as well as a spiritual concept. Within this framework, land functioned as "a commodity owned by individuals to be bought and sold as they saw fit," in contrast with the Indian perception of land as a "sacred phenomenon" (Salisbury, 238–239). But land represented far more than commercial gain. In the Puritan psyche land functioned as the currency of culture. The elaborate imagery of "plantation" and "transplantation" commonly used to describe the settlement and migration experiences reflects this equation. John Cotton, in "God's Promise to His Plantations," explains the metaphor in his response to the question, "What is for God to plant a people?": "It is a metaphor taken from young imps [saplings]; I will plant them, that is, I will make them to take root there; and that is, where they and their soil agree well together, when they are well and sufficiently provided for, as a plant sucks nourishment from the soil that fitteth it" (11).

Anticipating the spiritual trials that awaited them in the New World, Cotton goes on to exhort the Puritans to preserve the faith for their children: "have a tender care that you look well to the plants that spring from you, that is, to your children, that they do not degenerate as the Israelites did; after which they were vexed with afflictions at every hand.... if men have a care to propagate the ordinances and religion to their children after them, God will plant them and not root them up. For want of this, the seed of the repenting Ninevites was rooted out" (14). Thus, in the Puritan world view, land was not simply a place to settle. Rather, agriculture was the emblem of civilization, the *sine qua non* without which their faith, their community, and their families could not survive. It was as if the ownership and cultivation of land represented spiritual enclosure of their society within stable borders that protected it from the anarchy of the wilderness and, by extension, from spiritual orphanhood.[4]

The subject of land ownership also figures prominently in early Puritan tracts and legislation pertaining to land claims. For example, the author(s) of the *Planter's Plea* (1630) assert that the earth is God's gift to "men" (of the right religious persuasion) and that they have a divine (and proto-imperialist) mandate to appropriate it:

> Besides, the gift of the earth to the sons of men, *Psal.* 115. 16. necessarily enforceth their duty to people it: It were a great wrong to God to conceive that he doth ought in vain, or tenders a gift that he never meant should be enjoyed: now how men should make benefit of the earth, but by habitation and culture cannot be imagined.... If it were then the mind of God, that man should possess all parts of the earth, it must be enforced that we neglect our duty, and cross his will, if we do it not, when we have occasion and opportunity: and withal do little less than despise his blessing. (White 2)

The ever pragmatic Winthrop, in his "Reasons to Be Considered for... the Intended Plantation in New England," is interested in the religious argument also as a springboard to the economic: "the whole earth is the Lord's garden, and he hath given it to the sons of men.... Why then should we stand here striving for places of habitation... and in the meantime suffer a whole continent, as fruitful and convenient for the use of man to lie waste without any improvement?" (72).

The Puritans wasted no time enacting legislation to support their mandate. Among the original "Records of the Governor and Company of the Massachusetts Bay in New England" (1629) is a provision for the allotment of land: 200 acres to each adventurer who invested fifty pounds in the common stock and a "plot of ground" set aside for the town (197–198). There is no mention in this official text of the Indians, but the question of Indian "ownership" of land is a sticky one that the Puritan leaders uncomfortably acknowledge in their religious writings and other legislation. Among their various faults Puritans were consummate sophists, and their Indian land policy is a prime example of their ability to deceive themselves and manipulate others. Consider, for example, Winthrop's ingenious rationalization in "Reasons to Be Considered..." that the appropriation of Indian lands is a civil right:

the first right was natural when men held the earth in common, every man sowing and feeding where he pleased, and then as men and the cattle increased, they appropriated certain parcels of ground by enclosing and peculiar manurance, and this in time gave them a civil right.... The natives in New England, they inclose no land neither have any settled habitation nor any tame cattle to improve the land by, and so have no other but a natural right to those countries. So as we leave them sufficient of their use we may lawfully take the rest, there being more than enough for them and us. (73)

Winthrop imposes his own culture-bound value system on the Indians by privileging civil right over natural right and thereby justifies taking Indian lands on the grounds that they don't "own" them by civil right, the measure of which is agricultural use. He then goes on cavalierly to assert that the benefit the Indians will accrue from the Puritans' presence will be of greater value than the land they lose. Finally, he notes that it really doesn't matter if the colonists take the land since God has conveniently killed off most of the Indians anyway: "God hath consumed the natives with a great plague in those parts so as there be few inhabitants left." The "plague," of course, is the series of epidemics caused by diseases the Europeans transmitted, which infected the Indians and broke their resistance to settlement and colonization (73).

The fact that the Puritans enacted laws pertaining to the purchase of land from the Indians would seem to indicate that they felt at least some compunction about wholesale appropriation. However, a close examination of the laws suggests that whatever acknowledgment the Puritans made of Indian land "rights" was contingent upon the Puritans' interpretation of the warrant for those rights. The first laws of Massachusetts pertaining to the Indians, enacted in 1633, stipulate that whatever lands "any of the Indians in this jurisdiction have possessed and improved, by subduing the same, they have just right unto," according to Genesis 1:28 (*Colonial Laws*, 74). Of course, the fact that the notion of subduing the earth and having "dominion" over its creatures was foreign to the Indian world view completely escaped the Puritans, who went on to elaborate that if any English person or plantation "shall offer injuriously to put any of the Indians from their planting grounds, or fishing places," the Indians "upon their complaint and proof thereof" shall have recourse through the courts (*Colonial Laws*, 74). But again the problem is similar. The Indians' concept of the earth was communal rather than proprietary. They believed that the earth belonged to everyone to roam freely, so the idea of protecting only "their planting grounds and fishing places" misses the point. Moreover, it is highly ambiguous what kind of proof of ownership the Indians could possibly have offered, or the Puritans would have accepted.

According to the law, the remaining tracts of land "shall be accounted the just right of such English as already have, or hereafter shall have grant of lands from this court, and the authority thereof from that of Genesis 1. 28. and the invitation of the Indians" (*Colonial Laws*, 74). What this boils down to is that the Puritans have the right to any and all of the land, with the ambiguous exception of planting grounds and fishing places. The right of the Indians to sell land is also carefully circumscribed through a regulation that prohibits the Puritans from buying land without a license from the court, a provision designed not only to regulate ownership but also to encourage acquisition through means other than purchase (*Colonial Laws*, 74–75). Guided by a faith not only blind but blinding, the Puritans offer the Indians *allotments* of what even they would have to acknowledge, according to their premises, is the Indians' *own* land for both individuals and towns, provided the Indians convert and become civilized (*Colonial Laws*, 74).

In making land ownership contingent upon Christianization and civilization, this provision of the law underscores the importance of property as a reification of Puritan cultural identity. But what is crucial to understand about the Puritans' hypocritical attitude toward the Indians is that even allotments do not guarantee "adoption" into the Puritan "family." The subtext of the law on allotment encodes segregation, not integration or even assimilation. The Indians will receive land to reside in their own township, not Puritan towns; these "praying towns," as they came to be called, were the prototype of the reservation.

Further evidence of the reluctance to accept Indians into Puritan culture is policies toward the adoption of Indian children into Puritan families. Indian children were admitted to Puritan families only as servants, and this restriction epitomizes the hypocrisy underlying Puritan efforts at conversion. As in most imperialist ventures, conversion of the heathen was one of the professed motives behind the Great Migration. To mitigate their guilt and mask their commercial motives, the Puritans spewed forth a continuous stream of high-flown rhetoric not only about the covenant but about the need to convert the "heathen," whom they construed as the incarnation of the devil. For example, the official seal of Massachusetts actually depicts a scantily clad Indian with a bow and arrow, pleading, "Come over and help us." Conversion of the Indians was one of the primary excuses the Puritans used for leaving England, settling in the New World, and appropriating Indian lands.

Winthrop's confusion of religious and secular justifications in "Reasons to Be Considered..." reflects his own inner conflicts as well as a desire to manipulate his readers. The very first reason on Winthrop's list pertains to conversion of the Indians, which seems motivated less by an interest in their salvation than a desire to beat the Catholics to it: "First, it will be a service to the church of great consequence to carry the gospel into those parts of the world, to help on the coming in of fullness of the Gentiles and to raise a bulwark against the kingdom of Antichrist, which the Jesuits labor to rear up in those parts" (71). The Catholics enjoyed far greater success in converting the Indians than did the Puritans, who did not even begin their efforts in earnest until the middle of the century. Conversion was never a serious goal of more than a handful of the Puritans and is consistent with the circular reasoning that governed the exclusionary policy on "adoption," or church membership.

Puritan attitudes toward conversion intertwine with those toward land ownership and suggest a similar "bad faith." A perfect example of this conflation occurs in John Eliot's "The Day-Breaking of the Gospel with the Indians" (1646). Eliot was a Puritan minister who became celebrated as the "Apostle to the Indians," and in the following extract he applies the familiar agricultural metaphor to conversion:

> But me thinks now that it is with the Indians as it was with our New-English ground when we first came over, there was scarce any man that could believe that English grain would grow, or that plow could do any good in this woody and rocky soil. And thus they continued in this supine unbelief for some years, till experience taught them otherwise, and now all see it be scarce inferior to Old English tillage, but bears very good burdens; so we have thought of our Indian people and therefore have been discouraged to put plow to such dry and rocky ground, but God having begun thus with some few it may be they are better soil for the Gospel than we can think: I confess I think no great good will be done till they be more civilized, but why may not God begin with some few, to awaken others by degrees? (14–15)

In a similar vein, "New England's First Fruits" numbers among the colonists' successes conversion of the Indians. Part of their purpose is to "declare what *first fruits* he [the Lord] has begun to gather amongst them, as a sure pledge, (we are confident) of a greater *harvest* in his own time" (4; italics and parentheses in original).

The Puritans symbolically "converted" the Indians to an agricultural civilization in their texts by identifying them with the earth and its fruits, but this conversion was emblematic of colonization rather than adoption. The metaphor was, in effect, an expression of mastery over a culture, a circumscription of it within fixed and determined boundaries, comparable to the containment of the wilderness within borders that rendered it controllable. The most striking example of the appropriation of land under the guise of conversion occurs in Cotton's "God's Promise...." Cotton resorts to intricate typological examples of God's "casting" out the heathen to "give a foreign people favor" (5–6). Yet Cotton's conscience is obviously troubled by appropriation of their lands, so he, like Winthrop, adds justifications based on a specious interpretation of natural law—namely, that there is a meaningful moral distinction between inhabited land and vacant soil, between the civilized and the uncivilized use of land: "It is a principle in nature, that in a vacant soil he that taketh possession of it, and bestoweth culture and husbandry upon it, his right it is" (6). His ultimate rationalization is that God decides who lives where and that it is God's will that the Puritans inhabit this "land of promise," in part so that the Indians can receive the "benefit" of conversion: "offend not the poor natives, but as you partake in their land, so make them partakers of your precious faith: as you reap their temporals, so feed them with your spirituals: win them to the love of Christ, for whom Christ died.... *Who knoweth whether God have reared this whole plantation for such an end?*" (14–15; italics mine).

Here, land is clearly a medium of exchange, the currency of identity. The Puritans took the Indians' land and halfheartedly offered them Christianity in return. In taking away the Indians' land, the Puritans preserved their own identity as a culture and pretended to adopt the Indians into it, while in reality turning them into cultural orphans. For example, although Eliot professes a sincere desire to "educate and train up those children which are already offered us" and hopes that other Indians will "send their children to us when they see that some of their fellows fare so well among the English," his plan is not to place them in Puritan homes but in schools "among them or very near to them [the Indians]"—in other words, in segregated Indian boarding schools (21–22). This policy is in keeping with the Puritans' reluctance to adopt Indian children, whom they regarded not only as savages but as racial inferiors.

Since the Puritans regarded the family as the ultimate bulwark against pernicious influences, the thought of adopting Indians was anathema to them. Thus, boarding schools established at a safe distance from Puritan communities played the role of strict surrogate parents who attempted to inculcate Puritan values while avoiding the risk of contamination (Axtell, 215).

This practice derives from the same prejudice that consigned the Indians to praying towns and their own churches rather than allowing them to join the Puritan religious community. For example, Richard Mather, in his letter "To the Christian Reader" introducing *Tears of Repentance* (1652), a collection of Indian conversion narratives on which he collaborated with John Eliot, justifies, with the cultural condescension typical of a missionary, the delay in the "inchurching" of an Indian congregation in Natick on the grounds that they were not spiritually ready: "no marvel if the building of a spiritual temple, an holy church to Christ, and a church out of such rubbish as amongst Indians, be not begun and ended on a sudden; it is rather to be wondered at, that in so short a time, the thing is in so much forwardness as it is" (n.p.). One reason for the delay is the absence of a pastor, which was admittedly a problem even for an English congregation. Mather continues, "And if it be so amongst the English, who usually have better abilities, how much more amongst the Indians, whose knowledge and parts must needs be far less?" (n.p.).

Although the Puritans were not entirely hypocritical in their desire to convert the Indians, their evangelical desire to "save" them was significantly compromised by their desire to exterminate them in order to keep the community free of their influence and even their presence. The exclusionary impulse prevailed, and as Gary B. Nash acerbically comments, "with significant exceptions such as Roger Williams, the Puritans held the natives in contempt and would have preferred them all dead or removed from the region where they were building their 'city on the hill' " (6).

A policy of extermination, initiated by the Pequot War in 1637, was the final solution to the Indian problem and a tacit acknowledgment of the general failure to enslave, convert, and civilize. As a last resort, extermination offered several advantages. From a practical standpoint, it facilitated the process of land acquisition. But equally important was its symbolic function in terms of Puritan identity formation. Extermination was a form of scapegoating that preserved the community by displacing the Puritans' orphanhood onto the Indians. The Indians, as a demonic personification of the wilderness, functioned as a common enemy or scapegoat against whom the colonists could unite, thereby strengthening their own cohesiveness as a community. According to Richard Slotkin in *Regeneration Through Violence,* "The first colonists saw in America an opportunity to regenerate their fortunes, their spirits, and the power of their church and nation; but the means to that regeneration ultimately became the means of violence, and the myth of regeneration through violence became the structuring metaphor of the American experience" (5).

The wars against the Indians were motivated not simply by the Puritans' desire for conquest but also by their opposition to Indian acculturation. By differentiating themselves from the Indians, the Puritans could affirm their own "Englishness" and their precarious cultural and religious identity, which was threatened not only by the migration experience but by religious dissenters and nonconformists.

The polarization of heathen and Christian was an extreme version of the distinction between the Puritans and other religious groups, notably the Antinomians, Catholics, and Quakers, who not only constituted a threat to Puritanism but provided another construction of difference against which the struggle for identity could be played out. The Puritans reaffirmed their sense of identity as God's children by scapegoating these groups and turning them into cultural orphans. The Puritans, like the Anglicans in Virginia, adopted the English code of laws that treated religious dissent and blasphemy as crimes and enacted laws against religious groups — particularly the Quakers, who were subject to imprisonment, banishment, and even death. Vagabond Quakers were singled out for a special humiliation. A law of 1656 states that they shall "be stripped naked from the middle upwards and tied to a carts tail, and whipped through the town, and from thence immediately conveyed to the constable of the next town toward the borders of our jurisdiction, as their warrant shall direct; and so from constable to constable till they be conveyed through the outwardmost towns of our jurisdiction" (*Colonial Laws,* 61–62). The Puritans also falsely accused the Quakers of violating Puritan laws to manufacture an excuse to punish them. Similarly, the Puritans tried to justify their persecution of the Catholics on the grounds that the Jesuits were, in their efforts to convert them, inciting the Indians against the Puritans.

Scholars have traced the roots of antipapal prejudice in the colonies back to England, where Catholics were persecuted because Catholicism was looked upon not only as a corrupt faith but as a threat to the nation. The British tradition of equating all Irish Catholics with barbarians and cultural inferiors influenced colonial attitudes and fostered a predisposition to intolerance among the settlers who came to New England (Canny, 35). This predisposition to intolerance was intensified by competition with the French over land and converts.

Ironically, the greatest threat to the Puritans was posed by those dissenters who most closely resembled them, the Antinomians. The so-called Antinomian Controversy practically tore the colony asunder from 1636 to 1638. Whereas the heathen, the Quakers, and the Catholics were aliens who embodied radical forms of religious difference, the Antinomians, as dissenters from orthodox Puritanism, represented a more insidious threat from within. Considered an offshoot of Familism, Antinomianism also discredited law, scripture, and good works in favor of a belief in divine revelation and the indwelling of the Holy Spirit as evidence of grace. The principal fomenter of this heresy in New England was Anne Hutchinson, who was subsequently tried, convicted, and banished.

The Familist heresy had followed the Puritans all the way across the ocean and continued to haunt the Puritan community, as evidenced in their texts. For example, the title of Winthrop's account is "A Short Story of the Rise, reign, and ruin of the Antinomians, Familists & Libertines" (1637), and John Cotton, who was accused of being sympathetic to Hutchinson and the Antinomians, responds in "The Way of Congregational Churches Cleared" (1648) to the charge of "pretended Antinomianisme and Familisme" (Hall, 397).

Interestingly, both men also use familial imagery in their statements. Cotton defends himself against blame for the "fathering" of Hutchinson's tenets, or the origin of the heresy (Hall, 399), and Winthrop in "A Short Story" gives a "taste," or partial list of Antinomian heresies and promises, a distinctly familial flavor: "afterwards you shall see a litter of fourscore and eleven of their brats hung up against the sun and besides many new ones of Mistress Hutchinson's, all which they have hatched and dangled" (Hall, 202). Venting his spleen against the "American Jezebel," Winthrop even singles out her family as especially deserving of divine punishment at the hands of the Indians. Hutchinson was slaughtered by the Indians, along with most of her family, in 1644, prompting Winthrop to comment, "I never heard that the Indians in those parts did ever before this, commit the like outrage upon any one family, or families, and therefore God's hand is more apparently seen herein, to pick out this woeful woman, to make her and those belonging to her, an unheard of heavy example of their cruelty about all others" (Hall, 310, 218).

In both instances, the heretical opinions are metaphorically described as bad or evil offspring, and it is no coincidence that "A Short Story" also includes an account of a "monstrous and misshapen" child born to Mary and William Dyer, "the highest form of our refined Familists, and very active in maintaining their party" (281). Winthrop also makes much of the fact that the birth was discovered the day Hutchinson was cast out of the church. His description of the birth is eerily prescient of the hysteria that attended the Salem witch trials, but what is significant is that the imagery in both his and Cotton's texts places a familial construction on the beliefs as well as the believers, as if Puritan beliefs were the good children, i.e. God's children, and the heretical beliefs were the bad children, or orphans.

The anxiety the Puritans felt about the influence of other sects was not unfounded, and by mid-century signs of "backsliding" were already making themselves apparent. Moreover, the outcome of the Civil War in England, which was unprecedented religious tolerance, further shook the Puritans' confidence in their identity as God's children. As a result, religious leaders, feeling increasingly compelled to return the Puritans to orthodoxy, fell back on typology and traditional family imagery. For example, William Stoughton, in "New Englands True Interest...," stresses the honesty and fidelity of God's children. In recounting the grounds of God's expectations of his people, Stoughton declares: "A parent expects more from a child than from any other, because of the relation... if Israel had been no more than a servant or a home-born slave, the Lord had not expected so great things from him; but now being a son, yea a first born... this makes the judgments of God executed upon him for rebellions and backslidings to be, though more strange and astonishing, yet most just and righteous" (8). He goes to stress the importance of genealogy and heredity in maintaining the community of the faithful. God's expectations derive from "the extraction of a people, or their descent from such and such parents and progenitors; when they do not only stand in relation to God, but are born and grow up into covenant with him, as the seed and posterity of the Lords faithful ones" (9).

Stoughton's sermon reflects, in part, the failure of the wave of legislation in the middle of the century intended to protect the community from corrupting religious influences. Perhaps the single most important document of the early colonial period that illustrates the extent of Puritan paranoia about nonconformist religious groups is Winthrop's "A Defense of an Order of Court," an edict he issued in 1637 in response to the Antinomian crisis. "A Defense" is based on the premise that the government exists to preserve the safety and welfare of the citizens of the commonwealth. Winthrop declares, therefore, that "none should be received to inhabit within this jurisdiction but such as should be allowed by some of the magistrates" (164). The significance of this provision is that it empowers the magistrates to exclude arbitrarily any stranger or outsider (e.g., a nonconformist) who poses a threat to the commonwealth, which Winthrop variously compares to a body and to a family. His analogies to physical and social organisms reveal the degree to which Winthrop conceives of the Puritan community as self-contained and complete, defined as much by what it excludes as what it includes. "The Massachusetts Act Against Heresy and Error" (1646) turns prejudice into law by stipulating "that if any Christian within this jurisdiction shall be about to subvert and destroy the Christian faith and religion by broaching and maintaining any damnable heresies [which it goes on to itemize at length], every such person continuing obstinate therein, after due means of conviction, shall be sentenced to banishment" (*Colonial Laws*, 59).

With these edicts, the Puritans took the tradition of Puritan intolerance to new heights and set the stage in the New World for repeated waves of antagonism toward any group the dominant culture construed as "Other." The desperate need to find scapegoats reflects the degree to which the Puritans' sense of familial identity was provisional and dependent on the orphanhood of others as a means of self-preservation. Policies of exclusion subsequently extended to non-English immigrants, particularly the Irish, whom, like the Negroes and the Indians, the Puritans regarded as aliens, foreign in appearance, culture, and often in religion. In time, the religious persecution in which the Puritans engaged became inseparable from their xenophobia, in keeping with the fact that they equated America with Protestantism.[5]

One can see in the transition from Winthrop's "Model" to the "Defense" how the construction of the Puritans as God's children sowed the seeds for future waves of bigotry that resulted in the orphanhood of ethnic as well as religious groups. Certainly the "Defense" had the effect of codifying xenophobia toward foreigners who practiced a nonorthodox form of worship, notably French Huguenots, Scots-Irish, and Germans, and initiated the negative association between foreignness and religious dissent that fueled nativism in the nineteenth century. In short, religious and cultural conformity was an issue in American life as early as the colonial period, and it both reflected and influenced the homogeneity of the New England population, which was still primarily of English origin, with only a sprinkling of Irish, Scots-Irish, Scots, Huguenots, Jews, and Negroes.

The clearest early evidence of xenophobia is the colony's laws against strangers, which required strangers to be registered and approved by the court: "No town or person shall receive any stranger resorting hither with intent to reside in this jurisdiction, nor shall allow any lot or habitation to any, or entertain any such above three weeks, except such person shall have allowance under the hand of some one magistrate" (*Colonial Laws,* 143). Vagabonds were singled out for particularly harsh treatment (corporal punishment, followed by return to their "abode" or imprisonment) because they posed a threat to the family, the community, and the faith. In a preamble to a 1662 law justifying this treatment, the court specifies their offense as "the increase of profaneness and irreligiousness" they spread among the population by wandering "from town to town, thereby drawing away children, servants, and other persons, both younger and elder, from their lawful callings and employments, and hardening the hearts of one another against all subjection to the rules of God's holy word, and the established laws of this colony" (*Colonial Laws,* 152–153).

The fact that these outsiders consisted of criminals, rogues, vagabonds, foreigners, and political enemies cast out by the British as undesirables partly accounts for the vehemence of the Puritan reaction. But an equally important consideration was their poverty. In fact, poverty constituted legal grounds for the exclusion of outsiders and strangers from the community, underscoring the fact that the Puritans' motives for exclusion were not only religious and cultural but also economic and an offshoot the English Poor Laws. Given the circumstances of the Great Migration, the Puritans quite naturally felt somewhat embarrassed by their wholehearted embrace of religious intolerance, and it was convenient to have other excuses, such as poverty and vagrancy, on hand to mask the real reason. But this statement oversimplifies the fact that sometimes the reverse was true—religion was also used as an excuse to exclude outsiders who posed an economic threat to the colony. This slippery alliance in which one could cover up for the other as the occasion warranted is an outgrowth of the intimate relationship in Puritan ideology between the doctrine of election and the attainment of worldly success.

Puritan ideology, like Puritan theology, was relational, based on the acceptance and even the necessity of socioeconomic differences that drew other distinctions between God's children and orphans. Winthrop's "A Model of Christian Charity" is predicated on the notion of hierarchy on the grounds that inequality of station reflects the variety of God's creation and the work of his spirit in allowing the members of all social strata to demonstrate their Christianity in different ways and band together in a cooperative manner. He draws an analogy to the body in which all the parts act together for the good of the whole. Thus, the government, administered by a theocracy, a small, select group of God's elect, was dedicated to keeping all members of society in their place and perpetuating the hierarchy as a reflection of divine order. Within this hierarchy the poor had their place, as long as they belonged to the community.

Although the Puritans acknowledged their obligation to care for the "deserving poor" within their own community and even regarded them as a blessing because they gave the wealthy an opportunity to demonstrate their salvation through charitable intervention, their attitude toward the poor, like their attitude toward orphans, was quite different if the poor were outsiders and strangers. In fact, "fixity and stability of residence" was a more important criterion for charity than moral character; local communities categorically refused to accept responsibility for any poor outsiders and also enacted legislation to exclude them from the community. The Puritans revised the British poor laws to suit their own exclusionary ends, enacting provisions that protected the poor and the needy from within their own community and eliminating charitable provisions for those from outside the community, to the extent that there was even punitive legislation directed toward vagrants and dependent strangers (Rothman, 20).

Legislation directed specifically at the poor states that the court "shall have power to dispose of all unsettled persons into such towns as they shall judge to be most fit for the maintenance and employment of such persons and families, for the ease of this country" (*Colonial Laws*, 123). The fact that most rogues, vagabonds, and vagrants were not only poor but also of a different religion, race, or nationality established an early connection between religious, ethnic, and racial difference and poverty that influenced nativism and persists today.

In summary, the Puritans reacted to their sense of orphanhood by excluding groups that represented difference to preserve their identity as God's children. The differences between these groups were subsumed by the common denominator of poverty, which they came to share by virtue of their ostracism. Justifying the existence of poverty on religious grounds, the Puritans could easily sanction the poverty of those whom they classified as outsiders and even use their poverty as an excuse to exclude them.

Thus, the exclusion of outsiders from Puritan society was as inseparable from economics as it was from religion because most outsiders were both poor and heretical. The best way to divest these groups of their disruptive power was by keeping them outside the "family," the model for the church and the community. Tactics were land appropriation, in the case of the Indians, and simple exclusion, in the case of everyone else.

The irony is, of course, unmistakable. The Puritans left England imbued with faith in the covenant and their identity as God's children. But the unforeseen effect of the migration and settlement experiences was that it shook their belief in their chosenness and created the identification with orphanhood that underlies many Puritan texts. In reaction, the Puritans not only displaced their orphanhood onto others but unconsciously appropriated the identity of the oppressors who drove them from England in the first place.

In retrospect, it is clear that the Puritans' identification with God's children provided a model for the republic. Winthrop laid the foundation in his *Arbella* sermon idealizing "the city upon the hill," and Peter Bulkeley, who settled in Concord, extended the concept of Winthrop's city to other parts of New England. In his sermon, "The Gospel Covenant" (1651), written to recall the Puritans to the orthodoxy and spirituality of the early settlement, Bulkeley echoes Winthrop's elitism in calling upon

> the people of New England... to shine forth in holiness above other people.... we are as a city set upon a hill, in the open view of all the earth, the eyes of the world are upon us, because we profess ourselves to be a people in covenant with God.... Let us study so to walk that this may be our excellency and dignity among the nations of the world among which we live; that they may be constrained to say of us, only this people is wise, a holy and blessed people; that all that see us may see and know that the name of the Lord is called upon us; and that we are the seed which the Lord hath blessed. (212)

Bulkeley also uses the famous image of the shepherd separating the sheep and the goats to represent Jesus' separation of the holy from the unholy at the Final Judgment. It is an image that links national elitism with provincial exclusionism and sets the stage for the Revolution. He warns:

> Consider a time of separation must come wherein the Lord Jesus will divide and separate the holy from the unholy, as a shepherd separates the sheep from the goats. It is good to be found among the saints at that day, and to stand in the assembly of the righteous. Woe, then, unto all those that are secluded from them, to all those that must stand without and be among dogs and devils, having no fellowship with Christ nor with his saints. It is good, therefore to be holy. It will be found so then; woe unto the profane and ungodly at that day. (211–212)

As the colonies metamorphosed into a republic in the eighteenth century, it became clear the extent to which the identity of the burgeoning nation depended on just such arbitrary distinctions, and the task of its leaders, in their role as parents, was not only to give birth to the next generation of children but to create the next generation of orphans.

CHAPTER THREE

The Revolution

> But Britain is the parent country, say some. Then the more shame upon her conduct. Even brutes do not devour their young, nor savages make war upon their families....
> —THOMAS PAINE

F ollowing the Great Migration, the next major episode in American history to inspire an effusion of family imagery was the American Revolution. The rupture between England and America revived old memories of the traumatic separation between parent and child and sharpened the distinction between children and orphans, those who belonged to the family of the new republic and those who were effectively excluded from meaningful participation, and even citizenship, through a variety of legal and socioeconomic restrictions.

This development can best be understood within the context of the familial rhetoric that pervades Revolutionary and post-Revolutionary texts.[1] In the most thorough analysis to date of the family imagery projected onto the relationship between England and America, Edwin G. Burrows and Michael Wallace document what they describe as the *lingua franca* the Revolution: "Over and over again—in letters, diaries, newspapers, pamphlets, proclamations, and formal debates—they likened the empire to a family, a family in which England enjoyed the rights and duties of parental authority over the colonies while the colonies enjoyed the corresponding rights and duties of children" (168).

Conflating the patriarchal functions of God, king, and father, a variety of primarily religious sources inspired the belief of the Stuarts in the divine right of kings. James I, who ascended the throne after Queen Elizabeth's death in 1603, was the first monarch presumptuous enough to compare himself to God and, by extension, to the "Fathers of families, for a King is truly *Parens patriae*, the politique father of his people" (quoted in Burrows and Wallace, 170). As noted in chapter 1, in the mid-seventeenth century Sir Robert Filmer codified the religious basis for the absolute authority of the monarch by tracing his lineage back to Adam, the original man and the original father.

It followed inevitably from the perception of the king as a divine father that his subjects should be ideal children who would give him absolute filial obedience and devotion, in return for which they would be protected and nurtured. This patriarchal bond shaped the relationship between King George and not only his domestic but his colonial subjects. But for the American colonists, it was a submissive and degrading relationship that rationalized subjection on the grounds of dependency and need. As "wards of the empire," Americans were like young children who could not survive without the discipline and support of their parents and who would not even consider rebelling against or breaking away from them (Burrows and Wallace, 190).

So influential was the familial rhetoric that even after rebellion became a consideration in the American colonies, the loyalists continued to invoke the family analogy as justification for clinging to the status quo. For example, Thomas Bradbury Chandler in the *American Querist* (1774) poses one hundred rhetorical questions that "stated with peculiar force the traditional case for authority in the state, in society, and in the ultimate source and ancient archetype of all authority, the family" (Bailyn, 313). In his pamphlets, Chandler uses the family as his standard of judgment, castigating children who do not show respect to parents and by extension, colonies who fail to show proper respect to Great Britain. Chandler asks "whether *Great-Britain*, bears not a relation to these colonies, similar to that of parent to children; and whether any parent can put up with such disrespectful and abusive treatment from children, as *Great-Britain* has lately received from her colonies?" (4–5; italics in original).

Similarly Isaac Hunt, in his essay "Political Family" (1775), argues that the colonists owe a debt of gratitude to the "mother country" and also need her protection to assure their prosperity: "Colonies... are the children of more ancient nations.... they receive from the hands of their parents, protection from the insults and injuries to which their feeble, infant state is exposed. They ought, therefore, when they have attained their state of youth, or manhood, to evidence their gratitude, by a pious love and filial obedience" (29–30). Going even further, loyalist Jonathan Boucher, who revived Filmer's ideas in

America, uses the family analogy to justify rule by divine right and heredity, as opposed to any form of republican government based on consent and principles of equality (Bailyn, 314–318).

What made rebellion conceivable was, of course, taxation, the precipitating event in the Revolution that forced definition upon the ambiguous relationship between the king and the colonies. The colony actually functioned almost independently of the crown prior to the Revolution, and the imposition of parliamentary taxes, while consistent with the theory of monarchical rule, was inconsistent with colonial practice and created a crisis. What the colonists feared was that taxes would transform the colony into a quasi-feudal society in which "a few great lords" would gain control of all the lands currently held by freeholders because the latter would be unable to pay the taxes. In other words, taxation could force them into not only foreclosure but poverty and tenantry on what was once their own property (Bushman, 247–248).

The colonists could not help but recognize that their benevolent father was not so benevolent anymore. Not only was he suddenly trying to control them in a manner to which they were unaccustomed but he was trying to control them in a way that was patently self-serving and at odds with their own interests. (If one considers the colony to be now at the developmental stage of adolescence rather than childhood, as was typical during this period, it is as if parents give their son a car and require him to pay the expenses, which he does by working hard after school. Then they suddenly demand of him room and board and thereby make it impossible for him to keep the car because he can no longer cover the cost. Imagine the reaction!) Inevitably this crisis forced an agonizing reappraisal of the familial relationship between the king and his children, and no one rose to the occasion with greater pith and passion than Thomas Paine.

The single text that most strikingly realigned the familial relationship between the colony and the crown was Thomas Paine's *Common Sense*. Published in 1776, Paine's pamphlet sold more than half a million copies and was the first major document of the Revolution that openly advocated separation from England. The "genius" of the pamphlet, according to Eric Foner, was that it publicly expressed revolutionary sentiments that had seethed within the colonies for a long time and pertained to the economic, moral, and spiritual corruption of the Old World in contrast with the innocence of the New (79–80).

The overwhelming popularity of *Common Sense* derived not only from its ideas but from Paine's emotionally charged familial rhetoric. For example, he compares England to a bad parent and America to an abused child, analogies obviously calculated to incite reactions of outrage and rebellion. Paine also uses agricultural metaphors to reinforce the family imagery he sprinkles throughout the fertile soil of his polemic. Paine's metaphors of natural growth processes set the standard for judging the conflict between Great Britain and America and for predicting its outcome. For example: "Now is the seed-time of Continental union, faith and honor. The least fracture now will be like a name engraved with the point of a pin on the tender rind of a young oak; the wound would enlarge with the tree, and posterity read it in full grown characters" (16). The agricultural imagery is an obvious legacy of the Puritans, and Paine's appropriation of it is significant because it suggests a religious warrant for his concern with the violation of natural processes.

Three paragraphs later he rebuts the argument that because America "flourished" in the past by virtue of her connection with Great Britain, she will continue to do so in the future. His rhetorical device is an analogy to nurturing a child: "We may as well assert that because a child has thrived upon milk, that it is never to have meat, or that the first twenty years of our lives is to become a precedent for the next twenty" (17). In the same vein, Paine goes on to repudiate the claim that Great Britain has protected America from hostile powers by subtly characterizing her as a selfish parent: "We have boasted the protection of Great Britain, without considering that her motive was *interest* not *attachment*; and that she did not protect us from *our enemies* on *our account*; but from *her enemies on her own account,* from those who had no quarrel with us on any *other account* and who will always be our enemies on the *same account*" (17; italics in original).

Having thus cast the familial roles, Paine seizes upon the stereotype of England as the "parent country" and uses it as an excuse to both condemn her as unnatural and strip her of her parental prerogatives:

> But Britain is the parent country, say some. Then the more shame upon her conduct. Even brutes do not devour their young, nor savages make war upon their families; wherefore, the assertion, if true, turns to her reproach; but it happens not to be true, or only partly so, and the phrase *parent* or *mother country* hath been jesuitically adopted by the King and his parasites, with a low papistical design of gaining an unfair bias on the credulous weakness of our minds. Europe, and not England, is the parent country of America. This new world hath been the asylum for the persecuted lovers of civil and religious liberty from *every part* of Europe. Hither have they fled, not from the tender embraces of the mother, but

from the cruelty of the monster; and it is so far true of England, that the same tyranny which drove the first emigrants from home, pursues their descendants still. (18; italics in original)

Paine's attack on the parental relationship between England and America builds to a crescendo in which he rejects its basis on moral grounds: "Wherefore, I reprobate the phrase of Parent or Mother Country applied to England only, as being false, selfish, narrow and ungenerous" (19).

In the remainder of the essay, Paine takes the offensive, arguing that the relationship with England is deleterious to America's interests because it involves her in European wars and quarrels and hurts her trade. It is at this juncture that Paine makes the appeal to nature for which he laid the groundwork earlier in the essay: "Everything that is right or reasonable pleads for separation. The blood of the slain, the weeping voice of nature cries, 'TIS TIME TO PART.' Even the distance at which the Almighty hath placed England and America is a strong and natural proof that the authority of one over the other, was never the design of Heaven" (20).

Paine skillfully develops the idea that the relationship between England and America is an unnatural one, like that between a parent and child whose only bond is hatred: "Your future connection with Britain, whom you can neither love nor honor, will be forced and unnatural, and being formed only on the plan of present convenience, will in a little time fall into a relapse more wretched than the first.... Nature hath deserted the connection, and art cannot supply her place" (20). Once again, Paine conflates human nature and nature through an agricultural metaphor about the kind of conditions propitious for growth. The implication is that for the colonists, imperialism in the form of land ownership is not just a socioeconomic but a moral issue that links the physical and spiritual worlds.

Paine cleverly weaves into his neo-Shakespearean conceit about the unnatural parent/child relationship an appeal to his readers who, as real parents, are responsible for the future well-being of their children: "As parents, we can have no joy, knowing that *this government* is not sufficiently lasting to insure anything which we may bequeath to posterity; and by a plain method of argument, as we are running the next generation into debt, we ought to do the work of it, otherwise we use them meanly and pitifully. In order to discover the line of our duty rightly, we should take our children in our hand" (21–22; italics in original).

By looking at the differences between Britain and America through the lens of parental responsibility, a metaphor he further develops in his *American*

Crisis papers (1776), Paine provides a moral perspective that is flattering to America and consistent with the Puritan tradition of child-centeredness. Moreover, through a literary sleight-of-hand, he enacts a textual version of the Revolution by replacing the traditional parent, England, with a new patriarchal figure, the American "husband, father, friend, or lover" who will genuinely care for his family (20–21). This composite male "head of the household" is clearly the figure Paine has in mind when he writes in the appendix to *Common Sense*: "It is *now* the interest of America to provide for herself. She hath already a large and young family, whom it is more her duty to take care of, than to be granting away her property to support a power who is become a reproach to the name of men and christians" (31; italics in original).

Although no one approached his ability to milk the parental analogy for its full revolutionary implications, Paine was not the only leader to describe the colonial relationship to England in familial terms. The infamous Stamp Act (1765) prompted an outpouring of dismay and reproach to the "mother country" that justified disobedience on the grounds that England was an unfit parent. As John Adams writes in his *Dissertation on the Canon and Feudal Law* (1765), "But admitting we are children ... have not children a right to complain when their parents are attempting to break their limbs, to administer poison, or to sell them to enemies for slaves? ... will the mother be pleased when you represent her as deaf to the cries of her children ... ?" (quoted in Burrows and Wallace, 194). He then goes on to liken "the mother" to Lady Macbeth, a comparison that lingers in his imagination. In 1818 he reflects upon the meaning of the Revolution and recalls that "cruel Beldam" willing to "dash their brains out" and pronounces, "it is no wonder that their filial affections ceased and were changed into indignation and horror. *This radical change in the principles, opinions, sentiments and affections of the people, was the real American Revolution*" (292; italics in original).

Even the Declaration of Independence encoded familial imagery. In the second section, the statement of independence, the document records the appeal of the colonists to their British "brethren" for support and warns that the relationship is at stake. Unresponsive "to the voice of justice and of consanguinity," the British denied this appeal, and the result was a breach between the brethren as well as between the patriarch and his sons (Jefferson, *Autobiography*, 963).

The familial rhetoric used to dramatize the ideology of the Revolution intertwined with new attitudes toward the family that appeared in both England and America during the eighteenth century. John Locke was instrumental in reinterpreting the patriarchal authority that had long dominated British family and political life. Basing it on natural rather than divine law, Locke maintained that patriarchal authority is both limited and temporary and attacked its traditional association to political authority. Locke's point was that children have the right to grow up and become independent; that while children may owe their parents a debt of gratitude, they do not owe them everlasting obedience. In other words, the basis of the relationship between parents and children, like that between government and the people, should be a voluntary and contractual agreement among equals (Burrows and Wallace, 178–179).

Locke's theory replaced the authoritarian model with a contractual one and reflected the diminution of patriarchal authority within the family. A dramatic shift in family roles had taken place on both sides of the Atlantic by the mid-eighteenth century, replacing the hierarchical patriarchal structure with a comparatively egalitarian one that emphasized the importance of each individual member and is the prototype of contemporary model.

The new contractual model of the family became the model for the relationship between government and the people. While scholars have written copiously about the reasons for the Revolution, the most convincing interpretations are those that acknowledge the affective power of the family as a paradigm linking the political and the personal spheres, just as it did during the colonial period. Not only did the family provide the imagery for the Revolution, but it also inspired much of the intense emotion, as people inevitably projected their own experiences as children and even parents onto the political perception of England as the mother country and King George III as the father of his people (Greven, 339). The question of which influenced the other—whether changes in the family influenced political attitudes or vice versa—is moot because the two developments seemed inseparable both from each other and from the larger ideological context. What is certain is that the liberalization of attitudes toward the family inevitably made itself felt in the political sphere.

The erosion of patriarchal authority also coincided with economic changes. Fathers no longer had as much control over their land, which, according to the custom of partible inheritance, was now divided among all their sons. Moreover, new opportunities for nonagricultural work were drawing children away from home and giving them more freedom. Fathers had less control over their children's sexual behavior and choice of marriage partners. The result was that children now had more power and autonomy, and they were viewed as more unpredictable and less controllable (Mintz and Kellogg, 16–17).

Changing religious attitudes in the eighteenth century also had a major influence on the family. Puritans imbued with the fervor of the Great Awakening and concerned about preserving their heritage continued to focus on children as the salvation of the culture and pressured them to convert. Parents, however, now placed conversion within their children's control and thereby conferred upon them responsibility not only for their own "adoption" but for the future of the faith. In other words, children now held an unprecedented degree of power because they had to act in ways that could have a major effect on not only the religious but the political future of the colonies (Hiner, 256–257).

Eighteenth-century youth had also acquired characteristics we associate with modern adolescents—the rebelliousness, overvaluation of peers, and confusion about identity that Erik Erikson so insightfully documented in *Childhood and Society* (262–263). The appearance of adolescence as a discernible stage of child development during the eighteenth century introduced into the family issues of identity formation and generational conflict that were predicated on the revolutionary assumption that children were autonomous individuals who had the right to assume their independence in adulthood. Feeling both rebellious and oppressed, the adolescent became the personification of the unruly colony, and coming of age, as a rite of passage or initiation into adulthood, became "a quintessential motif" of the Revolution that linked family politics to the political quest for independence and self-government (Fliegelman, 3–4).[2]

The empowerment of the adolescent hardly mirrored the situation of all colonial children, however; some enjoyed less status than they had in the previous century. The Puritans in the seventeenth century insisted that everyone, even orphans, be attached to a family as a form of social control, but conditions had changed, and orphans now depended increasingly on public support, assuming they could meet the strict requirements for settlement and thereby become eligible for relief (Bremner, *Children and Youth in America*, 262). The Puritans' prejudice against strangers, especially if they were poor, persisted and influenced exclusionary attitudes toward orphans during this period.

In the eighteenth century, even orphans from within the community began to pose a pressing social problem. First, there were more of them as a result of Indian wars, epidemics, and natural disasters. Second, young children were considered a greater burden because the increased availability of indentured servants, slaves, and redemptioners made the investment in raising them less worthwhile. These changes necessitated innovations in the care of young dependent children, ranging from maintenance in their own homes or boarding out, both at public expense, to placement in almshouses, which were becoming increasingly widespread by the end of the century. At a suitable age, children were bound out as servants or laborers, but as Bremner wryly observes, "The practice of consigning free born boys and girls to involuntary servitude simply because they were poor hardly squared with the political philosophy of the Revolution and the young republic. The practice continued, but under the legal fiction that the children were being apprenticed" (Bremner, *Children and Youth in America,* 263). The point is that orphans or dependent children who were outsiders in the community were completely ostracized, and even some orphans from within the community experienced a form of social exclusion in the form of servitude or institutionalization. A shift from private to public responsibility was gradually taking place, and the exclusion of unadoptable children from the family signified a form of cultural as well as personal orphanhood that was the consequence of poverty.

Thus, the adolescent male child who represented the "Sons of Freedom" and the "Sons of Liberty" was hardly representative of all American children. As a genealogical descendant of a known father, he served as a symbol of spiritual rebirth, a reincarnation of Puritan millennialism that perpetuated the idea of a "national covenant" that Winthrop introduced in his *Arbella* speech.[3] The implication of this "rebirth" is that Americans were recapitulating their colonial identity as God's chosen, i.e. his children, and preserving the connection between church and state in their vision of a special American destiny (Ferguson, 20). Like the Puritans, Paine and other revolutionaries construed the physical act of leaving England as far more drastic than a mere migration; but while the Puritans dealt with the trauma of separation by transforming the migration into a religious mission, the revolutionaries collapsed the religious element into the larger struggle for national identity and used the former to serve the ends of the latter.

The Puritans' belief that Christ's sacrifice transformed the relationship between God and man into that of parent and child is central to the imagery of the period and at the root of the conflation of religious and political values. It is important to remember that in the Puritan world view, adoption belonged only to the converted and the regenerate, those who could satisfactorily prove that they were in a state of grace. As Fliegelman points out, the state of grace preceding final sanctification is "adoption," which confers upon the converted the privileges of sonship and membership in God's redeemed family (173).

The concept of adoption derives from the New Testament and is predicated on the sacrifice of Jesus Christ, who enabled the faithful to be adopted as the children of God the Father. As Paul wrote to the Ephesians, "He [God] destined us for adoption as his children through Jesus Christ, according to the good pleasure of his will, to the praise of his glorious grace that he freely bestowed on us in the Beloved. In him we have redemption through his blood" (Ephesians 1:5–7, 11). Through his blood, God's children are joined in a redeemed family, as if this spiritual adoption had established bonds of consanguineous kinship.

The religious significance of adoption readily translated itself into the political sphere insofar as the "Sons of Liberty" were joining a new family and a new kinship structure, modeled after the true religion of Protestantism—not Catholicism, as Paine's derisive allusions to "jesuitically adopted" rhetoric and the "papistical design" of England would indicate (15). The redemptive love of this "adoptive parent," as Crèvecoeur described America, was the religious basis of the postmillennial vision of America as a republic and the ultimate Christian community in which not everyone was "adoptable."

In order to be adopted, the "sons" needed an ideological parent to adopt them, a role obligingly filled by George Washington, who readily embraced the epithet "father of his country." Biographer Richard Brookhiser suggests that, lacking descendants, Washington eagerly turned to substitutes, among them his stepchildren and step-grandchildren, members of his staff, and, most importantly, the American people, present and future (165–166). He frequently voiced concern for the unborn generations of Americans, and Brookhiser infers that even "mentioning them was an act of adoption" (167).

The interesting question about George, the American patriarch, is how much he actually differed from George III, the English monarch who preceded him. George Washington was, after all, a product of the "natural aristocracy," a concept formulated by Adams and Jefferson that played a key role in shaping Washington's attitudes and values. Based on the assumption that virtue and talents are hereditary, Jefferson in his famous letter to John Adams distinguished the natural aristocracy from the "artificial aristocracy founded on wealth and birth, without either virtue or talents" and recommended members of the natural aristocracy as those best suited for political office: "The natural aristocracy I consider as the most precious gift of nature for the instruction, the trusts, and government of society" (*Writings*, 1305–1306). Building on the Lockean model of the contractual family, the natural aristocracy also postulated a reciprocal relationship between government leaders and the people.

But an awkward problem was the hereditary nature of the natural aristocracy. The rub was that although Jefferson theoretically placed a higher value on talent, he observed that most men of talent belonged to old families that had played leading roles in government and were linked to each other by bonds of marriage and kinship (Rogin, 21). In other words, despite Adams and Jefferson's rhetoric about the importance of self-education and meritocracy in shaping an individual, their underlying standard was nature, not nurture. Their racial attitudes corroborated this biological bias by comparing class differences to racial differences and thereby suggesting an inherent difference. Both likened "the subtle difference of social class to the simple and striking difference that divided whites from Indians or blacks." In drawing this analogy, they were suggesting a biological basis for class differences. In fact, the only real difference between the natural and the traditional aristocracy was that republican rhetoric made the hereditary bases of economic and political power less obvious.

The heroic image of George Washington helped to conceal this contradiction. Given his role as the ideal father, it seems less relevant that he belonged to the "natural aristocracy" than that he reinvented the patriarchal tradition. His mythic presence also perpetuated the Christian belief that children were not only born to their natural parents but were born again to a higher spiritual family headed by their heavenly father. Fliegelman infers that this doctrine "provided the kernel of a revolutionary insight: the title of father was transferable" (197). Representing the values of education, nurture, and Christian benevolence, Washington was also the embodiment of a new heroism, a perfect patriarch who justified the transfer of filial affection from King George. There were also trivial factors that enhanced the resemblance. Not only did the two men have the same first name but their profiles were so similar that coin collectors were unable to distinguish between them (Brookhiser 171–172).

Washington was, in short, exactly the kind of ideal father Paine wanted as a parent for himself and his fellow orphans, and orphans indeed they felt themselves to be. As Candidus wrote in 1776, "America was not sent out a Colony at the charge of *Great Britain*, and, for all the protection afforded her, might well be esteemed an orphan instead of a child" (quoted in Burrows and Wallace, 211). The obsessive identification with "sons" after the Revolution is clearly a reaction to an intensified sense of orphanhood that is reminiscent of the Puritans' attempts at denial. Like the Puritans, the "sons of liberty" also shifted the burden of orphanhood onto scapegoats whom they blamed for their internal problems and conflicts. These common enemies, mostly Indians and immigrants, enabled them through processes of differentiation and exclusion to affirm their identity as the adopted children of the republic.

In the aftermath of the Revolution, the systematic exclusion from the republic of those who represented religious, ethnic, and racial difference resulted in their cultural orphanhood and stemmed from the gradual identification of the "Sons of Liberty," who became the "Founding Fathers," with the oppressive patriarch and monarch, King George III.[4] The Oedipal implications are obvious, and the temptation to interpret the patriarchal imagery of the Revolution in Freudian terms is supported by its violent undercurrent. For example, Paine wrote about his reaction to the king after the battles of Lexington and Concord in April 1775, "I rejected the hardened, sullen-tempered Pharaoh of England forever; and disdain the wretch, that with the pretended title of FATHER OF HIS PEOPLE can unfeelingly hear of their slaughter, and composedly sleep with their blood upon his soul" (24).

Winthrop Jordan is the most persuasive of the critics who subscribe to a parricidal interpretation of the Revolution: "One can propose that in 1776 George III was killed in his American provinces vicariously but very effectively by an anonymous hand and that this act of murder constitutes a legitimate subject for historical inquiry" ("Thomas Paine...," 294). While praising Paine's *Common Sense* for its "subliminal" appeal in suggesting not only the superfluity and corruption of the monarchy but also the "chosenness" of the American people, Jordan also deconstructs the homicidal message embedded in the synecdoche of the "demolished" and "scattered" crown (298). Clearly echoing Freud's narrative of the transformation of the primal horde into the fraternal clan, Jordan compares Paine's image of the breaking of the crown into pieces to a "political eucharist" that recapitulates prehistoric ceremonies in which "men sometimes not only killed their father, the leader of the horde, but ate him in order magically to acquire his power" (298).[5] Jordan connects this rite to the significance of the tree in the Revolutionary imagination, which culminated in the symbol of the Liberty Tree, "a new sovereign," around which the sons gathered in a newly constituted brotherhood (305).

Obviously sons exist only in relation to a father, and in the case of the Revolution the sons derived the image of the new father in part from the old. It is significant that although the revolutionaries took great delight in contrasting the two Georges and in venerating Washington as if he were their new king, their veneration also eerily echoed Puritan typology. Timothy Dwight's epic poem *The Conquest of Canaan* (1785) is a post-Revolutionary version of the Puritans' typological vision that glorifies Joshua's (Washington's) success in leading the Israelites into Canaan and conquering the Canaanites (the Pequots). Dwight revives the idea of America's sacred mission in distinctly secular and prophetic terms as the founding of a new and mighty empire.

In construing Washington as the "Saviour of his Country" who would wash away the sins of the past and set his children upon a new mission, Dwight collapses the past into the present—not only the colonial past but the monarchical past as well (*Conquest of Canaan*, dedication). Following the Oedipal paradigm, Washington and the Founding Fathers had not only overthrown the father but they had assumed aspects of the father's identity as well. To be sure, America represented liberty and freedom, but the fraternal ideal was unattainable, and its failure resulted in a recapitulation of the family paradigm, with the father as a newly conceived authority figure needed to control his unruly sons, who abused their newfound liberties. Thus, America, the oppressed, gradually became the oppressor under the leadership of a "natural aristocracy" that sought to perpetuate its political and economic hegemony. Rogin sums it up: "The natural aristocracy... fell back upon that fatherhood, supported by state instead of society, which characterized colonial rule. 'The tyranny of Philadelphia may be like the tyranny of George III,' charged the Anti-Federalists" (34).

Thus, even though the American Revolution was predicated on the rejection of England and George III, the Founding Fathers emulated their former enemy by incorporating oppression into their rhetoric as well as their politics. The political rhetoric of the Revolution encoded policies of exclusion and discrimination that instilled a sense of self-conscious elitism and cohesion among the governing class, or natural aristocracy (Ferguson, 26). For example, the famous statement in the Declaration of Independence that all men are created equal clearly defined humanity in a very narrow sense. The most egregious example of those excluded from classification of humanity were, of course, the Negroes, whose status as slaves precluded them from mention, much less protection, in the Declaration.[6]

Despite the high-minded ideals of equality and inalienable rights propounded in the Declaration of Independence, it rapidly became apparent that not everyone belonged to the family of the republic and that the Founding Fathers were practicing an elaborate form of bad faith in relegating certain members of the human race to political and economic orphanhood. The need for political unity in the face of the temptations of republicanism was not the only reason for this exclusion. The rise of capitalism also threatened to set the sons against each other. Prior to the Revolution, it was easy to blame England for domestic problems such as social inequality and greed, and the Revolution helped the revolutionaries avert their eyes from burgeoning factional conflicts growing out of the rise of commodity capitalism (Rogin, 28). Instead of alleviating the problems created by capitalism, the Revolution exacerbated them in a way that threatened not only the social order but the sacred institution of the family, as individual members began to compete among themselves for wealth and property. By extension, the republic was vulnerable to the same divisiveness, as the land-owning natural aristocracy felt the challenge of a rising middle class aggressively pursuing economic gain.

The most compelling evidence of the natural aristocracy's effort to preserve its political leadership and economic hegemony is that the right to vote was contingent upon the ownership of property. This provision established a clear precedent for the equation of political power with socioeconomic elitism by ensuring that the only "citizens" of the new republic were members of a white male, neofeudal landed aristocracy. As Robert Berkhofer explains, "Under republican ideals of the period, property was connected with life and liberty because its ownership was the surest guarantee of those other inalienable rights. To perpetuate the social hierarchy, leading Americans deemed desirable to preserve public virtue as well as to provide the stake in society thought necessary for responsible decision-making, republican constitutions restricted the franchise to property holders" (137). The Founding Fathers were thus taking the Puritans' secular attitude toward property, with its emphasis on agriculture as an emblem of civilization and its conflation of land ownership and cultural identity, a giant political step further by connecting property directly to citizenship.

This restriction politicized the meaning of adoption and had the desired effect of excluding, without specifically naming, unwanted "children" from the family of the republic: those members of the middle class who were too poor to own property, as well as Negroes, Indians, and immigrants (many of whom were Catholic).[7] This economic criterion implemented an ethnic, racial, and religious discrimination that entrenched the power of landowners and the natural aristocracy and orphaned everyone else. As James Thomas Flexner points out in his analysis of the conflict between Jefferson and Hamilton, the underlying conflict was between rival economic systems vying for dominance (241).

The ancillary effect of this conflict was that it legitimized the exclusion of undesirables from the political process and hence from "adoption" into the American family (i.e., citizenship) and confirmed the Indian as the archetypal orphan and the primary target of oppression in the aftermath of the Revolution and the early years of the republic.

Far from being an unintentional byproduct of class conflict, the scapegoating of the Indian continued to be fundamental to the project of national identity formation. There was, for example, a chilling parallel between the abusive treatment of colonists by their corrupt British father and the cruel, and at times sadistic, treatment of the Indians by their American fathers, whether Washington, Jefferson, or Andrew Jackson, in the nineteenth century. The revolutionaries wished to appropriate not only King George's power but the Indians' nativeness by seizing their land which, in the "civilized" form of property, constituted the reification of citizenship. Land was also a potential source of private wealth, and land speculation, as "the major investment opportunity in early America," played a major role in shaping not only Indian removal policies but political destinies, including Washington's (Rogin, 18). Jefferson believed that the growth of the nation and the avoidance of class conflict depended on the availability of large quantities of cheap land. Thus, from a socioeconomic point of view, dispossessing the Indians of their lands was integral to the rise of capitalism and the economic growth of the new republic (Rogin, 13).

The need to obtain land at any cost, human as well as financial, shaped government policy toward the Indians from the time of the Revolution into the nineteenth century and resulted in ludicrous efforts at deception as well as self-deception to disguise that policy as benevolent. Daniel M. Friedenberg summarizes, "The bedrock on which rests early American history is the use of land to gain wealth and reach high political office" (356). The image of the Indians in the minds of the Founding Fathers is consistent with their ulterior motives. For example, although Washington recommended in his celebrated letter of 1783 to James Duane "the propriety of purchasing their lands in preference to attempting to drive them by force of arms out of their Country," his reasoning seems to be based more on practical than on moral considerations, for he goes on to compare "coercion to driving the wild Beasts of ye forest which will return as soon as the pursuit is at an end and fall perhaps on those that are left there; when the gradual extension of our Settlements will as certainly cause the Savage as the Wolf to retire; both being beasts of prey tho' they differ in shape" (Allen, 266).[8]

In that same letter, Washington repeatedly advocates drawing "a boundary line between them and us beyond which we will *endeavor* to restrain our People from Hunting or Settling, and within which they shall not come, but for the purposes of Trading, Treating or other business unexceptionable in its nature" (261–262; italics in original). The significance of this "line" is far more than geographical and suggests that a division based not only on rights and status but on common humanity separates the citizens of the republic from the "savages" (261).

Washington's acquisitive, expansionist attitude toward the land set the standard for the new republic and grew out of his personal background as one raised in plantation society in which land was the currency of belonging. To Washington, land signified not only wealth but status. Men without property could not participate in civic affairs, and full political rights were enjoyed only by those who owned sufficient property. Landed wealth was also the prerequisite of leadership, and the roles of landed gentlemen merged with that of father ruling over his estate, his community, and even his country (Longmore, 6).

Washington began a concerted policy of land acquisition at an early age, provoked in part by his father's premature death. His first job as a young man was as an intern in 1745 mapping land grants in the back country. He subsequently became a surveyor on the frontier and began buying property. During the Seven Years' War he continued to gobble up land, to the extent of exploiting poor soldiers in his army by purchasing their bounty lands. By the 1760s Washington owned 20,000 acres of frontier land, which he increased over the course of his life.

Given his mindset about the importance of land ownership, it is hardly surprising that he regarded the Indians, whom he dubbed more accurately than he realized in his letter to Duane "a deluded people" (261), as little more than an obstacle to be gotten round with as little inconvenience as possible. This is not to say that Washington did not show a certain grudging respect for the Indians, gained during his years of fighting against them, but this was not enough to alter his racist view of them or to make him take seriously any claim they might have to rights that infringed on those of American "citizens."

Jefferson seemed to take a more benign view of the Indians, but only in defense of the nation and at the expense of the Negroes. Jefferson needed to refute the claim that the American environment produced human degeneracy (i.e., Indians) because of the negative image it conveyed of America. So he vaguely attributed to "circumstances," such as lack of exposure to the civilizing effects of numbers and letters, whatever apparent inferiority the Indians represented. He even forced himself to compare the Indian favorably to the white man in *Notes on the State of Virginia*, praising him for his sexual prowess, bravery, fortitude in the face of death, affection for his children, capacity for friendship, keen sensibility, and a "vivacity and activity of mind...equal to ours in the same situation" (184–185, 188).

But there are racist underpinnings to the comparison, which profits the Indian at the expense of the Negro. Applying the principles of natural history, Jefferson rates the Indian higher than the Negro on the racial scale and distorts the reality of racial differences by exaggerating them in the Negro and ignoring them in the Indian. As Jordan sardonically observes, "Confronted by three races in America he determinedly turned three into two by transforming the Indian into a degraded yet basically noble brand of white man" (*White over Black*, 477). In other words, he uses the more positive image of the Indian to abase the Negro as the ultimate Other, the embodiment of such extreme difference that he is no longer even human. For example, in a letter to another plantation owner, Jefferson remarks, "[Potatoes and clover] feed every animal on the farm except my negroes" (Regis, 91).

Jefferson also invokes the principles of natural history to argue that blacks are an inferior race based on physiological differences, such as color, as well as deficiencies in reason and imagination. In extolling the superior beauty of whites, he makes the infamous assertion of "the preference of the Oranootan [*sic*] for the black women over those of his own species" (*Notes*, 265). The point is that although Jefferson is committed to emancipation and education for Negroes, he is nevertheless deeply wedded to the concept of their racial inferiority, and he uses his image of the Indians to reinforce it.

Yet Jefferson's Indian policies made a mockery of his higher regard. The implication of his democratic goal of making land available to all free individuals was dispossession of the Indians, or removal to the West. And although he publicly espoused alternatives to extinction, paying lip service in his *Notes* to the ideas of Indian assimilation and even amalgamation, his actual policies made orphanhood, and even extermination, inevitable (Slotkin, *The Fatal Environment*, 70). In short, his commitment to expansionism ultimately overrode his principles.

The hypocrisy that underlay the posture of paternalistic concern in Jefferson's attitude for the Indians eventually became apparent through his actions. With the great wave of expansionism, beginning with the Louisiana Purchase in 1803, the problem of what to do with Indians in both the overcrowded east and the newly acquired western territories became an increasingly pressing one. While professing a desire to protect the Indians and integrate them into white society, Jefferson's actions reveal that he was determined to keep them physically, culturally, and racially separate from the family of the republic. For example, although he proposed incorporating the Indians into the republic in his 1805 inaugural, Jefferson privately recommended removal to a Chickasaw delegation later that year. In general, Jefferson seemed to regard the land gained in the Louisiana Purchase as a dumping ground for unwanted natives, first the Chickasaws in 1805, then the Choctaw and the Cherokees in 1808. Moreover, Jefferson defined citizenship on the basis of color, a policy foreshadowed by his recommendation that the Negroes be shipped back to Africa to avoid granting them citizenship and running the risk of miscegenation. Drinnon correctly infers, "colonizing reds in the West was the internal counterpart of his external 'expatriation' scheme for blacks" (Drinnon, 84).

Early in his presidency, Jefferson fell into the habit of addressing Indian delegations in paternalistic terms, as "children," "my children," or "my son." However, he clearly regarded them as neither his natural nor his adopted children, but as orphans in need of protection from their all-powerful white "father." Similarly, although Indians were commonly referred to in other writings of the period as "brothers" or "red brethren," it was also clear that they were not "blood brothers" but rhetorical brothers. "The unfortunate sons of nature," as John Quincy Adams disparagingly dubbed them, had nothing in common with the civilized sons of the republic other than cohabitation of the continent (Rogin, 5). The Founding Fathers consigned the Indians to a state of perpetual childhood in order to distinguish them from the whites, who were growing out of their symbolic childhood as colonials into their symbolic adulthood as citizens of the republic and, not incidentally, as imperialists (Rogin, 6). Another way of looking at it is that insofar as American "national" identity was predicated on a form of colonization, which entailed the appropriation of Indian land and Indian identity as indigenous, dispossession of the Indian "children" resulted in their cultural orphanhood.

That they were encouraged to see themselves as dependent children predisposed the Indians to further psychological manipulation. Under the façade of paternal benevolence, Jefferson fostered this dependent self-image by instilling concepts of "good" children who were submissive to whites and "bad" children who rebelled. Drinnon bleakly concludes, "Nestled under Jefferson's philanthropy was an ominous will to exterminate" (95). To mask that desire, Jefferson rationalized extermination on the grounds that Indians were not only merciless savages but children vulnerable to dangerous outside influences from European nations.

The process of extermination took insidious as well as blatant forms that reflect the ulterior motives behind Indian policy. The importance of deconstructing the myth of the Founding Fathers as egalitarian lies in connecting Revolutionary consciousness to both the colonial past and the expansionist future through the channel of racism that, Jefferson's demurrals to the contrary, shaped post-Revolutionary attitudes toward the Indians. Indian policy in post-Revolutionary America was driven by bad faith, a combination of expansionist greed and dread of the dark Other. Lurking beneath the professed goal of assimilation was the unexpressed goal of racial and cultural annihilation, either by transforming the Indian into a model white American or by transporting white Americans to Indian lands. The point was to substitute an "American" for an "Indian," a ploy that "eliminated the latter in favor of the former" (Berkhofer, 136).

The ambivalent attitude of Jefferson and his successors toward the Indians not only served the purpose of obscuring the reality of government policy but also gave rise to illusions about the Indians that conveniently justified the failure of professed assimilationist goals. As Brian Dippie argues, the image of the Indians as a vanishing people, lurching inevitably toward extinction, became a self-fulfilling prophecy that was used to rationalize their dispossession, just as the image of the Indians as culturally deficient served as an excuse for the appropriation of their lands. Thus, the government's official policy of converting and educating the Indians was belied by the unofficial assumption that the Indians were destined never to be Christianized or civilized and would eventually decay and become extinct. This fatalistic theory had the effect of placing the blame for their own demise on the victims rather than the oppressors, and it became a particularly appealing explanation after the War of 1812 in which the Indians fought on the side of the British. After 1814, the theory of the Vanishing American became a convenient rationalization for extermination (Dippie, 10).

Despite the apparent collaboration between the government and the missionaries to assimilate the Indians into white society, the hidden agenda was always exclusion and separation of the races, as in Puritan times. The ironic rationalization was that until the Indians were converted and educated, they needed to be isolated from white society to protect them from its vices. Thus, Indian children were segregated in missionary schools and Indian tribes were subjected to removal, a policy James Monroe revived in 1817.

By the end of his administration, Monroe recommended the removal of all tribes east of the Mississippi and paved the way for Andrew Jackson's dispossession of the Cherokee, who had made the mistake of assimilating all too well in the state of Georgia. Both Monroe and Jackson protested that they were acting in the Indians' best interests, basing their policy on the supreme rationalization that by removing the Indians from the East, where "their 'degradation and extermination' would be inevitable and by transplanting them in the West, they were saving them from extinction and enabling them in time to become a 'civilized people' capable of integration" (Dippie, 61). The Indian Removal Act of 1830 resulted not only in the displacement of the Cherokee but in the infamous "trail of tears" and the dispossession of thousands of native peoples. As a result of Indian removal policy, seventy-five percent of the 125,000 Indians living east of the Mississippi in 1820 were removed to the West. By 1844 most eastern tribes, except those living in the remote regions of Lake Superior, had been forcibly relocated, leaving less than 30,000 Indians in the east (Rogin, 4).

In short, in the early years of the republic, as in colonial New England, the Indians played the role of scapegoat and served as a model for the cultural orphans created by the "family of the republic." Gradually, immigrants also became implicated in the processes of scapegoating and cultural orphanhood. The nature of this connection is particularly evident in the writings of Benjamin Franklin and J. Hector St. John de Crèvecoeur. Despite his apparent sympathy for the Indians and apparent tolerance of and even hospitality toward immigrants, there is another side of Benjamin Franklin that reflects his identification with the oppressive power he fought so hard to overthrow. To set his attitudes in a psychological context, it is worth noting that Franklin's own personal history reflects a troubled relationship with paternal authority.[9] For example, in Franklin's depiction of his early life in his *Autobiography*, he draws a parallel between his own experience and his "aversion to arbitrary power." Working as an apprentice to his older brother in a Boston printing house, Franklin bitterly notes, "Tho' a Brother, he considered himself as my Master," and he chronicles the abuse he received at his brother's hands: "my Brother was passionate & had often beaten me, which I took extremely amiss." In fact, Franklin took it so amiss he adds in a footnote, "I fancy his harsh & tyrannical Treatment of me, might be a means of impressing me with that Aversion to arbitrary Power that has stuck to me thro' my whole Life" (21).

The combination of his brother's "unfairness" and "the Blows his Passion too often urg'd him to bestow" were eventually vexing enough to provoke Franklin into running away, an act of elective orphanhood that induced a mixture of self-pity and pride, as the following summation suggests: "I found myself in New York near 300 Miles from home, a Boy of but 17, without the least Recommendation to or Knowledge of any Person in the Place, and with very little Money in my Pocket" (23). Next Franklin wended his way toward Philadelphia. He describes in waiflike terms the hunger, thirst, exhaustion, and sickness he endured: "It rain'd very hard all the Day, I was thoroughly soak'd and by Noon a good deal tir'd, so I stopped at a poor Inn, where I stayed all Night, beginning now to wish I had never left home" (25). Striking a deliberately plaintive note, his narrative culminates in his description of his entry into Philadelphia: "I was in my Working Dress, my best Clothes being to come round by Sea. I was dirty from Journey; my Pockets were stuff'd out with Shirts & Stockings; I knew no Soul, nor where to look for Lodging. I was fatigued with Travelling, Rowing & Want of Rest. I was very hungry, and my whole Stock of Cash consisted of a Dutch Dollar and about a Shilling of Copper" (27).

Fliegelman sees Franklin's account "of the fortunate fall of yet another prodigal son" as a reflection of antipatriarchal tendencies running rampant within the colony, which validated youth as a time of education and exploration rather than subjugation (107, 109). Also illustrating Locke's optimistic view of human development as experiential, the first part of the *Autobiography* implicitly challenges assumptions about the importance of a father's influence and authority in forming a son's character.

Franklin's personal animus toward authority helps explain the mystery of why he even became a "Founding Father." He was, after all, much older and had an established reputation. Moreover, he was an Anglophile with aristocratic and imperialist leanings, and was one of many Americans in the 1760s loyal to England and the king. Gordon Wood has termed him "one of the most loyal of all" (48). Why then did this "least likely of revolutionaries," who once imagined Pennsylvania a royal colony with himself as royal governor, reverse himself (47, 49)? The ostensible reason was the Stamp Act, but the underlying explanation is that he was denied a role in imperial politics. In short, Franklin appears to have been guilty of sour grapes! Thwarted as in his youth by "arbitrary power," Franklin seized upon the Revolution with a vengeance.

It is evident from his *Autobiography* that Franklin did stage his own personal "revolution" at an early age and that this legacy remained with him all his life. Certainly it makes more comprehensible his emphasis on the self-made man as a reaction to his self-made orphanhood. It also explains his tendency to equate his own personal odyssey toward identity with that of the emerging nation. Sacvan Bercovitch recognizes this, suggesting: "Through all his provisional *personae*, Franklin, as even his first readers saw, assumes an identity representative of the rising nation. The link between the Franklins of the particular moments in his career and the 'essential' Franklin is the *exemplum* of corporate selfhood, ascending from dependence to dominance" (234). What is most interesting about this identification is its reciprocity. Just as Franklin mythologizes himself to give identity to the nation, he mythologizes the nation to create an identity for himself. It is an ingenious solution to the problem of orphanhood and a recapitulation of Puritan strategies that collapses the private into the public self.

But the identification of the rebellious son with the revolutionary nation was complicated by the previous identification of the "son" with the "father," the oppressor, King George. The most persuasive evidence that Franklin internalized the ideology of oppression exemplified by the "bad parent" lies in his neocolonial attitudes toward Indians and immigrants. Although Franklin professes commitment to the ideals of republicanism, he is not always consistent, and his disturbing expressions of racism, xenophobia, and economic elitism indicate that his lifelong "aversion to arbitrary power" has "stuck" as both a negative and a positive standard.

In "On Claims to the Soil of America" (1773), a letter version of "An Edict by the King of Prussia" which succinctly satirizes the colony's grievances against England, Franklin uses the prior occupancy of the New World by the Indians as an argument to challenge the legitimacy of British claims to property and ownership of the colonies: "Now the Fact is well known, that Britain had not a foot of Land in New-England; and that when the first Settlers went into that Country, they found it possessed by various Tribes of Indians, from whom they either purchased or conquered what they now enjoy" (227). That he is also impugning by logical implication the legitimacy of colonial claims to Indian lands is an issue he neatly bypasses. Despite his sensitivity to Indian culture and to the injustices committed against the Indians, Franklin blithely tosses off Indian property rights as a matter of little consequence in his analysis of population growth, "Observations Concerning the Increase of Mankind, Peopling of

Countries, &c." (1751): "The *Europeans* found *America* as fully settled as it well could be by Hunters; yet these having large tracts, were easily prevailed on to part with Portions of Territory to the new Comers, who did not much interfere with the Natives in Hunting, and furnish'd them with many Things they wanted" (368; italics in original). As in the justifications written by his Puritan forebears, Franklin's assumption is that the colonists will make better (i.e., more civilized) use of the land than the Indians.

Even an apparently sympathetic text such as "A Narrative of the Late Massacres" (1764), which protested the massacre of a peaceful community of Indians (the remains of the Six Nations) by a band of frontiersmen, is tinged with racism. Franklin attacks the notion that all Indians are alike because they look alike by distinguishing between the Six Nations, who have kept faith with the English and have "Notions of Honour," and the "Rum-debauched, Trader-corrupted Vagabonds and Thieves on Sasquehannah and the Ohio, at present in Arms against us" (803). But he clearly judges their differences on his own culture-bound terms. That he regards them in general as an inferior civilization is obvious in such passages as the following: "This [the massacre] is done by no civilized Nation in Europe. Do we come to America to learn and practise the Manners of *Barbarians*? But this, *Barbarians* as they are, they practise against their Enemies only, not against their Friends" (804). Moreover, the *Narrative* is implicated in capitalist ideology, employing emotional rhetoric that would appeal to a middle-class, Christian audience who appropriated Indian lands and wished to maintain the status quo rather than to express genuine sympathy for the dispossessed Indians (Mulford 347).

In fairness, however, one should acknowledge a post-Revolutionary document, "Remarks Concerning the Savages of North America" (1784), in which Franklin shows himself to be aware not only of the principles of cultural relativism but of the abuses of capitalism: "Savages we call them, because their Manners differ from ours, which we think the Perfection of Civility; they think the same of theirs. Perhaps, if we could examine the Manners of different Nations with Impartiality, we should find no People so rude, as to be without any Rules of Politeness; nor any so polite, as not to have some Remains of Rudeness" (96). He praises the Indians for their politeness, hospitality, generosity, and even their manliness, contrasting their virtues with the defects of his own culture, such as its materialism, as illustrated in an anecdote about cheating the Indians in the purchase of beaver. Moreover, his stand during the Constitutional Convention against property qualifications for voting and holding office suggests a more genuine commitment to principles of republicanism than that of the other Founding Fathers, and casts at least a shadow of a doubt over the political justification for appropriating Indian lands. For example, in 1776 Franklin proposed a resolution to the Pennsylvania constitution that would give the state the right to discourage individuals from amassing property because they would thus infringe the happiness of others (Lemay, "Franklin...," 332).

The point is that Franklin's attitude toward the Indians cannot be reduced to a simple formula. A careful reading of his writings on the Indians suggests that he was ultimately interested in manipulating both their positive and negative qualities to promote his own values and the welfare of the nation. This is perhaps nowhere more apparent than in his comments on immigrants and foreigners in which the Indians play the role of the baseline. For instance, in an effort to analyze why some nationalities are lazier than others, he implies an equation between Indians and indolence, whites and industry: "The proneness of human Nature to a life of ease, of freedom from care and labour appears strongly in the little success that has hitherto attended every attempt to civilize our American Indians in their present way of living, almost all their Wants are supplied by the spontaneous Productions of nature, with the addition of very little labour, if hunting and fishing may indeed be called labour when Game is plenty" (Letter to Peter Collinson, 470).

That Franklin pretends to praise the Indians for their "few but natural wan*s and those easily supplied," which contrast with our "infinite Artificial wants, no less craving than those of Nature, and much more difficult to satisfy," seems even more hypocritical in view of the fact that he elsewhere advocates controlling the Indians through trade by manipulating their desire for rum and other luxuries (471). His attitude seems to reflect an uneasy mixture of irony and insincerity, as evidenced in such statements as: "if it be the Design of Providence to extirpate these Savages in order to make room for Cultivators of the Earth, it seems not improbable that Rum may be the appointed Means. It has already annihilated all the Tribes who formerly inhabited the Sea-coast" (*Autobiography*, 135–136).

The ambivalence underlying Franklin's attitude toward the Indians typifies his attitude toward immigrants as well. For example, in his letter to Peter Collinson, he praises the Germans as hard workers, even though "those who come hither are generally of the most ignorant Stupid Sort" (472). One gets the feeling that Franklin almost wishes they weren't so industrious since he fears their numbers and influence and urges increased efforts to assimilate them into Anglo-American culture. Obviously, Franklin's desire to embrace the "cultivators of the earth" and displace the savages does not extend to all immigrants, and he draws a distinction between those he wishes to adopt as Americans and those he groups with the Indians as aliens. In his most startling eruption of racist and xenophobic invective, Franklin makes clear that he regards certain races — i.e., the Negroes and the Orientals — as far less desirable than the Indians.

The conclusion of "Observations," a list of twenty-five principles concerning population growth, is splenetic in its invective toward those who embody cultural, racial, and ethnic difference: "why should the *Palatine boors* be suffered to swarm into our Settlements, and by herding together establish their Language and Manners to the Exclusion of ours? Why should *Pennsylvania*, founded by the *English*, become a Colony of *Aliens*, who will shortly be so numerous as to Germanize us instead of our Anglifying them, and will never adopt our Language or Customs, any more than they can acquire our Complexion" (374).

Franklin then goes on to distinguish among the peoples of the world on the basis of their color: Africans are black or "tawny," Asians "chiefly tawny," Indians "wholly" tawny, most Europeans "swarthy," whereas Germans and the English "make the principal body of White People on the Face of the Earth." Franklin laments the fact "that the Number of purely white People in the world is proportionally very small" and wishes "their Numbers were increased." Noting that we are brightening America by clearing it of woods, he asks, "why should we in the Sight of Superior Beings, darken its People? Why increase the Sons of *Africa*, by Planting them in *America*, where we have so fair an Opportunity, by excluding all Blacks and Tawneys, of increasing the lovely White and Red? But perhaps I am partial to the Complexion of my Country, for such Kind of Partiality is natural to Mankind" (374; italics in original). Resonating with racism and ethnocentrism, this passage reveals that Franklin believes in his own version of Jefferson's "natural aristocracy" and racial hierarchy, which ranks the Negroes even lower than Indians on the racial scale.

In evaluating Franklin's attitude toward immigrants, it is important, just as in the case of the Indians, to consider each document within the context of his other writings on the same subject to uncover the complexity and even the contradictions. For example, Franklin's much later "Information to Those Who Would Remove to America" (1784) is a promotional tract *encouraging* immigration on the basis of its potential benefit to the nation ("people do not inquire concerning a Stranger, *What is he?* but, *What can he do?* If he has any useful art, he is welcome" (976–977; italics in original). But built into this overarching capitalist criterion for acceptance are hidden biases. The fact that so many of the immigrants pouring into the nation were indigent alarmed him, and he was willing to embrace only those who showed promise of success. Only certain kinds of Europeans fulfilled his requirements, and it is revealing that Franklin's examples fall into this category: e.g., "Multitudes of poor People from England, Ireland, Scotland and Germany have by this means in a few Years become wealthy Farmers" (978). Thus, as in the case of the Indians, Franklin's attitude toward immigrants seems to have been shaped primarily by practical considerations—those who possess qualities that will further the growth of the republic are adoptable, whereas those who undermine the prosperity of the established order are orphaned, like the Indians who threaten the stability of the "family."[10]

For Crèvecoeur as well as Franklin, economic considerations linked the destinies of Indians and immigrants in the new republic and determined their status as children or orphans. The explicit connection for Crèvecoeur was the land, and he saw the relationship in strictly sacrificial terms. The clear if unstated message behind Crèvecoeur's *Letters from an American Farmer* (1782) is that the Indians must surrender their lands to the immigrants and the agrarian ideal. In a region between border and coast, Crèvecoeur situates the American dream and his hero, the American farmer. He erects a mythology around the farmer and agriculture as emblems of civilization, clearly echoing the significance of Puritan imagery of "planting" and "transplanting" in the wilderness.

Through his spokesman, James, Crèvecoeur rhapsodizes about America as a land of opportunity, as a utopia that has the magical power to effect not only an economic but a cultural and even a spiritual transformation based on the ownership and cultivation of property. According to Crèvecoeur, the purchase of two hundred acres of land has the power to produce the following transcendent state in the immigrant: "What an epocha in this man's life! He is become a freeholder, from perhaps a German boor—he is now an American, a Pennsylvanian, an English subject. He is naturalized, his name is enrolled with those of the other citizens of the province. Instead of being a vagrant, he has a place of residence; he is called the inhabitant of such a country, or such a district, and for the first time in his life counts for something; for hitherto he has been a *cypher*" (78–79).

In other words, ownership of land confers upon the "cipher"—the immigrant *qua* vagrant *qua* orphan—not only a home but a sense of *being*, as if he did not even exist before arriving here. Crèvecoeur credits America with giving the immigrant a new identity by giving him land as a mother satisfies the basic needs of her child: "What attachment can a poor European emigrant have for a country where he had nothing? The knowledge of the language, the love of a few kindred as poor as himself, were the only cords that tied him: his country is now that which gives him land, bread, protection, and consequence: *Ubi panis ibi patria*, is the motto of all emigrants" (54). Building on her interpretation of the land as a maternal symbol, Annette Kolodny places the *Letters* within the context of the "American pastoral experience, the metaphor of the land as woman. The landscape experienced as feminine allowed, indeed invited, the newly arrived immigrant to feel himself reborn, transformed into something that had never been possible in the bosom of a cruel 'stepdame'" (54).

How can the adopted child not be loyal to this nurturing new mother: "What love can he entertain for a country where his existence was a burthen to him; if he is a generous good man, the love of this new adoptive parent will sink deep in his heart" (77–78). The farmer even imagines himself adopted, reborn into another family. Crèvecoeur links "being received into the broad lap of our great *Alma Mater*" with the national destiny, as if it created "a new race of men" who would form a utopian community reminiscent of Winthrop's "city upon a hill": "Americans are the western pilgrims, who are carrying along with them that great mass of arts, science, vigour, and industry which began long since in the east; they will finish the great circle" (55). Like Winthrop, Crèvecoeur also invokes the family model, but his emphasis is entirely different. Crèvecoeur foreshadows the ethos of the Revolution by rejecting the hierarchical model of society to which the Puritans subscribed and advocates instead a fraternal model in which the adoptable immigrant shares the land and its bounty equally with his "brothers" who have preceded him "and becomes as it were a member of the family" (77).

The culmination of the immigrant's labor is that he is eventually able to purchase the magical two hundred acres, which ensure his adoption into the American "family." Clearly property is tied up with identity in Crèvecoeur's mind—the orphaned immigrant is born to a new Self that he acquires from his new parent, America, who gives him a new name, *American*, and what he most needs to survive, land. What Crèvecoeur fails to acknowledge is that the immigrant acquires this land, and with it a new identity, only at the expense of the Indian, whose land he seizes and whose indigenous identity he appropriates. The fact that over the course of colonial history so much rhetoric is expended in *denying* the identification with "the savages" merely reveals how deeply implicated the settlers were in *all* aspects of Indian identity, especially their "nativeness."

The denial of this reality is reflected in Crèvecoeur's exaggerated fear of Indian influence, despite the fact that he, like Franklin, also expresses admiration for them. Crèvecoeur warns against the dangers of the woods and the frontier, for even if settlers move west with the intent to establish agricultural communities, they inevitably become hunters and degenerate to a savage state: "once hunters, farewell to the plough. The chase renders them ferocious, gloomy, and unsociable; a hunter wants no neighbour, he rather hates them, because he dreads the competition. In a little time their success in the woods makes them neglect their tillage" (66–67). The worst of what Crèvecoeur calls "our bad people . . . are those who have degenerated altogether into the hunting state"; in short, frontiersmen who have become like the Indians. "As old ploughmen and new men of the woods, as Europeans and new made Indians, they contract the vices of both; they adopt the moroseness and ferocity of a native, without his mildness or even his industry" (69).

The Revolution forces an identity crisis upon James, who must now choose between his family loyalties to his birth parent, England, and the parent that has newly adopted him: "If I attach myself to the Mother Country, which is 3000 miles from me, I become what is called an enemy to my own region; if I follow the rest of my countrymen, I become opposed to our ancient masters: both extremes appear equally dangerous to a person of so little weight and consequence as I am, whose energy and example are to no avail" (287–288).

Confused and disillusioned, James falls back upon the immigrant experience and the agrarian ideal and flees westward toward the frontier, which he believes offers him the best chance of reestablishing his identity as a farmer in an agricultural community. Of necessity, he now romanticizes the Indians as the children of nature: "They most certainly are much more closely connected with nature than we are; they are her immediate children, the inhabitants of the woods are her undefiled offspring" (308).

But he cannot shake himself completely free of his old apprehensions. Aware through captivity narratives of the susceptibility of white children to Indian influences, James secretly fears that despite the fact that he has chosen to live with a peaceful tribe of Indians, his family, particularly his children, will succumb to savage ways. His solution is agriculture: "I have but one remedy to prevent this great evil; and that is, to employ them in the labour of the fields, as much as I can; I am even resolved to make their daily subsistence depend altogether on it. As long as we keep ourselves busy in tilling the earth, there is no fear of any of us becoming wild; it is the chase and the food it procures that have this strange effect" (316).

James's fears illustrate the extent to which Crèvecoeur equated agrarianism with the formation of civilization and American identity. James worries that both he and his family could turn into the dark Other and equates survival of the self, as well as the country, with a specific way of life and a specific environment (Regis, 126, 130–131). The inland freehold farmer is the prototypical American, and this prototype excludes not only Indians but immigrants who fail to conform to the agricultural ideal of owning and cultivating land (Regis, 126). In other words, a man does not become an American, or an adopted child of the American family, simply by emigrating. He must own and cultivate land or run the risk of cultural orphanhood, like the Indian.

In welcoming Americans to the classless, egalitarian society he imagines America to be, Crèvecoeur, like Franklin, is nevertheless guilty of his own form of prejudice because he clearly favors those immigrants who make the best farmers, i.e. the Germans, followed by the Scotch, with the Irish at the bottom of the list (81–82).[11] In order to understand the wave of anti-immigration sentiment that erupted in the 1790s, it is important to recognize that Crèvecoeur's apparently wholehearted embrace of immigrants was in fact highly qualified, contingent upon their conformity to an agricultural ideal and a code of socioeconomic behavior that harked back to Puritan times. Crèvecoeur's answer to his own question, what is an American, was far more prescriptive than descriptive and contained the seeds of discrimination against those who, in deviating from the civilized norm, became identified with the Indians as purveyors of alien values. In fact, American leaders tried to deny asylum to immigrants they suspected of still being loyal to their country's values and institutions and sought to replace Indians with "proper" Americans on their native soil (Berkhofer, 139).

As Crèvecoeur's biases suggest, territorial conflict was not the only factor in the complex relationship of the white community to the Indians. The Indian served as the scapegoat that protected the familial identity of the "children" of the republic and also was the model for immigrants and other dangerous outsiders who joined him in collective orphanhood. Ironically, the Founding

Fathers revived the colonial drama that Crèvecoeur naively thought they had rewritten, changing only the cast. The "fathers" were now playing the role of the neocolonial oppressors and the Indians the role not only of scapegoats but of neocolonial orphans who, by surrendering their land and with it their identity, made possible the adoption of elite, property-owning immigrants into the family of the republic. Clearly the example of King George was not so much rejected as ingested, and this identification had far-reaching effects on attitudes toward immigrants as well as Indians.

Prior to the American Revolution, colonial attitudes toward immigration could best be described as ambivalent and even contradictory. While immigrants were sought after as laborers and settlers to increase revenue, expand borders, and defend the frontier, they were also denigrated as bad elements that jeopardized the economic and religious stability of the colonies. Legislation reflected the specific fears: "Colonial immigration restrictions, it will be noticed, took no account of the nationality of newcomers. Instead, religious affiliation, economic status, and moral standing were the yardsticks by which the desirability of immigrants was measured" (M. Jones, 37).

Whereas the American Revolution brought the colonies' diverse ethnic groups together in an impressive display of the kind of unity idealized by Crèvecoeur, that unity was nevertheless prone to cracks and fissures. By the time of the Revolution, the population of the colonies had become far more ethnically diverse. During the eighteenth century, there was a fourfold increase in the colonial population, with emigrants coming here for such diverse reasons as poverty and economic oppression, religious persecution, and banishment in the case of social outcasts. Although the population of New England was still relatively homogeneous and primarily of English origin, with but a sprinkling of Scots-Irish, Scots, Huguenots, and Jews, the population of the middle and Southern colonies was distinctly heterogeneous, with the English comprising only about fifty per cent. In Pennsylvania, those of English origin numbered only about one third, barely more than the Germans. Large minorities of Germans, Scots-Irish, and Scots, along with Negroes, diluted the predominantly English character of the Southern population.

Despite these regional differences (as well as internal friction between the ethnic groups), the influence of English institutions and language that resulted from "the overwhelming predominance of Englishmen during the first two generations of settlement" drew the colonies together and created conditions propitious for Revolution (M. Jones, 31). But underlying the façade of cohesiveness, there were tensions waiting to erupt, and they lodged in minds as illustrious as those of the Founding Fathers, such as Franklin, who resented the German immigrants, those "Palatine boors."

It is significant that the reason for the xenophobia directed toward the Germans and other immigrant groups was often economic rather than religious or cultural. The largest single group of eighteenth-century immigrants were the Scots-Irish (approximately 250,000) who left Ireland because of discontent with the land system. Because of their numbers and their poverty far more than their religion, they were reluctantly received in both New England and Pennsylvania, which were suffering from the inflation and scarcity of food that plagued the early eighteenth century. In short, many of the British, Irish, Scots-Irish, and German immigrants who came to these shores were driven by want and destitution, which placed distinct economic pressure on the new nation.

It is important to recognize that the extent to which the Puritans' policy toward the poor established a precedent for the xenophobia that emerged so forcibly during the aftermath of the Revolution. According to Douglas Lamar Jones's history of the eighteenth-century poor, the Massachusetts settlement and Poor Laws of 1637, 1646, and 1659 basically stipulated that only those who were members of the community were eligible for poor relief. "Strangers" were not automatically admitted to the community, had to apply for residency, and could remain for only three weeks except by permission of the Council and two magistrates, after which they would be "warned out." Furthermore, there was a three-month residency requirement before they were entitled to poor relief.

Obviously the purpose of this legislation was twofold: to minimize the economic burden to the community by keeping out the poor, and to protect the community from the dangerous influences of strangers (i.e., foreigners, dissenters, etc.). Moreover, the responsibility for care of the poor fell to families, who were naturally more inclined to take care of their own indigent relatives than to look after outsiders. But in the eighteenth century families began shirking their responsibilities, and a custodial system of poor relief that consisted of a combination of almshouses and compensation to families for care of the poor replaced the traditional system. With this gradual shift from the private to the public sector, legislation against "transients" focused particularly on the poor. In 1701 the settlement law extended the residency requirement for poor relief to twelve months and set the standard for the remainder of the century.

Residency also became harder to obtain and depended on the consent of the town. This legislation was directed not only at transients with legal residences elsewhere in Massachusetts but also at foreign immigrants, and it had the effect of equating "outsiders" with the poor. Jones summarizes: "Practically speaking, this right to select town members in mid-eighteenth century Massachusetts was the power to exclude the transient poor. The warning-out system — the enforcement arm of the settlement law — became the focal point for town officials and migrants alike, as transiency and poor relief became identified with each other" (D. Jones, 176).

Although the settlement laws and warning-out system were originally intended to exclude only paupers, wealth had become an explicit criterion for residency by the late eighteenth century (181). Certainly the influence of Franklin's philosophy, with its emphasis on worldly success, the accumulation of wealth, and the self-made man is apparent in the thrust of this legislation. The Massachusetts settlement law of 1789 "contained an explicit test of residence based on wealth. In addition to the usual methods of gaining legal residence by approbation of the town, birth, marriage, the law provided two standards of residence based on property ownership" (D. Jones, 188–189). Clearly those least likely to own property or wealth were immigrants, and the Massachusetts legislation, despite the liberalization of its attitude toward poor relief in 1794, epitomized the xenophobic posture of the federal government during the 1790s.

Of course, some of the prejudice against immigrants was based on religion. Another "father" of his country, John Adams, perpetuated with Paine the long-standing tradition of anti-Catholicism, warning against "popery" in his *Dissertation of the Canon and Feudal Law* (1765) and regarding Catholicism as a threat to the nation because of its powerful influence and ties to foreign governments. Adams took great pride in the size of his prolific family, which spanned five generations and attributed its vitality to a combination of "industry, frugality, regularity and religion," especially the last: "What has preserved this race of Adamses in all their ramifications, in such numbers, health, peace, comfort, and mediocrity? I believe it is religion, without which they would have been rakes, fops, sots, gamblers, starved with hunger, frozen with cold, scalped by Indians" (quoted in Drinnon, 73)

Adams is obviously not referring to religion in general but to the "right" religion, Protestantism. The widespread opposition to Catholicism had the effect of unifying a large portion of the population around a single issue, much as it did during the early colonial period when the various sects agreed only on their opposition to Catholicism. The fact that Adams regards his proper Protestant family as a microcosm of the nation suggests the degree to which the family model served as a marker of hereditary inclusion and exclusion in the minds of the Founding Fathers. The children of his family, he states, "multiplied like the sands on the seashore or the stars in the milky way, to such a degree that I know not who there is in America to whom I am not related. My family, I believe, have cut down more trees in America than any other name!" (quoted in Drinnon, 73).

The major difference in anti-Catholic prejudice before and after the Revolution is that the basis became more political than religious, as Ray Billington points out in *The Protestant Crusade*. Whereas Catholicism had always been a patriotic as well as a religious concern to the Puritans in both England and the colonies, it acquired a fresh impetus in the eighteenth century because of foreign wars, alliances, and revolutions. For example, in 1690 with the outbreak of French and Spanish wars, anti-Catholicism increased as the threat to national existence was perceived. More restrictions were placed on Catholics, and only non-Catholic immigration was encouraged. In the mid-eighteenth century after war with France had broken out, Catholics were suspected of plotting with the French and Indians, and during the Revolution the paranoia shifted to a suspected alliance between the English king and the Catholics.

Anti-Catholicism was too deeply rooted to expire after the Revolution. Despite the fact that federal and state constitutions codified religious tolerance, subtle ways were found to exclude Catholics and aliens from public office. During the 1790s, bigotry against Catholics was fed by political events in Europe, which resulted in an unprecedented wave of immigration. The French Revolution prompted an influx of refugees from France and Santo Domingo, followed by British and Irish radicals, and the fact that so many of these immigrants were Catholics seeking political asylum generated a parallel wave of anti-Catholic sentiment in the new republic.

The Revolution had supposedly given new meaning to the concept of America as an asylum for fugitives from tyranny, as Paine had idealistically characterized it in *Common Sense*. But while America was professedly hospitable to immigrants and the Congress enacted the Naturalization Act of 1790 requiring only a two-year period of residency before citizenship could be obtained, the Federalists became increasingly apprehensive about revolutionaries and radicals during the succeeding decade and tightened restrictions. The notorious Alien and Sedition Acts enacted by the Federalist Congress in 1798 under the presidency of John Adams increased the naturalization period to fourteen years; authorized the President to expel dangerous aliens from the country and to banish or arrest them in wartime; and made assembly, conspiracy, or riot crimes against the government punishable by fines and imprisonment. This oppressive legislation reflected both Federalist resentment of aliens who were loyal to Jefferson and the fear that aliens might influence foreign policy and embroil Americans in European conflicts (Billington, 23).

Thomas Jefferson and the Republicans denounced the Alien and Sedition Acts as an encroachment on states' rights, encouragement of executive tyranny, a threat to civil liberties, and a betrayal of the ideals of the Revolution, but they too were ambivalent about immigration, on the one hand wanting to welcome victims of tyranny and on the other fearing the influence of royalist emigrés accustomed to despots and reared by the principles of absolutism. Jefferson had even predicted their effect on the body politic would be to "infuse in it their spirit, warp and bias its directions, and render it a heterogeneous, incoherent, distracted mass" (quoted in M. Jones, 68). Nevertheless, after Jefferson came to power in 1801, the Republican Congress changed the residency requirement back to five years and allowed the Alien and Sedition Acts to expire.

But a dangerous precedent had been set. Although naturalization laws permitted the adoption of immigrants, the Alien and Sedition Acts made sure that only those immigrants who met certain standards for citizenship were eligible. The result was that although naturalization had both broadened and politicized the Puritan definition of adoption, it still tended to remain the privilege of the elect, an economic elite who could afford property and a spiritual elite who could demonstrate their conversion to the ideology of the republic. Even with the liberalization of the laws under Jefferson, the mere distinction between native-born and naturalized citizens signified an emotionally charged difference between "natural" and "adopted" children that fed the nativist frenzy during the mid-nineteenth century.

In summary, the newly formed nation experienced a crisis in the aftermath of the Revolution whereby the sons of the Founding Fathers were confronted with the challenge of identity formation in the absence of a common enemy such as King George. Despite the authority of the Constitution, which was intended to control disruptive behavior, the sons experienced a lack of purpose and showed signs of dissipating their energies in just the kind of competition, materialism, and acquisitiveness that would make a mockery of Crèvecoeur's idealized fraternal community. In other words, the sons were losing sight of the identity conferred upon them by the fathers, and Indians and immigrants served as convenient scapegoats for this crisis. By orphaning these scapegoats from American culture, the sons could rid themselves once and for all of the legacy of orphanhood, grow from adolescents to adults, and become fathers of the republic's next generation.

During the early nineteenth century, the family of the republic continued to express its ideology in metaphorical terms, with the child as a symbol of inclusion, as distinct from the excluded orphan, whose spectral presence began in the early nineteenth century to haunt the literary imagination.

CHAPTER FOUR

Tales of Captivity and Adoption

> The white man's God cannot love our people or
> He would protect them. They seem to be orphans
> who can look nowhere for help.
> —CHIEF SEATTLE

As the previous chapter explained, the xenophobia that manifested itself at the end of the eighteenth century was inseparable from racist attitudes toward the Indians. For the new nation struggling in the aftermath of the Revolution to define the meaning of America, the Indians represented a threat from within whereas the immigrants represented a threat from without. Both also served the purpose of scapegoats who, through their differences, consolidated the unity and power of the "natural aristocracy" — the white Anglo-Saxon Protestant landholders who constituted the dominant culture. Displacing their postrevolutionary identification with orphanhood onto these scapegoats, the republican "fathers" resembled the oppressive monarch they had recently overthrown and institutionalized that resemblance in the form of the federal government. Both the dispossession of the Indians and the repression of the immigrants reflected the neocolonial posture of an insecure and frangible nation struggling to assert its identity, like an adolescent striving for manhood.

As the citizens of the republic struggled to carve out a new identity for themselves as Americans rather than colonial subjects, certain novels of the early nineteenth century expressed the dream life of the republic, transforming the quest for identity into a family drama that used the metaphor of orphanhood to raise the question of what it means to be American. The first major novel in this category is Charles Brockden Brown's *Edgar Huntly; or, Memoirs of a Sleepwalker* (1799), in which the orphanhood of the protagonist encodes tensions surrounding national identity formation by making his identity depend upon the annihilation of Indians and immigrants.

Born in 1771 in Philadelphia, Brown is widely touted as the first major American novelist, an epithet he earned not only because he published six novels in three years (1798–1801) but because he set himself the task of forging a national literature. His first novel, *Wieland; or, The Transformation* (1798), he subtitled *An American Tale*, which represents an attempt to adapt European literary influences, particularly the gothic, to a specifically American context. In 1799 Brown published three more novels, one of which, *Edgar Huntly*, is his most deliberate and self-conscious attempt to write a distinctively "American" novel. He clearly expresses that intention in his prefatory notice "To the Public":

> America has opened new views to the naturalist and the politician, but has seldom furnished themes to the moral painter. That new springs of action and new motives to curiosity should operate, — that the field of investigation, opened to us by our country, should differ essentially from those which exist in Europe, — may be readily conceived. The sources of amusement to the fancy and instruction to the heart, that are peculiar to ourselves, are equally numerous and inexhaustible. It is the purpose of this work to profit by some of these sources; to exhibit a series of adventures, growing out of the condition of our country and connected with one of the most common and most wonderful diseases or affections of the human frame. (29)

Renouncing the classic European literary devices of "puerile superstition and exploded manners; Gothic castles and chimeras" for "calling forth the passions and engaging the sympathy of the reader," Brown adduces instead "incidents of Indian hostility, and the perils of the western wilderness [as] far more suitable... for a native of America" (29).

The result, according to Leslie Fiedler's classic analysis, is that in *Edgar Huntly* "the American gothic, that is to say, the heathen, unredeemed wilderness and not the decaying monuments of a dying class, nature and not society becomes the symbol of evil" (147). On this basis, Fiedler lauds *Edgar Huntly* over *Wieland* as "the most successful and characteristic of his gothic romances" (156). Whereas *Wieland* depicts madness and malevolence within an idealized, agrarian society that embodies the values of the Enlightenment, *Edgar Huntly* shifts the locus of the irrational to the frontier, specifically to the wilderness, an alien environment teeming with Indians, wild animals, and the hostile forces of nature that epitomizes the American experience.

Considering Brown's professed chauvinist intention in writing it and its obvious indebtedness to the captivity narratives, *Edgar Huntly* would presumably invite the kind of political interpretation given to Brown's other novels, particularly *Wieland*, which Jane Tompkins reads "not as an object to be analyzed in modern psychological or aesthetic terms, but politically, as a plea for the restoration of civic authority in a post-Revolutionary age" (*Sensational Designs*, 61). But in her analysis of the "cultural work" Brown's novels perform, Tompkins inexplicably ignores *Edgar Huntly*, his most indigenous novel, which uses the wilderness and its inhabitants to address the issue of national identity.

Nevertheless, Tompkins's analysis of *Wieland* is relevant to a cultural interpretation of *Edgar Huntly*. In the story, Brown chronicles the descent of Wieland and his sister Clara, who represent Enlightenment ideals, into degrees and kinds of madness, as a result of irrational forces that intrude upon their agrarian utopia. Tompkins treats *Wieland* as an implicit critique of Jeffersonian democracy and of Republican confidence in the people's ability to govern themselves with a minimum of institutionalized authority. Just as the Reign of Terror cast a dark shadow over the ideals of the French Revolution, Wieland's sudden eruption into homicidal mania plunges his utopia into chaos.

Tompkins attributes the catastrophe to the "vacuum of authority" that forces Wieland to invent "a source of authority outside himself whose 'commands' he feels bound to obey," and also to the guilt-ridden legacy of Calvinism: "The Wielands' catastrophe does not stem from anything they have done or neglected to do, but from their history, which is to say from their position as *orphans* of civilization in the New World" (54; italics mine). The fact that Wieland and his sister Clara were orphaned in childhood suggests both social isolation and alienation from the fundamental sources of identity, and their orphanhood is consistent with the extreme suggestibility that proves their downfall.

Brown made clear in his other activities and writings his interest in politics. He regularly attended political gatherings, wrote political pamphlets, and even designed a plan for a utopia. Raised as a Quaker, he almost became a lawyer but veered toward literature instead and developed a didactic theory of narrative that was explicitly directed toward social and political change. For example, in "Walstein's School of History" (1799) Brown, through a fictional alter ego, contemplates the "ways in which genius and virtue may labor for the public good" and compares the rhetorical efficacy of argumentation and narration in bringing about political change (150). He concludes, "an eloquent narration, a model of right conduct, is the highest province of benevolence" (151).

Political statements were a dominant theme in American writing during the Revolutionary and post-Revolutionary decades, and Brown's novels epitomized the tendency to encode ideology in literary texts (Tompkins, 44–45). The fact that Brown sent a copy of *Wieland* to Jefferson when he was vice president supports interpretations of the novel as a disguised political tract. Appalled by the aftermath of the French Revolution, Brown was politically a conservative who believed in the fallibility of mankind and the need for strong governmental control. After giving up fiction because of the poor response to his novels, Brown turned directly to a series of political pamphlets that reflected his conservatism, particularly his distrust of and aversion to "aliens" within (Negroes and Indians) and outside (immigrants) the nation's borders, which led to his support of the Alien and Sedition Acts.[1]

If the characters of *Wieland* are "orphans of civilization in the New World," Edgar Huntly, the orphaned protagonist who succumbs to savage and foreign influences, is even more bereft than they. Because of the novel's preoccupation with mental states (and the predisposition of certain twentieth-century literary critics reared on Freud), *Edgar Huntly* has traditionally inspired Freudian and even Jungian interpretations that minimize its historical context. For example, Richard Slotkin writes, "Like the protagonist of the Puritan confession, Edgar Huntly is a hero isolated in space and time; his acts relate essentially to the drama of his self-discovery and only tangentially to social conditions and issues" (*Regeneration*, 376). Yet the novel is most comprehensible as a political allegory.

A Gothic murder mystery set in the Pennsylvania wilderness, the novel features an almost hopelessly convoluted plot, implausible contrivances and coincidences, and an endless sequence of mistaken, merged, and ambiguous identities or "doubles." The novel's complexity and ambiguity goaded Fiedler to describe it as "a charmingly, maddenly disorganized book, not so much written as dreamed" (144). To summarize a plot that is nearly impossible to summarize, Edgar is a young man who lives with his uncle and sisters in the woods of Solesbury [sic] in Bucks County, Pennsylvania. He is also an orphan whose parents were massacred many years before by the Indians, an obvious trauma that left him with "lasting and terrific images in my fancy. I never looked upon or called up the image of a savage without shuddering" (165).

The form of the novel is epistolary, consisting of Edgar's letters to his betrothed, the sister of Waldegrave, his best friend, who was recently shot and killed under a large elm tree not far from Edgar's house. Feeling it his duty to try to apprehend the murderer of his friend and his fiancée's brother, Edgar returns one night to the scene of the crime and espies beneath the tree a man weeping and burying a mysterious object. When the man passes him by, Edgar realizes he is sleepwalking and also recognizes him as a laborer from a nearby farm who recently emigrated under mysterious circumstances from Ireland. Edgar leaps to the conclusion that this man, Clithero Edny, is Waldegrave's killer and that his somnambulism is a symptom of his guilty conscience. Most of the novel is taken up with Edgar's obsessive pursuit of Clithero during his nocturnal rambles through the wilderness. Edgar's desire for revenge quickly shifts from curiosity to compassion, and by the end of the novel he has come to identify so closely with Clithero that he has acquired Clithero's appearance, his habit of sleepwalking, and his wild, woodland ways.

Right from the beginning of the novel, Edgar's responses to Clithero are conditioned by the fact that Clithero is an "emigrant from Ireland," and it is largely on that basis that Edgar seizes upon Clithero as Waldegrave's murderer, although he acknowledges there is nothing in his character that arouses suspicion: "But, as I conned over the catalogue, I perceived that the only foreigner among us was Clithero. Our scheme was, for the most part, a patriarchal one. Each farmer was surrounded by his sons and kinsmen. There was an exception to the rule. Clithero was a stranger, whose adventures and character, previously to his coming hither, were unknown to us" (39).

There is clearly a value judgment implied in this passage—that the societal norm is a patriarchal family structure and that one who lives outside of that norm is an ungoverned (and ungovernable) character. It is noteworthy that Huntly even twists Clithero's positive qualities, such as his obvious "cultivation" and "the standard of his intellectual attainments," into grounds for suspicion about his motives for "abandoning" his country. There is also the intimation that an orphan such as Edgar, even though he is nominally attached to a family, is a renegade who, because he lacks the governing influence of a father, is susceptible to negative outside influences.

Edgar's prejudicial attitude toward one who has "come hither" is understandable within the context of the anti-Irish sentiment that was prevalent during the 1790s on the part of political conservatives, who frequently identified the Irish with savages and barbarians. The fact that the Irish population in eastern cities like New York and Brown's own Philadelphia supported the Republicans, "instinctively hated the Federalists as would-be aristocrats and tools of the British," and enjoyed staging rowdy mob protests did little to endear them to the federal government, and efforts to restrict enfranchisement by levying taxes on certificates of naturalization and to extend the waiting period for naturalization were directed largely against the Irish (M. Jones, 84). As Harrison Gray Otis of Massachusetts wrote, "If some means are not adopted to prevent the indiscriminate admission of wild Irishmen and others to the right of suffrage, there will soon be an end to liberty and property" (quoted in Jones, 86).

Moreover, through the nexus of anti-Catholicism, fear of the French in the wake of the French and Indian wars helped feed anti-Irish sentiment, especially in Pennsylvania because of its proximity to Canada. The Pennsylvania Council even considered forbidding Irish immigration to stem the flow of Catholics, but nothing was done until the outbreak of the Seven Years War when fear of French attack from Canada reached a peak. An avalanche of anti-Catholic legislation ensued in Pennsylvania, as a result of which Catholics were overtaxed and censored, forbidden to bear arms or serve in the militia, and registered in the colony so their activities could be observed (Billington, 13). The Alien and Sedition Acts were a direct response to the Irish insurrections, notably the Irish Rebellion of 1798, as well as the French menace (Billington, 23).

Given this xenophobic climate, the fact that Brown makes Clithero an *Irish* immigrant seems hardly coincidental. Not only does Clithero epitomize the alien but, as a madman, he embodies the forces of anarchy. As the novel progresses, the reader learns that although Clithero is not guilty of Waldegrave's murder, he did commit one back in Ireland and believes himself guilty of two more. Consumed with guilt and depression, Clithero exiles himself from his native Ireland to America, where he becomes orphaned from civilization as well as his country. An accusation from Edgar plunges him deeper into confusion, and he reverts to a barbaric state: "His scanty and coarse garb had been nearly rent away by brambles and thorns; his arms, bosom, and cheeks were overgrown and half concealed by hair. There was somewhat in his attitude and looks denoting more than anarchy of thoughts and passions. His rueful, ghastly, and immovable eyes testified not only that his mind was ravaged by despair, but that he was pinched with famine" (111).

Part of the novel's irony is that Edgar, who inexplicably identifies with Clithero and pursues him through the wilderness, comes more and more to resemble him. Like Clithero, Edgar also becomes orphaned from civilization, and the sleepwalking disorder they both share becomes a metaphor for the irrational state into which Edgar, as well as Clithero, descends. Edgar's transformation is so extreme that he even degenerates into bestiality and savagery. In one of the novel's most suspenseful and disturbing sequences, Edgar mysteriously awakens in a cave into which he has fallen while sleepwalking. Edgar describes it as a pitch-black "dungeon" and "tomb" in which he feels himself to be buried alive, but to a post-Freudian reader it suggests not only the unconscious but the womb (155–156). Prompted by mounting panic and inordinate hunger, Edgar squeezes his body through a narrow passageway, only to stare into the eyes of a panther. Edgar kills the panther with a tomahawk he conveniently found in the cave (Edgar is proud of his prowess with his own tomahawk, an *Indian* weapon) and then proceeds to *eat* the panther raw: "The first suggestion that occurred was to feed upon the carcass of this animal. My hunger had arrived at that pitch where all fastidiousness and scruples are at an end.... I will not shock you by relating the extremes to which dire necessity had driven me. I review this scene with loathing and horror" (160). In short, he "becomes" a wild animal through a primitive act of ingestion.[2]

The nature of Edgar's transformation into savagery is similar. He finally manages to find his way out of the cave, only to encounter four Indians guarding the entrance and a captive woman. He describes the "brawny and terrific figures" as "naked... uncouth figures [whose] mocassins... were adorned in a grotesque manner" and perceives them as alien to the point of constituting a foreign, even subhuman species. Edgar wonders, "Had some mysterious power snatched me from the earth, and cast me, in a moment, into the heart of the wilderness? Was I still in the vicinity of my parental habitation, or was I thousands of miles distant?" (164). In other words, his geographical removal serves as a metaphor for his psychological removal from civilization.

This episode in the novel is evocative of the captivity narratives that began to appear in New England during the seventeenth century and raised similar identity issues. The historical genesis of the captivity narratives was King Philip's War, but they continued well beyond it as the locus of hostilities shifted to the northern frontier where Indians from as far north as Canada allied themselves with the French and preyed upon the Puritans in southern New England. Puritan authors attempted to illustrate in their narratives the working of God's plan in their lives and community by imposing a metanarrative of sin, punishment, and redemption.

Richard Slotkin believes that the migration experience was the indirect inspiration and that the rupture of the families caused by capture played upon the Puritan imagination as a symbolic reenactment of the colony's rupture with England. He maintains that the captivity narratives expressed the Puritans' guilt about leaving England and exposing themselves and their children to the corrupting influences of the wilderness by casting the Indians as "the instruments of God for the chastisement of his guilty people" (*Regeneration,* 98–99).

Whatever their motivation, captivity narratives were ideally suited for expressing didactic sentiments and venting vindictive feelings, and the formidable Puritan minister Cotton Mather, who dedicated himself at the turn of the century to reviving the orthodoxy of the "backsliding" Puritans, used them to play upon their emotions. It was obvious to him that demonization of the heathen Indians (and the papistical French) was a fruitful rallying point, so in *Decennium Luctuosum* (1699) he describes "the Dark places of New-England, where the Indians had their Unapproachable Kennels... of Cruelty" and narrates in the most lurid terms several stories of captivity that focus on the killing of weeping, screaming children who were tortured before their brains were dashed out (597–598). Similarly, in *Good Fetch'd out of Evil* (1676), he recounts how the captives were "detained with the *Indians* in their horrid and howling *Wigwams*... among those *Dragons of the Wilderness*" and interprets the eventual escape or rescue of the more fortunate as evidence of Divine Providence (4).

The religious intention of the captivity narratives diminished, along with Puritan zealotry, as the eighteenth century unfolded, but writers were deft in exciting the personal and secular passions that the drama entailed (Vaughan and Clark, 24). Mather's tone of hatred and hysteria reverberated, and the captivity narrative in the eighteenth century typically depicted in gory, gothic detail life and death struggles between Indians and helpless captives, often female. Within the context of the Indian-hating tradition and the "capture-escape-flight theme," *Edgar Huntly* situates the conflict between rational and irrational forces in the protagonist's mind in the same wilderness setting that provided the context for the conflict the Puritans experienced between the spiritual and physical worlds (Vaughan and Clark, 26).

The other context in which the captive's struggles unfold is the family, which represents the values of civilization and Christianity. Despite the permutations of the captivity narrative as a genre, the thread that unites its various versions is the emphasis on family, not only the pain of separation but the *danger* of separation, which can mean the loss of cultural identity. Edgar's literal and figurative orphanhood exemplifies this metamorphosis. Removed from the patriarchal control of family and then from the control of civilization, Edgar loses control psychologically as well. Despite his professed "aversion to bloodshed [which] was not to be subdued except by the direst necessity," Edgar dispatches the savages with surprising dexterity, ill-concealed relish, and even pride. One of his weaker excuses for his enthusiasm is the trauma of his childhood: "Let the fate of my parents be, likewise, remembered. I was not certain but that these men were the assassins of my family, and were those who had reduced me and my sisters to the condition of orphans and dependents" (169–170). (Since in Edgar's taxonomy all Indians belong to the class of the undifferentiated Other, i.e. the Enemy, the question of whether these particular Indians were his parents' murderers is academic.)

The legacy of the captivity narratives is clearly relevant to this transformation. There was a significant cultural difference in Puritan and Indian attitudes toward adoption of captives. As discussed in chapter 2, Indian captives were taken into Puritan families only as servants. There is virtually no record of their numbers or the extent of their acculturation, and the common assumption is that they were probably released after a few years of servitude (Vaughan and Richter, 30). In contrast, there is ample evidence from the captivity narratives that the Indians treated their captives very differently and that the attitude of the captives was also markedly different.

In general, Indian culture was far more inclusive and permeable than that of the Puritans. To replace lost family members, the Indians adopted captives, gave them Indian names, and treated them as their own. One captive, Susanna Hastings Johnson, reproachfully recorded for posterity her opinion of this cultural difference that redounded to the moral credit of that "untutored race": "Can it be said of civilized conquerors, that they, in the main, are willing to share with their prisoners, the last ration of food, when famine stares them in the face? *Do they ever adopt an enemy and salute him by the name of brother?*" (75–76; italics mine). Significantly enough, Johnson's son Sylvanus, who was "redeemed" in 1758, "retained certain Indian habits and often expressed regret for having been redeemed" (Coleman, 311–312).

The Indians enthusiastically tried to incorporate captives into their tribes, and to the consternation of the Puritans they were frequently successful, prompting Crèvecoeur to wonder nervously why so many Europeans chose to become Indians and not even one Indian chose to become European (Vaughan and Richter, 23). One reason the Indians took prisoners was to replace family members who had died in warfare or from disease. The Indians also did not share the Puritans' racist prohibitions against intermarriage, so Puritan women were looked upon as suitable wives and children were eagerly sought after to replace the Indians' own dead offspring. Even male captives were considered desirable as workers and desirable replacements for fallen braves. The Indians treated the adoptees like their own family, and a Shawnee speech made when relinquishing captives in 1764 gives a sense of the Indians' sincerity and depth of familial feeling: "Father—Here is your Flesh and Blood... they have been all tied to us by Adoption, although we now deliver them up to you. We will always look upon them as Relations, whenever the Great Spirit is pleased that we may visit them.... Father—we have taken as much care of these Prisoners, as if they were [our] own Flesh, and blood" (quoted in Axtell, 306).

The result of this inclusive attitude on the part of the Indians and the kindness with which they often (though not always) treated their captives inevitably had an unsettling effect on Puritan culture, particularly when the captives "went Indian" and decided not to return home. Returned captive Titus King sums up this cultural nightmare: "[Captivity is] an awful School for Children When We See how Quick they will Fall in with the Indians' ways. Nothing Seems to be more taking. In Six months' time they Forsake Father & mother, Forget their own Land, Refuse to Speak their own tongue & Seemingly be Wholly Swallowed up with the Indians" (Demos, *Captive* frontispiece).

The best available statistics indicate that of the known captives taken to Canada less than half returned to New England. Of 451 captives held in civilian Canada as opposed to military prisons, 117 returned to New England while 202 chose to remain. Of those choosing to remain most were young and female. Axtell summarizes: "Nearly a third of the female captives but less than a tenth of the males stayed. In short, girls between the age of seven and fifteen were most susceptible to conversion, but all ages and sexes turned their backs on their natal homes" (289).

John Demos focuses on just such an adoption. In 1704 Eunice Williams, the daughter of Puritan minister John Williams, was captured by the Indians along with her family, taken to Canada, and adopted by her captors. She subsequently married an Indian and when given the opportunity to return to the Puritans elected not to. Even Williams's son Stephen, who lived with the Indians for fourteen months, showed signs of succumbing to Indian influence, and

Demos sensitively chronicles the ambivalence toward his own and his sister's captivity that haunted him throughout his life.

Such incidents were all too common, and a great source of embarrassment to the Puritans. Even Mary Rowlandson's famous *A Narrative of Captivity and Restoration* (1677), which chronicled her captivity and eventual rescue and at first seemed to be a model of orthodoxy, was tinged with ambivalence. Such narratives left a disturbing legacy of cultural vulnerability that persisted throughout the eighteenth century, a deeper fear of the Other based not on difference but on identification. If the captivity narratives taught Americans anything, it was that the stakes of the most important Indian war were not just territorial but psychological, and that the real meaning of conquering the Indians was not becoming like them.

Set against this backdrop, Edgar's demonization of the Indians becomes more comprehensible, as does his horror at his bloodthirsty "transformation." He not only makes excuses but tries to disassociate himself from it by projecting the blame onto the Indians, as if they had taken possession of him: "Think not that I relate these things with exultation or tranquility. All my education and the habits of my life tended to unfit me for a contest and a scene like this. But I was not governed by the soul which usually regulates my conduct. I had imbibed from the unparalleled events which had lately happened, *a spirit vengeful, unrelenting, and ferocious*" (182; italics mine).

What Edgar is really describing here is a psychological form of captivity based not on abduction by the enemy but on the "victim's" appropriation of the enemy's identity. The collapse of Edgar's identity into the savage world, in the form of wild animals and Indians, is simply an exaggerated version of the fusion that takes place with Clithero, and it dramatizes both Edgar's instability and his susceptibility to irrational and primitive influences.

It is significant that the novel is written in the first person and that Edgar describes his character in terms that further reinforce the reader's impression of instability. He admits to "wanderings of my reason and my freaks of passion" (42), which he relies upon his uncle to temper (151). Edgar seems to have no specific *work*, other than the "labour and rustic obscurity" that leave him too poor to marry. Even more significant, Edgar has no land, the currency of identity and civilization, in American society. The Delaware Indians seized his father's farm when they killed his parents; ironically, the farm was part of a tract of land illicitly taken from the Delawares in the first place. The implication is that is lack of property contributes to Edgar's lack of a stable identity by putting him in the same category as the Indians who do not "own" property. So when Edgar asks himself, with regard to Clithero, "why should my whole attention and activity be devoted to this man?", the question underscores the orphanhood that impels him to pursue surrogate fathers who can confer upon him at least a cultural inheritance (131).

Among these were his uncle and his tutor, Sarsefield, who "treated me with paternal tenderness, and insists upon the privilege of consulting for my interests as if he were my real father" (251). They provided him with positive role models, but their influence was not enough to offset Edgar's inner chaos, and Brown seems to be suggesting that there is no substitute for real paternity and real property. Edgar's attachment to Clithero has similar filial overtones, but the problem is that Clithero is a fellow orphan, not a father figure, who represents disintegration rather than integration, which Brown dramatizes by the doubling of their identities.

The impression of Edgar's instability is reinforced by the pattern of his mental processes. He is on the one hand impulsive, leaping to conclusions, and on the other indecisive, wavering in his judgments. While he is rashly meddling in the affairs of others, usually on the basis of mistaken inferences, he is simultaneously questioning motives, and the relationship between intentions and actions. In short, he acts without understanding and reasons without concluding. It becomes apparent very quickly that Edgar is a highly suggestible and impressionable young man. The skin of his identity, like the boundary between civilization and the frontier, is thin and permeable, and there is an alarming amount of absorption into the selves of others. He is also, by extension, a highly fallible narrator who legitimately questions his ability to tell his story in a coherent fashion. His blatant fallibility has, in fact, led some critics to interpret the novel as a critique of Lockean empiricism.[3]

But like *Wieland*, *Edgar Huntly* can be read more convincingly as a critique of republicanism, or the confidence in man's ability to govern himself without strong patriarchal authority. The key to Edgar is that he is like Crèvecoeur's cipher. As an orphan, he has no familial structure, no source of stability in the form of land or work, and no sense of Self. Driven by an infantile, Lacanian sense of a lack, he identifies with fragmentation in the form of the chaotic, anarchic wilderness and continually tries to define himself in terms of his relationship to those with whom he has no natural relationship. It is no wonder that even his best intentions result in the destruction not only of his enemies, the Indians, but of Clithero, whose death he inadvertently causes, and even of those against whom he intends no harm. Toward the end of the novel, Edgar pronounces despairingly about the human condition: "Disastrous and humiliating is the state of man! By his own hands is constructed the mass of misery and error in which his steps are forever involved.... How little cognizance have men over the actions and motives of each other! How total is our blindness with regard to our own performances!" (250).

If one interprets Edgar as a personification of the newly formed nation trying to establish an identity, then his experience of running amok through the wilderness assumes a new dimension. His rampage robs him of whatever tenuous identity he possesses as a civilized being and makes a mockery of both the Puritans' "errand into the wilderness" and Enlightenment ideals of freedom and progress. Instead of taming the wilderness within himself and overcoming his enemies, Edgar becomes them, the savage Indian and the barbaric immigrant, and the novel suggests that in contrast with utopian dreams of innocence, the New World has corrupted rather than saved its new inhabitants. If a relatively normal, decent fellow like Edgar is so vulnerable to irrational influences and can stray so deeply into error, then the unavoidable implication is, as Crèvecoeur would have agreed, that the American exposed to the wilderness becomes a caricature of the "new man." What Edgar lacks is the stabilizing influence of family structure, specifically the authority and legacy of a father. By implication, then, one can read *Edgar Huntly* as going beyond Brown's other novels in its pessimism about man's ability to regulate himself and in its endorsement of a strong, centralized government to keep the dark forces in human nature under control.

But there is another, more subtle political implication to the novel that pertains directly to Edgar's orphanhood. Insofar as the orphanhood serves as a metaphor for personal and national identity formation in the novel, Edgar dramatically illustrates the extent to which identification with and destruction of the Other, the Indian and the immigrant, are inextricably related.[4] In his desperate search for an identity which, as an orphan, he could not derive through identification with his parents and the acquisition of property, Edgar tries to acquire one by differentiating himself from his real and imagined enemies. But because, as an orphan, he has such a weak sense of self, he cannot complete the process of separation. The boundaries break down and he becomes the Other, the creature of the wilderness rather than the man of property. The loss of Self in the Other in turn requires the destruction of the Other in order to reinvent the independent Self. In cultural terms, the irony is that Edgar, an orphan who represents white civilization, must destroy those "outsiders," scapegoats on whom his provisional sense of identity depends, in order to create an "adopted" identity at their expense. Edgar hardly succeeds in becoming a child of the republic. At the end of the novel he is alone, without property, and remorseful at the havoc he has wreaked through his "misguided, indeed, but powerful benevolence" (259). Brown's message is clear: there is no substitute for patriarchal authority within the family and the government.

A different situation exists for yet another "orphan," Natty Bumppo, who willingly partakes of Indian culture, but who, unlike Edgar, successfully displaces this identification in order to affirm himself as an adopted child of the republic. The irony of Natty Bumppo's many names — Deerslayer, Hawkeye, Leatherstocking, Pathfinder, Long Rifle, and Trapper — is that they reflect his lack of a stable identity. The more names he acquires, the more mutable and elusive he seems, as if he were constantly shaking off one cloak of identity and trying to replace it with a better fit. In the course of James Fenimore Cooper's Leatherstocking series, which comprises five romances written over the course of almost twenty years (1823–1841), the reader learns almost nothing about Natty's past other than that he was born to a family of simple, hard-working Christian people, as his given name reflects. Like a mythic figure, he springs fullblown into the action, and Cooper provides us with the only important fact we need to know about his personal history — that he rejects it.

At the core of the Leatherstocking tales is the close relationship between Natty and the Indians, specifically his friendship with Chingachgook in *The Pioneers* (1823), Uncas and Chingachgook in *The Last of the Mohicans* (1826), and Hard Heart in *The Prairie* (1827). This friendship represents, according to Fiedler, not only an adolescent ideal of male bonding but an "archetypal relationship" between the "dark-skinned" man and the white (152). These Indians are noble savages who personify the innocence of nature, as Natty's praise of the Pawnee in *The Prairie* suggests: "if you had seen as much good and evil as I have seen in these nations of redskins, you would know of how much value was a brave and simpleminded warrior. I know that some are to be found who both think and say that an Indian is but little better than the beasts of these naked plains. But it is needful to be honest in oneself to be a fitting judge of honesty in others" (384).

Illustrative of Cooper's ambivalence is that Natty also views the Indians as "but little better than the beasts of these naked plains." *The Prairie* is riddled with pagan, animal, and even demonic imagery (e.g., demons, wolves, hounds, vermin, and the hands-down favorite, reptiles) that recalls Mather's rhetoric; Cooper uses it to describe the ignoble savages who seem far more abundant than their idealized counterparts. The liberal sprinkling of negative epithets throughout the novel denotes a basically dehumanized view of the "savages" and reflects a deep-seated racial prejudice underlying Natty's professions of good will. Moreover, Natty's friendship with elite Indians is superseded by his abiding allegiance to his racial and cultural origins. For example, Natty ultimately identifies with the values of white civilization by defining himself in no uncertain terms as "a man without a cross" (whose blood is unmixed with that of other races) and as a Christian.

Because of his conflicting loyalties, Natty incarnates what Slotkin calls the "myth of concern" about the moral dilemma posed by the Indians. In this respect, Natty appears to differ from the "military aristocrats," such as Duncan Heyward in *The Last of the Mohicans* and Captain Middleton in *The Prairie*, who serve as one-dimensional ideological symbols through whom social and racial tensions are glibly resolved in favor of white civilization and the natural aristocracy. The "ideological resolution" these characters represent contrasts with the "mythic resolution" that *The Last of the Mohicans* offers to the problem of miscegenation (Slotkin, *Regeneration*, 103–105). Depicting a relationship and potential intermarriage between an Indian (Uncas) and a mulatto (Cora), who is tainted with a mere drop of Negro blood, the novel poses the possibility of miscegenation, but ultimately rejects it by killing off Uncas. A limited form of cultural miscegenation does take place, however, in the friendship between Natty and Chingachgook.

The "mythic resolution" that interracial male bonding represents is hollow at best, and its artificiality highlights more than conceals Cooper's racism. Miscegenation is a theme that recurs with almost obsessive frequency throughout the Leatherstocking tales and is particularly charged in *The Last of the Mohicans* because of Cora's alleged negritude, her "drop" of Negro blood, which in Cooper's bizarre racial economy makes her unworthy of marrying a white but too good to marry an Indian (a prejudice distinctly reminiscent of both Franklin's and Jefferson's). For example, responding to Magua's proposal to Cora, Major Heyward exclaims, "Cora! Cora! You jest with our misery! Name not the horrid alternative again; the thought itself is worse than a thousand deaths" (109). That Cooper feels an equally visceral antipathy toward white/red miscegenation is evident in *The Deerslayer* (1841), the last novel Cooper wrote in the Leatherstocking series but the first chronologically. Natty rejects an Indian girl who is otherwise an appropriate choice for him simply because he is white, and a white man cannot "in reason" love an Indian woman.

In his other novels, the outcome of white/red relationships also reflects Cooper's aversion to the "horrid alternative." For example, in *The Pioneers* (1823), the first published in the series and the next to last in the narrative sequence, the presumed Indian Young Eagle (a.k.a. Edward Oliver Effingham) is not eligible to marry Judge Temple's daughter until it is revealed that he is actually a white man who symbolically inherited his Indian blood from his father, an honorary member of their tribe. Yet there is a strong suggestion here and in Cooper's other novels that his aversion to intermarriage is not only racist but imperialist and based on the denial of Indian land rights.

Eric Cheyfetz in "Savage Law" perceptively reads *The Pioneers* against the historic Supreme Court case *Johnson and Graham's Lessee v. M'Intosh*, which was decided in 1823, the same year *The Pioneers* was published. The decision based title to land, or ownership of land, on the principle of discovery by "superior" nations, thereby effectively giving the government the right to make land claims and eliminating all Indian territorial rights. Supposedly the intent of the decision was to establish a principle that would resolve disputes between European governments over land claims, but the not-so-hidden agenda was dispossession of the Indians. In rendering the decision, Chief Justice John Marshall argues from the historical precedent that did not entirely disregard "the rights of the original inhabitants" but considerably "impaired" them:

> They were admitted to be the rightful occupants of the soil, with a legal as well as just claim to retain possession of it, and to use it according to their own discretion; but their rights to complete sovereignty, as independent nations, were necessarily diminished, and their power to dispose of the soil at their own will, to whomsoever they pleased, was denied by the original fundamental principle that discovery gave exclusive title to those who made it. (Cheyfetz, 111)

Viewing *The Pioneers* as a dramatization of this decision, Cheyfetz argues that the marriage of Effingham and Temple's daughter consolidates the "real" property Effingham inherited from his "real" white father and invalidates the "fictional" property to which, in his guise as Young Eagle, he laid claim because he believed Temple had defrauded him of his birthright. In Cheyfetz's view, Effingham's renunciation of his Indian land claims creates the illusion that in this "romance of property... the Indians alienated their land willingly" (125). Furthermore, it enacts a narrative of white hegemony, in which white identity and Indian identity are mutually exclusive, with the former depending upon the annihilation of the latter. Going even further, the suicide of Natty's beloved friend Chingachgook at the end of the novel suggests an interdependence not only between property and "American" identity but between property and life itself.

In Cooper's novels the theme of cultural and racial amalgamation serves as a metaphor for the massive expansionist thrust under Jefferson, Monroe, and Jackson during the early nineteenth century. It is in *The Prairie*, the last narrative of the series, that this connection is most explicit. The historical context of the Leatherstocking Tales was the Louisiana Purchase of 1803, which included a vast expanse of land that, in Cooper's own words, "made us masters of a belt of fertile country" even as it created a "barrier of desert to the extension of our population in the West" (*The Prairie*, 9). Cooper was fascinated by the exploration of this region and avidly read both Lewis and Clark's *History* and the more current and comprehensive *An Account of an Expedition from Pittsburgh to the Rocky Mountains; Undertaken in the Years 1819 and '20 . . .* (Elliott, xvii).

What particularly fascinated Cooper was the clash of cultures that the expansion caused not only between the Americans and the Spanish but between the new breed of emigrants and the Indians. *The Prairie* is in many respects a recapitulation of the Great Migration, a fictional chronicle of a westward migration that was this time inspired by dreams of prosperity and even affluence as emigrants pushed onward to the "Eldorado of the West" (11). The only real obstacle in their path was the Indians, but Cooper apparently did not regard them as a serious impediment, as evidenced by his cavalier statement that the purchase "gave us the sole command of the great thoroughfare of the interior and placed the countless tribes of savages who lay along our borders entirely within our control" (9).

In this respect, *The Prairie* is less about the clash of cultures than the passing of a people, and the most interesting tension in the novel grows out of the moral conflict within Cooper, who simultaneously rejoices in and laments the subjugation of the Indians. Certainly Cooper's concern with maintaining his own wealth and status helped to foster this ambivalence, which centered around the issue of land ownership. Cooper belonged to an almost feudal society of wealthy landowners in upper New York state, having inherited a portion of his father's huge estate and married a well-to-do woman. But Cooper's tenure as lord of the manor was short-lived because the inherited land was encumbered by legal disputes and mismanagement, which ultimately forced

Cooper to sell a portion of his holdings and even some of his household possessions. Living at times on the verge of arrest, Cooper was highly sensitive to the issue of property, particularly the dynamics of acquisition and dispossession, and these biographical circumstances help explain why he felt empathy for the Indians and a simultaneous desire to participate in their dispossession. Moreover, the legacy of Washington, Franklin, and Jefferson was idealization of progress, prosperity, and individualism as touchstones of the republic, and they depended directly or indirectly on the ownership of property. The unspoken corollary was that as a class, the wealthy, landed aristocracy depended for its identity on the denial of the rights, and even the humanity, of those who held the real power over the land: the Indians who possessed it and the Negro slaves who worked it.

It is within this context that Cooper's denigration of the Indians as animals, vermin, and reptiles makes sense as justification for the appropriation of property. While it violates the law to take another man's property, no one would question the right to seize the territory of a lower life form, such as "bad Indians" who not only justify but invite extermination. Although Natty is no Nick of the Woods, he does kill Indians and is, like Edgar Huntly, complicit with the values of white civilization that are ultimately destructive to Indian civilization.[5]

Philip Fisher in *Hard Facts* makes the case that certain popular novels of the nineteenth century perform the cultural work of making "ungraspable" and "unimaginable" social realities, such as extermination of the Indians, acceptable through a process of familiarization (8). This underlying motive makes obvious why Natty can embody only a "myth" of reconciliation. The challenge of creating a protagonist who could mediate between red and white and reconcile all manner of ethnic, racial, national, and even sexual tensions placed an enormous burden on Cooper and drove him inevitably into the realm of fantasy. It is tempting to conclude that beneath the myth, what we are dealing with in Cooper's romances is sentimentality, the kind of hypocrisy that feigns sympathy with the victim in the process of identifying with the oppressor. To the extent this is true, one can argue that Cooper is the literary counterpart of the Founding Fathers — of Franklin, Adams, and especially Jefferson — who paid lip service to assimilation while simultaneously conspiring to dispossess and perhaps exterminate the Indians.

Clearly the romance of interracial male bonding is no substitute for intermarriage, which entails not only the merger of property but the potential passing on of property through progeny. From this standpoint, the advantage of friendship between a white man and an Indian, in contrast with marriage, is that there is no merger of property and no issue as to who can lay claim to inheritance. The Indian is effectively precluded from any possibility of "owning" property under the law not only because he could not (and would not) "buy" his own land but because he could not acquire it through marriage or inheritance. Thus, just as the bestial imagery reflects the cultural exclusion of Indians from the human family, the orphan imagery that abounds in Cooper's fiction reflects the exclusion of the Indian from the family of the republic.

As previously discussed, the paternalistic attitude of the government typified by Jefferson was a reaction to the image of the Indians as uncivilized children who need the protection and ministrations of enlightened adults to raise them out of the primeval slime. That this stereotype persisted throughout the 1820s and influenced not only policy but legislation is evident in Chief Justice Marshall's next major decision related to Indian affairs, his ruling for the majority in *The Cherokee Nation v. the State of Georgia* (1831) following the passage of the Indian Removal Act. Although he was an opponent of Jackson's, Marshall argued that the Cherokee could not seek redress before the court because Indian tribes were the equivalent of "domestic dependent nations," or children: "they are in a state of pupilage. Their relation to the United States resembles that of a ward to his guardian. They look to our government for protection, rely upon its kindness and its power, appeal to it for relief of their wants; and address the president as their great father" (quoted in Berkhofer, 164).

The image of the Indians as "wards" was more than rhetorical and mirrored their treatment as real and cultural orphans. Dispossessed of their lands, to which they gave the attributes of parents, they were forced to rely instead upon their white "stepfather," who not only made them figurative orphans by depriving them of their lands but even made literal orphans of their children by separating them from their families. In the early nineteenth century "the government turned to what it called a civilization policy," according to Bremner, the goal of which was to transform the Indians into "white Americans, or at least...a manageable and partial facsimile" (*Children and Youth in America*, 438).

To this end, private missionary agencies established schools among the tribes, but with the exception of the Cherokee, their efforts proved largely unsuccessful because the Indian children clung to traditional tribal customs. Thus, emphasis turned before the Civil War to the boarding school, or separation from the family, as a more effective means of indoctrinating Indian children with "civilized" Christian values and annihilating their cultural identity. The assumption was that children who were taken away from their parents—i.e., orphaned of both family and culture—had the best chance of becoming civilized Christians and assimilating into white culture. Of course, part of the problem was that the effort to assimilate the Indians was not only ill-conceived but insincere insofar as it was predicated on a desire to tame them, like domesticated wild animals, rather than adopt them like children (i.e., potential citizens, with equal property rights in the family of the republic).

Of all Cooper's novels, *The Prairie* best illustrates that the racial taboo applied to all familial relationships, as reflected in the orphanhood theme that pervades the novel. It is important to bear in mind that Cooper's preceding romance, *The Last of the Mohicans*, is virtually predicated on the concept of orphanhood, with Uncas and Chingachgook representing the "orphans" of their extinct tribe. After the death of his son Uncas, Chingachgook laments, "As for me, the son and the father of Uncas, I am a blazed pine in clearing of the pale-faces. My race has gone from the shores of the salt lake, and the hills of the Delawares." Natty echoes the lament of his solitary friend: "The gifts of our colours may be different, but God has so placed us as to journey in the same path. I have no kin, and I also say, like you, no people" (349).

The Prairie, which depicts Natty's death and is the last of the tales chronologically, establishes Natty as an alienated figure, "a solitary who has lived for seventy years in the very open bosom of natur'..." (260) and is now fleeing even further from the settlements to "come into these plains to escape the sound of the ax, for here, surely the chopper can never follow!" (122). His loathing for the "choppers" is so profound that it drove him from all contact with white civilization: "I come hither to escape the wasteful temper of my people.... I live alone, and never do I mingle with men whose skins are white" (222). Natty's home is the forest, or the plains in *The Prairie*; in short, the wilderness in whatever manifestation, and he roams it like a wild creature or marks it like one of his beloved trees. As he nears death, Cooper compares him to a tree: "Though evidently so near its dissolution, his attenuated frame still stood like the shaft of seasoned oak, dry, naked, and tempest-riven, but unbending and apparently indurated to the consistency of stone" (244–245).

In *The Prairie*, the focus broadens from Natty's sympathy with the Indians to his identification, and their shared cultural orphanhood seems to form a profound basis of kinship. Foreseeing his approaching death, Natty proclaims, "I am without kith or kin in the wide world!... when I am gone there will be an end of my race" (399). The "seasoned oak" thus symbolically equates himself with the "blazed pine" in a wilderness decimated by the white man. Throughout the romance, Natty dwells on his lonely, solitary state, and Cooper, as early as the introduction, establishes a parallel between Natty and the Indians as fellow exiles: "The Great Prairies appear to be the final gathering place of the red men. The remnants of the Mohicans and the Delawares, of the Creeks, Choctaws, and Cherokees, are destined to fulfill their time on these vast plains.... The sound of the ax has driven him [Natty] from his beloved forests to seek a refuge, by a species of desperate resignation, on the denuded plains that stretch to the Rocky Mountains" (vii).

The connection between Natty and the Indians resides in their similar attitudes toward nature and their alienation from white civilization. But it also consists of the deeper affinity of orphanhood, epitomized by Natty's adoption of the Pawnee brave Hard Heart as his son. His act is motivated by a combination of loneliness, a desire to help the fatherless young brave who is now the leader of his tribe, and a sense of spiritual kinship that transcends cultural differences. In his initial overture to Hard Heart, Natty makes the following touching speech:

> I have never been father or brother. The Wahcondah [Indian God] made me to live alone. He never tied my heart to house or field by the cords with which the men of my race are bound to their lodges; if he had, I should not have journeyed so far and seen so much. But I have tarried long among a people who lived in those woods you mention, and much reason did I find to imitate their courage and love their honesty. The Master of Life has made us all, with *a feeling for our kind.* I never was a father, but I had even begun to fancy that some of his blood might be in your veins. But what matters that? You are a true man, as I know by the way in which you keep your faith; and honesty is a gift too rare to be forgotten. My heart yearns to you, and gladly would I do you good. (289; italics mine)

Part of Natty's feeling of kinship first with Uncas and then with Hard Heart is that he clearly identifies with their orphanhood, both literal and figurative, and sees himself also as cut off from the cultural family of which he was originally a part. In a romance that is strikingly modern in its exploration of alternative family structures; subversive in its endorsement of aspects of natural over institutionalized law; and progressive (for Cooper) in its sanction of an intermarriage between a Mexican Catholic and an Anglo-Saxon Protestant (though definitely *not* of a Mexican Catholic and an Indian), Natty's unusual proposal seems not that radical. Cooper lends it weight by contrasting the spiritual kinship of Hard Heart and Natty with the estranged relationship that exists between the other "real" orphan in the novel, Ellen Wade, and the patriarch Ishmael who has cared for her and proposes to adopt her. Because of their differences in values, Ellen rejects him: "You took me a fatherless, impoverished, and friendless orphan... when others, who live in what may be called affluence compared to your state, chose to forget me [but] I like not your manner of life; it is different from the ways of my childhood, and it is different from my wishes" (363).

The novel dramatizes the common practice of adoption among the Indian tribes. In *The Prairie* this custom is depicted in the effort of the old Sioux chief Le Balafré to adopt Hard Heart: "Le Balafré has come to look for a young arm on which he may lean and to find a son, that when he is gone his lodge may not be empty" (323). But Hard Heart, for reasons similar to Ellen's, spurns him: "My father is very old, but he has not yet looked upon everything.... He has never seen a buffalo change to a bat; he will never see a Pawnee become a Sioux!... Hard Heart is not without a grayhead to show him the path to the blessed prairies. If he ever has another father, it shall be that just warrior" (325–326).

In designating Natty rather than Le Balafré his "father," Hard Heart is also exemplifying the inclusiveness of the Indians, who freely adopted their kind (i.e., Indians) and had no compunctions about crossing racial lines through adoption (and even marriage).[6] On a certain level, Natty, in offering to adopt Hard Heart, is acting out a fantasy of being adopted himself, as if *he* were the orphan. This impression is reinforced by Natty's peculiar idea of the "good" that he would do to Hard Heart. Surmising that Hard Heart is about to be killed by the Sioux, Natty is proposing to become not only his "father" but his "son" as a kind of spiritual heir: "I have made him my son that he may know that one is left behind him," just as Chingachgook, the father, was left as the solitary witness to the life and death of his son Uncas (327). What we have here, then, is not only an arbitrary assumption of a paternal relationship but a duality and reciprocity that suggests union. In their ability to exchange roles on the symbolic plane, Natty and Hard Heart appear to be one.

But as the final scenes of the romance reveal, it is an illusory kinship founded on bad faith. Despite his apparent magnanimity and avowals of kinship with Hard Heart, Natty's paternity can be no more than symbolic, and the racial lines are as sharply drawn as ever. For example, Ishmael asks Natty the telling question, "to which people do you belong? You have the color and speech of a

Christian, while it seems that your heart is with the redskins." After equivocating about there being "little difference in nations," Natty reveals his true colors, in every sense: "Still *I am a man without a cross of Indian blood*; and what is due from a warrior to his nation is owing by me to the people of the States, though little need have they, with their militia and their armed boats, of help from a single arm of fourscore" (79–80; italics mine). Even during his initial, emotional overture to Hard Heart, in which a genuine union appears to take place, Natty continues to differentiate himself, as illustrated by the exchange in which Hard Heart asks him to deliver a message of unforgiveness to the Sioux and Natty replies, "Pawnee, I love you; but being a Christian man, I cannot be the runner to bear such a message" (290).

In the final scenes, as he is dying, Natty barely misses a beat between his denunciation of white civilization ("Settlements, boy! It is long sin' I took my leave of the waste and wickedness of the settlements and the villages") and his profession of loyalty to it ("Though I have seen so much of the wilderness, it is not to be gainsaid that my feelings as well as my skin, are white") (384–385). He even appears to reject his kinship with Hard Heart: "Pawnee, I die, as I have lived, a Christian man!... as I came into life, so will I leave it. Horses and arms are not needed to stand in the presence of the Great Spirit of my people. He knows my color, and according to my gifts will he judge my deeds" (396). And at the moment of his death Natty shows his true colors even more plainly. He says to Middleton, "I am glad you have come, for though kind and well meaning according to the gifts of their color, these Indians are not the men to lay the head of a white man in his grave" (398).

The manner of his burial obviously causes Natty some concern and conflict, not only its location but its commemoration. He proclaims, "Let me sleep where I have lived—beyond the din of the settlements!" but then muses, "Still I see no need why the grave of an honest man should be hid, like a redskin in his ambushment" (399). It is obvious he would like a headstone, but at first he denies it: "No, no, I have no son but Hard Heart, and it is little that an Indian knows of white fashions and usages" (399). When Middleton discerns his wishes and offers to perform the task, Natty responds, "I thought you might be willing to do it, but I was backward in asking the favor... seeing you are not of kin. Put no boastful words on the same, but just the name, the age, and the time of death, with something from the holy book; no more, no more. My name will then not be altogether lost on 'arth; I need no more" (400).

Thus, in his final moments as he gives Middleton burial instructions, Natty affirms his identity as civilized, white, and Christian, and his reference to Hard Heart as his son seems perfunctory at best. In fact, he treats Middleton more like a son than Hard Heart, and their intimacy amounts to a gesture of betrayal and a clear inscription of the limits of adoption. Cooper then stages a symbolic resolution that is meant to transcend the disappointing reality. As Natty gazes into the setting sun, utters the cryptic exclamation, "Here!" and expires, Hard Heart and Middleton are supporting him *together*. It is obviously intended to be a mythical moment, with Natty apotheosizing the American spirit and synthesizing the best of white and Indian values. But it comes across as phony—an artificial yoking together rather than a natural union that leaves one wondering about Hard Heart, who has been virtually *removed* from the narrative. His removal parallels the historical treatment of the Indians at the hands of white men, and as yet another instance of perpetual displacement it confirms that the *real* orphan in the narrative is not Natty but Hard Heart. It is Hard Heart, not Natty, who has lost his father; Hard Heart, not Natty, who is being driven from his homeland. Despite his maundering self-pity and lofty sentiments, Natty's orphanhood is a fiction, not a fact, a fantasy that Cooper has conjured up to shift attention away from the real victim.

Natty is a product of the genuine conflict between Cooper's acknowledgment of Indian rights and respect for Indian culture on the one hand and his self-interested embrace of the principles of Manifest Destiny on the other. Natty's identification with the Indian as an orphan is thus far more complicated than Edgar's. Edgar's identification with the Indians is an expression of the collective fear of not only the savage without but the savage within, and as an orphan, a cipher, he is particularly vulnerable to possession by the Other. Although Natty shares a similar degree of confusion about who he is culturally, his identification with the Indians arises out of a combination of guilt and admiration and expresses itself in the kind of sentimentality that *The Prairie* epitomizes. As a mock orphan, Natty appears to serve as an agent of reconciliation, a figure who can incorporate the best of both races and set an example of unity through the symbolic process of adoption (as opposed to biological union through marriage). But the ending of *The Prairie*, like that of *The Last of the Mohicans*, reinscribes the separation between the races that reflects Cooper's true values.

Proceeding from her observations that "figurative mothers and fathers certainly abound in historical discourses" and that in American fiction "adoption is a constant motif, an American structure of compromise between blood and symbolic parenthood," Alice Cagidemetrio sees Natty as mediating between white and Indian cultures and translating Indian myths into an American national myth: "the Indian as alien is turned into Native American, where native stands for the land, a geographical entity, but also for the new nation, as its symbolic natural ancestor" (31–32, 28). The irony is that Natty, as he is portrayed in *The Prairie*, is also a father figure to the Indian, the "symbolic natural ancestor." But the "father" he represents in his adoption of Hard Heart is really a false father who delivers betrayal. The problem is that Cooper takes what he needs from Indian culture to fashion Natty into a mythic figure uniting the two races and throws out the rest. It is a classic example of what ethnopsychoanalyst George Devereux describes as "antagonistic acculturation," which takes place when a group is trying to preserve its identity in the face of a threat from another culture. The group's survival strategy is to adopt the means and even the intermediate goals of the alien culture, but not the ends. This dissociation from the ends is what Devereux means by antagonistic acculturation — a culture's act of creation using appropriation of aspects of an alien culture to promote its own goals (246–247).

The relevance of this subterfuge to *The Prairie* lies in the way Natty appropriates the values of Indian civilization — i.e., the reverential attitudes toward the wilderness and nature — and then subsumes them to a national ideology based on exploitation and appropriation of land. To borrow from Joseph Conrad, Natty may seem to be "one of them" but in reality he never stops being "one of us," a member of the dominant culture. It is a pernicious kind of hypocrisy, echoing that of Jefferson and his successors who plotted destruction of the Indians while pretending to save them. In terms of identity formation, *The Prairie* enacts through the character of Natty how the identity of the children of the republic was constituted by acts of aggression that turned the Indians into orphans.

But perhaps the most depressing subterfuge of all in *The Prairie* is that Cooper cheats the Indians even of their identity as orphans by preempting that role for his protagonist. By focusing the reader's attention on Natty as an orphan, Cooper creates sympathy for him and diverts attention from the novel's real orphan, Hard Heart, and the nation's true orphans, the victims of the reconstituted errand into the wilderness. It is not only a sentimental ploy but a cheap trick that tries to cover up the bitter reality of cultural and spiritual orphanhood that Chief Seattle was to articulate some twenty-five years later. Responding in 1853 to the governor of the Washington Territory, who planned to confine Seattle's tribes, the Suquamish and the Duwamish, to a reservation in Washington, Seattle gave the following historic speech, encoding the conflict between Indians and whites in familial terms:

> Our good father at Washington—for I presume he is now our father as well as yours, since King George has moved his boundaries further north—our great and good father, I say, sends us word that if we do as he desires he will protect us.... Then in reality will he be our father and we his children. But can that ever be? Your God is not our God! Your God loves your people and hates mine.... The white man's God cannot love our people or He would protect them. They seem to be *orphans* who can look nowhere for help. How then can we be brothers?... No; we are two distinct races with separate origins and separate destinies. There is little in common between us. (1770–1771; italics mine)

Seattle's speech is an epitaph for the Indians and a judgment on their treatment in the new republic. Its poignancy lies in the sorrowful acknowledgment that no ties of kinship are possible between the white, adopted children and the red, orphaned children. They can never be brothers or share as brothers in the legacy of the land, a legacy defined by patriarchal codes of inheritance that, even had Indians not been excluded from marriage or adoption into white families, were alien to the matrilineal structure of Indian culture.

It is noteworthy that despite his prejudice against miscegenation, Cooper does depict it in a later novel, *The Wept of Wish-Ton-Wish* (1829). But although Fiedler called it the "first anti-miscegenation novel in our literature," it hardly purveys an enlightened attitude and falls instead squarely into the racist tradition of Cooper's earlier novels (205). Like Eunice Williams, upon whose captivity experience Cooper drew, Ruth, a young white woman captured by the Indians as a child, marries an Indian, Conanchet, and they have a child toward whom Ruth's mother feels a visceral repulsion Cooper clearly shares. When Conanchet and Ruth die together in a form of divine retribution for their transgression, the child disappears from the novel as if she had never existed, the benighted issue of an unholy union.

Miscegenation and interracial adoption are inextricably related issues that figure prominently in Cooper's fiction because they threaten both the purity and the property of the Anglo-American family. With no intermarriage or adoption, there are no half-breed children who can legally lay claim to the land that belonged to the Indians in the first place. Thus, Cooper subsumes his sympathy for and admiration of the Indians to the higher values of property ownership and manifest destiny, and rejection of the Indians as members of the white American family serves as a metaphor for denial of their legal rights as citizens and even as human beings.

Cooper's negative attitude toward miscegenation and adoption is typical of other fiction during this period, with the notable exception of two novels by women authors that suggest a significant gender difference in the perception of Indians. Lydia Maria Child's *Hobomok* (1824) and Catharine Sedgwick's *Hope Leslie* (1827) both depict a more inclusive version of the family in which interracial marriage and adoption are at least contemplated, if not condoned. Moreover, both are historical novels set in Puritan times that encode a critique of Puritan, and specifically patriarchal, culture as oppressive not only to Indians but to women.[7] For example, Carolyn Karcher in her introduction praises *Hobomok* for Child's "revolutionary insight into the connection between male dominance and white supremacy" and regards the central theme of interracial marriage as a symbol for "both the natural alliance between white women and people of color, and the natural resolution of America's racial and sexual contradictions" (xx).

Set in Naumkeak, or Salem, in 1629, the novel's plot focuses on the rebellion of young Mary Conant against her father, who epitomizes the rigid, authoritarian nature of Puritanism. Not only does Mary have the effrontery to fall in love with an Episcopalian, Charles Brown, but she also has the audacity to marry an Indian, Hobomok, as the result of the unexpected outcome of an experiment with witchcraft in which she drew a circle and vowed she would marry whoever jumped into it, expecting it to be Brown and encountering instead Hobomok. Believing Brown to be drowned at sea following her father's banishment and also severely depressed over her mother's death, Mary decides to marry Hobomok, a decision reached in a desperate but not deranged state. Child makes clear that Hobomok was neither her first choice for a husband nor an entirely rational one, but she also implies that rebellion against her father and the culture he represents were equally compelling reasons. Following Hobomok's leap into the circle, Mary ruminates: "A broken and confused mass followed; in which sense of sudden bereavement, deep and bitter reproaches against her father, and a blind belief in fatality were alone conspicuous" (121).

Hobomok exults in her decision, as does his mother (in contrast with Mary's father), and the difference in their reactions underscores the vastly different attitudes of the two cultures and genders toward mixing the races. Upon her marriage, Mary states, "'I love him better than any body living,'" and time adds "romantic fervor to her increasing affection" (136). With the birth of her son, she achieves a degree of happiness she could not have foreseen and confides to her friend Sally Oldham, "I speak truly when I say that every day I live with that kind, noble-hearted creature, the better I love him" (137). In short, not only has Child redeemed the mythic Hobomok from his original identity as a devil-god, whom a Puritan woman was hanged for "marrying" in 1653, but she has awarded the historical Hobomok, who was a trusted friend of the English, the status of a title character (Slotkin, *Regeneration*, 142).

Yet despite the fact that *Hobomok* goes far beyond Cooper's novels in depicting miscegenation positively, the novel cannot be read as an unqualified endorsement in light of its ending. Brown returns after an absence of three years, and racial ties prevail over emotional. Hobomok, in a supreme act of magnanimity, agrees to divorce Mary, "that Mary may be happie [*sic*]" (146), and Mary, although she feels what appear to be genuine compunctions ("if ever a wife owed love to a husband, heathen or christian, I do to Hobomok" [147]), she welcomes Brown back like her lost true love, begs his forgiveness, and proclaims, "but to this hour, my love has never abated" (148). Brown does not hesitate to marry her or to adopt her son, Charles Hobomok Conant (according to Indian custom he took the name of his mother). Brown ominously pronounces, "He shall be my own boy," a prediction that comes all too true, for the son becomes a favorite of his grandfather's, inherits half the legacy in England, and graduates from Cambridge.

The ending is disappointing because it renders Mary too inconsistent to be credible and subverts the ideological critique the novel has raised. Not only does Mary succumb to white patriarchal values but her son becomes totally their product, to the extent of abandoning the last vestige of his Indian identity, his name: "His father was seldom spoken of; and by degrees his Indian appellation was silently omitted" (150). He becomes, in short, a "white Indian" masquerading as an Anglo-Saxon whose ultimate validation (and badge of betrayal of his own culture) is his ownership of British property.

Thus, the novel ends on a note that sounds the death knell of the Indians. Intermarriage, once condoned and even celebrated, is dissolved, and the adoption of a half-breed by Indians is reversed and culturally corrected in a move that makes adoption tantamount to cultural annihilation. Karcher summarizes: "Child has succumbed her to the familiar white fantasy that the Indian will somehow disappear.... Only if Indians cease to be Indians... can they earn a place in the society that is dispossessing them" (Introduction, xxxii). But despite the ending, which reads like a conciliatory step back from the brink of radicalism, *Hobomok* is far more progressive in its attitudes toward miscegenation than Cooper's novels.

As in *Hobomok*, the family model depicted in *Hope Leslie* is extended rather than nuclear. Inspired by Mary Jemison's and Eunice Williams's captivity experiences (Jemison's narrative appeared in 1823, and Williams was a distant relative of Sedgwick's), the novel is also a thinly veiled critique of Puritan ethnocentrism and patriarchy. Hope and her sister Faith are orphans adopted by William Fletcher and his family around the time of the Pequot War, for which Sedgwick makes clear the Puritans' share of responsibility. But even though Fletcher is disillusioned with the Puritans' narrow-minded repressiveness and moves to Springfield to escape it, there is no escape from their influence. For example, two young Indian captives from the war, Magawisca and her brother Oneco, become servants rather than adopted children like Hope and Faith, in contrast with the Indian custom of adopting captive children into the family.

In general, Indian culture is depicted as being more appealing to Puritan women than their own. For example, the character who dominates the novel, Magawisca, is a model of courage and rebellion against authority, including that of her father, the chief of the Pequots. Magawisca defies Puritan magistrates, goes to jail for her convictions, and even sacrifices an arm to save Fletcher's son from execution by her people. Juxtaposed against the example of submissive Puritan women such as John Winthrop's wife, it is little wonder that Hope falls under the influence of Magawisca. Sedgwick uses the following contemptuous simile to describe the "unqualified obedience" of Winthrop's wife to "her appointed lord and master": "like a horse easy on the bit, she was guided by the slightest intimation from him who held the rein; indeed, to pursue our humble illustration still farther — it sometimes appeared as if the reins were dropped, and the inferior animal were left to the guidance of her own sagacity" (144–145).

Thus, in one of the novel's many inversions, the Indian woman becomes the role model for the white, and Magawisca leads Hope into similar acts of rebellion and defiance. The action of the novel turns upon a series of captivities and escapes, all of which serve as a model for not only female liberation but family relations. Hope and Magawisca have both lost their mothers, and at the site of their graves Hope ruminates, "Mysteriously... mysteriously have our destinies been interwoven. Our mothers brought from a far distance to rest together here—their children connected in indissoluble bonds!" (192). Here we have a female version of Natty and Chingachgook's friendship that goes beyond friendship and daringly suggests mutual adoption and sisterhood. We are also far removed from *Edgar Huntly*, which drew on the captivity narratives to suggest a nightmare of cultural breakdown rather than a dream of cultural harmony.

Sedgwick challenges the familial norm even further by reversing the power relations—it is not Magawisca who is assimilating to white culture but Hope who is assimilating to Indian. Moreover, the affinity Hope feels is surpassed by her sister's. Faith, who is taken captive by the Pequots during a surprise attack on the Fletcher family, adapts only too well, to the extent of marrying Oneco and totally rejecting her own culture. While Hope does not go to this extreme and is initially horrified by Faith's marriage ("God forbid!," exclaimed Hope, shuddering as if a knife had been plunged in her bosom. "My sister married to an Indian!"), she eventually reconciles herself to her sister's decision, particularly since Faith has chosen to remain a Christian (188).

But Faith remains childless, and miscegenation is thus condoned but not rewarded with progeny. Like Child, Sedgwick falters at the end, retreating from the radical position to which her novel was building by marrying Hope to Everell and keeping Hope safely ensconced within the fold of white culture, while Magawisca returns to her people and the forest. As Philip Gould summarizes, "Her revisionary history demonstrates the difficulty of carrying on simultaneous revisions of gender and race—of critiquing republican manhood and fully humanizing the Pequot for a largely racist audience" (652).

The evident attraction that both Child and Sedgwick felt toward Indian culture, like that of female captives, derives in part from their knowledge of the difference in how the Indians treated women. Sedgwick had studied Roger Williams's *A Key into the Language of America* (1643), as well as the histories written by the Puritan clergymen John Robinson and John Eliot, and Child acquired her almost encyclopedic knowledge from several sources, including accounts by Captain John Smith, Lewis and Clark, and John Heckewelder, whose *An Account of the History, Manners, and Customs of the Indian Nations Who Once Inhabited Pennsylvania and the Neighboring States* (1818) is a major anthropological source. In the essay "History of the Condition of Women, in Various Ages and Nations," Child acknowledges the general subjugation of women to men ("The power of Indian husbands is absolute"), but she also emphasizes ways in which women enjoy a higher status because of their greater physical strength and endurance, their role as healers and prophets, their occasional participation in tribal councils, and the matrilineal organization of certain tribes (176).

The difference in treatment impressed both Child and Sedgwick and clearly influenced the portrayal of their female characters. For example, Magawisca is certainly the epitome of a powerful woman who, although she was still under her father's authority, exemplified a degree of independence and influence unheard of in Puritan society. Moreover, Child and Sedgwick also recognized the parallel between oppression of women in their own society and the treatment of Indians by white patriarchy. Both constituencies were treated not as human beings, as citizens with equal rights, but as property and even domesticated or wild animals. The novels can thus be read both as protofeminist interpretations of the captivity narratives and as commentaries on, if not corrections of, the distorted history of white-Indian relations concocted by white male authors such as Brown and Cooper.

Both Child and Sedgwick, despite their submission to the demands of literary and cultural conventions at the end of their novels, made a courageous attempt to deal with the complex and emotionally charged issues of miscegenation and interracial adoption in a manner that exposed the underlying patriarchal values that oppressed women as well as Indians. In situating their drama within the family domain, they found themselves slightly seduced, like Mary Rowlandson and Eunice Williams, by the Indian, the Other, who mirrored their own oppression and tantalized them with the possibility of voluntary captivity, followed by elective orphanhood and adoption into families more congenial than their own.

But blood will tell, as it ultimately does in all the novels. Like marries like, heroes and heroines remain with their own kind, and complex issues of cultural identity are obscured in simplistic endings that encode the values of a natural aristocracy and reify exclusive "families" whose children are united by economic, ethnic, racial, and religious kinship bonds. Even for someone as enlightened in her attitudes as Child, the only way the culturally inferior Indians could be admitted to the family of the republic was through assimilation—in other words, the repudiation of their own culture. As Child writes in "An Appeal for the Indians," "How *ought* we to view the peoples who are less advanced than ourselves? Simply as younger members of the same great human family, who need to be protected, instructed and encouraged, till they are capable of appreciating and sharing all our advantages" (220; italics in original).

As the nineteenth century unfolded, the tenuous bonds of kinship to the Indians that Child and Sedgwick endorsed gave way to the harsher male view exemplified by Brown and Cooper. With the rise of capitalism, new lines were drawn between natural, adopted, and orphaned children, and membership in the family of the republic became inseparable not only from race, ethnicity, and religion but from the web of class structure.

CHAPTER FIVE

The Rise of the Republic

> For ye have the poor always with you;
> but me ye have not always.
> —MATTHEW 26:11

Metaphorically speaking, the Revolution entailed a reconfiguration of the family in which sons replaced fathers, first through violent overthrow and then through generational succession. With the formation of the republic, the notion of citizenship became fundamental, and the Founding Fathers distinguished between natural children who belonged by birthright to the family of the republic and unadoptable orphans, Indians and Negroes, who circled like restless shadows outside its narrow embrace. But there gradually appeared a third category of children, adoptable orphans, or foreigners, who could become naturalized citizens. While naturalization laws appeared to signify a liberalization of earlier Puritan attitudes toward "strangers," they reinforced and even fomented an extraordinary wave of xenophobia during the 1840s and 1850s that recapitulated the exclusionary policies of the Puritans. In short, the Federalists adapted the Puritan notion of election to the political sphere, and as the recipients of God's grace asserted their right not only to serve as spiritual leaders but to regulate political and social conduct (Griffin, 425–426).

During the first half of the nineteenth century, or the antebellum period, patterns of inclusion and exclusion became firmly established in the wake of the rapid social changes that were engulfing the fledgling nation. Industrialization, immigration, and innovations in transportation and technology were among the factors that created a second Revolution and destabilized the social order. The result was a republican ideology that was the product of the newly emergent middle class. It was an ideology that looked backward to the Puritans' organic view of society in which family, government, and religion intertwined; it also looked forward, insofar as its legacy persists today in the form of contemporary attitudes toward race, class, and gender that determine degrees and kinds of participation in American society.

The new social dynamic that shaped attitudes during the antebellum period was class conflict. As important as the Great Migration and the Revolution in shaping American national identity in the seventeenth and eighteenth centuries, the rise of capitalism in the nineteenth century gave birth to that many-headed hydra, the middle class. Class distinctions that had been amorphous and ill-defined emerged sharply, despite the effusion of democratic, egalitarian rhetoric intended to minimize them. The delineation of classes was, of course, the inevitable outgrowth of a market economy. Scholars such as James A. Henretta trace the formative period of American capitalism to the pre- and post-Revolutionary decades when the increased demand for commercial products at home and abroad created a new set of economic relations based on wage labor rather than the cooperation, barter, and self-sufficiency that characterized the earlier agricultural economy. For example, Henretta situates the formative period of American capitalism in the decades from 1770 to 1800.

The Revolution itself can be viewed in economic terms. For example, the leaders of the Revolution belonged to the so-called "ruling classes" — merchants, major landowners, and professionals (Foner, xvii). Another factor was that economic and social changes in urban centers attended the rise of capitalism and undermined allegiance to the British mercantilistic system (Nash, 200–201). While the extent of the changing economy's influence on the Revolution is debatable, there is little question that the aftermath of the Revolution provided impetus to the growth of capitalism by disrupting the import trade and stimulating domestic production and enterprise, as well as speculative and acquisitive instincts. Specific changes wrought by the Revolution included confiscation and redistribution of Loyalist property, as well as the destruction and creation of working opportunities. These changes generated a surge in social mobility that, according to Bernard Bailyn, caused the apprehensive gentry to remark, "When the pot boils, the scum will rise" (302).

Indirectly, the Revolution sharpened class distinctions and circumscribed the nature and range of social intercourse. Stuart M. Blumin, in *The Emergence of the Middle Class: Social Experience in the American City, 1760–1900*, explains, "the experience of class in the nineteenth-century city can be understood in no small degree as the process by which people were brought together and kept apart, attracted to one another and repelled, and as the effect that resulting social networks had on the way people lived and perceived themselves as living in society" (231). After 1840, class distinctions seemed to become more ambiguous, as evidenced by the proliferation of imprecise terms used to distinguish the "aristocracy" and the "upper class" from the "working," "producing," "laboring," or "lower" classes, and both from the middle class or "middling classes." But these distinctions were not so fine and reflected basic differences in kinds of work rather than class, with the lower class performing manual labor, the middle class working in a nonmanual capacity as vendors or merchants, and the upper class or "capitalists" managing businesses and inherited wealth.

Certainly the most significant social change in the nineteenth century was the establishment of the middle class as a recognizable, if ill-defined, entity. Although the urban term "middle class" was vague at best, it nevertheless denoted a hierarchical distinction that established the middle class as a coherent and ascending mass superior to both the working class and the poor (Blumin, 244–245). One reason for the slipperiness of the term is the scope of the category, which led Carroll Smith-Rosenberg to prefer the plural, "middle classes," as a more accurate description.[1] She summarizes the fragmentation and "extreme instability" of what she calls the bourgeoisie: "The beneficiary of the commercial and industrial revolutions, it [the bourgeoisie] consisted of an inharmonious grouping of quite disparate economic and social components: an older mercantile elite; new wholesale merchants only just risen from peddler to prince; smaller shopkeepers; the new industrial entrepreneurs; the equally new professionals" (*Disorderly Conduct*, 86).

The Panic of 1837 and the subsequent Bank War combined with the huge increase in the rate of immigration, the urban riots during the 1840s, and the mounting dissension over slavery to create an atmosphere of class instability that pervaded the Jacksonian period. But these crises, which resulted in widespread business failures, unemployment, and rampant inflation following a period of wild speculation, also had the ironic effect of ensuring the political hegemony of the middle class, represented by the Whigs who appealed to the traditional Franklinian philosophies of pragmatism and the self-made man (Sellers, 359–360).

The degree of middle-class hegemony is a matter of some debate among scholars, however, some of whom hold that it was far from absolute and partially eclipsed by the political role of the upper class, particularly in the local arena. In an essay entitled "Who Governed the Nation's Cities in the Era of the Common Man?" Edward Pessen debunks the assumption that "great political power [was] commanded by persons of little or no property" (243). He asserts instead that the wealthy were overrepresented in political office before 1838 and that any decline in their representation during the 1840s was attributable to lack of interest rather than lack of popular support (246, 251). Pessen concludes that in northeastern cities and even small towns during the second quarter of the nineteenth century, "the rich appear to have been a true 'governing class.' Despite his possession of the suffrage, the common man had little influence, let alone power, in the nation's cities during the [egalitarian] era named in his honor" (257).

The fact that the rich commanded such a disproportionate share of the wealth necessarily diminished the share of the middle class. The unequal distribution of wealth not only persisted but intensified as the century progressed, with a greater concentration of wealth in the hands of a smaller percentage of the population. This trend persisted throughout the 1850s and resulted in increasingly wide disparities by the time of the Civil War. Pessen grimly concludes: "Far from being an age of equality, the antebellum decades were featured by an inequality that surpasses anything experienced by the United States in the twentieth century" ("The Egalitarian Myth," 29).

If the economic power of the middle class was limited, so was its upward mobility. Pessen refutes the thesis that American society in the antebellum period was dominated by the "middling orders" and flanked by a proportionately small number of rich and poor. The fact that the rich were not only a much larger and more influential component of the socioeconomic population but obtained their wealth and status by inheritance, challenges the rags-to-riches fantasy that became so popular during this period ("The Egalitarian Myth," 29). The majority of the members of the upper class traced their origins not to the poor, the self-made, or even the middle class but to their wealthy forebears who combined wealth with high social status ("Myth," 27).

The consensus that can be drawn from all the scholarship is that although the middle class did indeed rise and prosper during the first half of the nineteenth century, there was a distinct limit on its upward mobility, a glass ceiling of hereditary privilege that constrained the ability of the middle class to penetrate the upper. Between the 1820s and the 1850s, the frightening reality for the middle class was that downward mobility exceeded upward, at least in cities.

This created a mood of apprehension that was at odds with the façade of optimism. In this respect, the middle class was reminiscent of Winthrop and the Puritan leaders after the migration who felt compelled to keep up a brave front despite their underlying doubts. Karen Halttunen uses an apt escalator metaphor to sum up the middle class's mood of social schizophrenia: "Members of the middle class imagined themselves on a social escalator to greater wealth and prestige. They lived suspended between the facts of their present social position and the promise, they took for granted, of their economic future. In reality... the middle class escalator was at least as likely to go down as up" (29).

Contributing to internal tensions within the middle class was the pressure from below. Although upward mobility was limited, members of the working class could readily ascend to at least the lower levels of the middle class and demand a share of its prosperity. As the number of craftsmen diminished with industrialization and the number of shopkeepers and clerks increased, the parameters of the middle class expanded to include them among the "mercantile elite" (Blumin, 136–137). The effect of this expansion was not only increased competition within the middle class but increased resentment between the middle and lower classes, distinguished from each other by a manual-nonmanual dichotomy. According to David Roediger, nonmanual labor came increasingly to be identified with exploitation and wage slavery, and former artisans, craftsmen, and mechanics metamorphosed by industrialization into wage laborers compared themselves to slaves oppressed by despotic masters (51). Roediger states, "a term like *white* slavery was not an act of solidarity with the slaves but rather a call to arms to end the inappropriate oppression of whites" (68).

The Jacksonian period, which shaped the sensibility of those female novelists who rose to prominence during the 1850s, was a time of social conflict and instability in which members of the middle class were squeezed from above and below and pitted against one another in a spirit of competition and a Darwinian struggle to survive. Even more alarming to the middle class than their restricted upward mobility and the twin perils of lower-class resentment and lower-class incursion was the specter of poverty. Poverty was a pit into which anyone could fall, and pauperism was considered a social evil that threatened the well-being of middle-class culture. The result was a grudging alliance of the classes that assumed the disguise of benevolence, the linchpin of middle-class ideology.

As a result of the expanding market economy, the family had become the symbol of the middle class and the bulwark of the republic (Rogin, 31).[2] To rewrite Winthrop: A family is a little republic, and republic is a great family. Now as a family is not bound to entertain all comers, no not every good man (otherwise than by way of hospitality) no more is a commonwealth. The idealization of the family, commonly known as the cult of domesticity or the Cult of True Womanhood, was a distinctly middle-class phenomenon that entailed a distinct shift in emphasis from the father's influence to the mother's. The nucleus of the family became the mother, whose responsibility it was to set the moral tone for the family. Harking back to Puritan times, the family was revered as the ultimate source of moral stability, with the difference that in the new republic the task devolved to the mother to uphold the political, economic, and religious values that were identified with the welfare of the republic.

For example, Catharine Beecher, daughter of Congregationalist minister Lyman Beecher, became a writer and educator best known for her national "best-seller," *A Treatise on Domestic Economy for the Use of Young Ladies at Home and at School* (1841). The book is a paean to the importance of women's influence in the home and a plea for educating women to increase that influence; as a historical document it is notable for its conflation of democracy, Christianity, and the middle-class family. Beecher equates the principles of democracy with the principles of Christianity and states, "The success of democratic institutions... depends upon the intellectual and moral character of the mass of people," which she in turn attributes to the influence of women within the home: "the formation of the moral and intellectual character of the young is committed mainly to the female hand. The mother writes the character of the future man; the sister bends the fibres that hereafter are the forest tree; the wife sways the heart, whose energies may turn for good or evil the destinies of a nation" (210).

In other words, not only the fate of the family but the welfare of the republic depends on the moral influence and suasion of women. Although Beecher seemingly embraces women of all classes and backgrounds within her vision of the "glorious temple," a republican version of Winthrop's "city upon the hill," the "family values" she professes are the purview of white, middle-class, Protestant, Yankee women: "It is the building of a glorious temple, whose base shall be coextensive with the bounds of the earth, whose summit shall pierce the skies, whose splendor shall beam on all lands, and those who hew the lowliest stone, as much as those who carve the highest capital, will be equally honored when its top-stone shall be laid, with new rejoicings of the morning stars, and shoutings of the sons of God" (211).

This enormous responsibility, tantamount to the Puritan mission in the New World, conferred an unprecedented amount of power on women that was strikingly at odds with the reality of their lives. The shift in focus from the father to the mother as the spiritual leader in the home was the indirect result of industrialization and related social changes. By altering the nature and patterns of work, industrialization created clear lines of demarcation in the roles of husbands and wives, mothers and fathers, that removed men to the marketplace where they engaged in income-producing work and restricted women to the home, where they performed non-income-producing domestic tasks. In the wake of religious revivalism and under the influence of the clergy, women fashioned for themselves a notion of moral superiority that gave them a new role and status and that mitigated their sense of social and economic marginalization. Evangelical ministers conspired in the elevation of women by turning a necessity into a virtue. In short, they transformed the restriction of women to the home, the so-called women's sphere, into a kind of holy calling, and the Cult of True Womanhood became the new piety (Smith-Rosenberg, *Disorderly Conduct*, 133).

It is relevant that the first half of the nineteenth century was a time when women could not vote and their property and earnings belonged to their husbands or fathers. Rather than lamenting their lack of economic power, women turned it to their advantage by regarding the marketplace with moral opprobrium. Sarah Hale, editor of the popular magazine *Godey's Lady's Book* in Philadelphia, pronounced, "Our men are sufficiently money-making. Let us keep our women and children from the contagion as long as possible" (Cott, 68). But as Ann Douglas astutely points out, the reality was that wives reaped the benefits of the marketplace and conspired with their husbands in the pursuit of wealth, playing with alacrity the contradictory roles of consumer and saint:

> Middle-class women, like those who counseled them, inevitably preferred to stress their moral and religious "influence" rather than their evolving importance as highly socialized and expert shoppers. In actual fact, however, the two roles, saint and consumer, were interlocked and mutually dependent; the lady's function in a capitalist society was to appropriate and preserve both the values and the commodities which her competitive husband, father, and son had little time to honor or enjoy; she was to provide an antidote and purpose for their labor. (60)

Another factor in the changing attitudes toward the male and female roles was the child-centeredness of the middle-class family. The most exalted task of the mother was to raise her children to be good Christians (specifically good Protestants) and good capitalists who would preserve the class into which they were born and justify its privileges. Epitomizing the efforts of evangelical revivalists to conflate Christian and capitalist values, Reverend Charles Finney urged support of the new capitalist gospel of optimism and self-help, virtues that assured spiritual as well as material rewards for hard work (Smith-Rosenberg, *Disorderly Conduct*, 153). The complicity of nineteenth-century American Christianity with capitalism is perhaps best illustrated by the fact that women directed their efforts toward improving, or at least maintaining, the status of their own children exclusively rather than raising that of the lower classes and thereby promoting an egalitarian society (Brady, 87).

Thus, within the context of religious revivalism, the nineteenth-century obsession with child-rearing becomes comprehensible as a reaction to socioeconomic pressure, specifically as the desire of the middle class to protect its own and ensure the future of the republic. Social historians have noted that one of the practical effects of the cult of motherhood was that mothers reduced the number of their offspring so they could concentrate more on each (Mintz and Kellogg, 50–52). Parents even prolonged the dependency of their children, particularly their sons, to ensure their entry into the middle class (Ryan, *Cradle*, 179).

The authority of the father declined with his ability to pass on land and craft skills to his children, and his power became chiefly symbolic. In other words, he was the role model who prepared his sons for life in the work force, whereas the mother was viewed as the epitome of unselfish devotion and nurturance. The reason for the apparent shift in importance from the father's influence to the mother's was purely expedient and predicated on "the belief that children were more effectively governed by persuasion than coercion and by rewards than by punishments (a belief that ties in with the growing conviction among laissez-faire economists that laborers could be encouraged to work harder by rewarding rather than by penalizing them)" (Mintz and Kellogg, 59).

The contrasting parental functions of the father and mother in the nineteenth-century middle-class family were more nominal than real, insofar as both were united in their goal of raising their children to perpetuate the middle class and preserve the values of the republic. The apparent difference in parental roles derived from the fact that the father was active in the marketplace and the mother was isolated in the home, a situation that distanced her from the harsh realities of commercialism and enabled her, without an inkling of bad faith, to cloak sentimental hypocrisy under the mantle of virtue.

There is a profound discrepancy between the current and the historical perception of the "woman's sphere." During the formative years of the republic, women perceived themselves and each other as saintly emissaries of Christian benevolence, whereas to contemporary critics of domestic ideology they were sentimental hypocrites. In their view, the husband acquired wealth, the wife spent it, and together they formed the core capitalist dyad. The practice of Christian benevolence was motivated less by a desire to help the poor and unfortunate than by the need to serve as undercover agents for capitalism advancing middle- and upper-class interests.

The alleged hypocrisy of nineteenth-century middle-class women is part of a wider controversy over social control that raises questions about the motives behind the women's benevolent movement. At the behest of the clergy, the surge of benevolent and volunteer activities undertaken by women during the Second Great Awakening was inseparable from the Cult of True Womanhood that inspired women to channel their religious zeal toward their children. Their involvement in charitable causes was clearly motivated by a desire to ameliorate the social ills that were wreaking havoc in the cities and on the orderly and harmonious functioning of society. But what did that mean? A society that supported the elevation of the poor as well as the prosperous, or a society that oppressed and repressed the poor in order to prevent them from having a disruptive influence on the privileged classes? In other words, was the women's benevolent movement propelled by a genuine, altruistic, Christian desire to help the less fortunate by improving their station, or was it a crypto-capitalist conspiracy to protect the interests of their own families and their own class by preserving the socioeconomic status quo?

The issue here is one of social control. Social control is an ambiguous, emotionally charged term that invites ideological interpretation and bias. It can simply refer to the effort to maintain social order in the face of threats to its stability, or it can take on polemical significance when used to attack those, such as nineteenth-century philanthropists and reformers, who under the mask of benevolence allegedly conspired to oppress the poor (Wright, 200). The current debate over welfare and welfare reform in this country gives the nineteenth-century controversy contemporary resonance. For example, a number of social historians have compared the current war on poverty to nineteenth-century benevolent movements, alleging that "members of the so-called ruling class, or specific elitist groups, manipulated and regulated the attitudes and behavior of members of the lower classes or other deprived groups, *in order to promote their own self-interest*" (Trattner, *Social Welfare or Social Control?*, 4; italics in original).

The fact that the success of capitalism is predicated on the existence of a class system is consistent with the idea that efforts to help the poor were inspired more by a desire for social meliorism than for social reform. In other words, the goal was to alleviate the suffering of the poor either through acts of charity or institutionalization, but not to eliminate "the poor" completely because, despite the threat they posed to the stability of the republic, the poor were a convenient distraction from the unsavory realities of capitalism, such as greed, materialism, and class conflict. Moreover, class is a relational concept that depends on the existence of hierarchy. Thus, the upper, middle, and lower classes needed the poor to maintain within the existing class structure their positions of relative superiority. In short, the poor were an intrinsic and essential part of the social hierarchy, and whatever real or imaginary threats they might pose to the classes above them were significantly less than the social reform required to eliminate them by raising their station.

The profound ambivalence of the privileged classes toward the poor was not only economic but religious in origin, in a way that is reminiscent of the Puritans' hierarchical construction of social differences, explained in chapter 2. According to Winthrop, the social hierarchy gives both rich and poor the opportunity to demonstrate their spiritual regeneracy, the rich by showing "love, mercy, gentleness, temperance, etc." and the poor by showing "faith, patience, obedience, etc." Not incidentally, he designates the poor the "inferior sort" (82–83). The nineteenth-century republican version of this is that benevolence will bring the classes together in a mutually edifying partnership whereby the rich will learn to be charitable and frugal and the poor will learn to be self-reliant and industrious (Banner, 39–40).

Winthrop also makes clear in "A Defense of an Order of Court," however, that there are very definite limits on the mercy, or charity a rich man is required to show a stranger: "a man is not a fit object of mercy except he be in misery. Second, we are not bound to exercise mercy to others to the ruin of ourselves. Third, there are few that stand in needs of mercy at their first coming hither. As for hospitality, that rule doth not bind them further than for some present occasion, not for continual residence" (166).

In the nineteenth century, not even misery was enough to earn mercy, and in some respects Winthrop's strictures took an even more severe turn. The poor were perceived as not only a drain on the nation's resources but a primary source of crime, insanity, and immorality. The privileged classes saw themselves as besieged by the poor and blamed them for corrupting and bankrupting the republic. According to David Rothman, "The poor stood as a separate, distinct, and hostile class. Rather than appear as brothers with a common bond of interest in the community, they became paupers, endangering the balance of the system" (155).[3]

Benevolent societies became increasingly judgmental as the century wore on, and the problem of the poor, worsened by the influx of immigrants, created a moral distinction between the "deserving" and the "undeserving," the "worthy" and the "unworthy poor." For example, in 1818, the *First Annual Report of the New York Society for the Prevention of Pauperism* clearly places the primary blame for poverty on nine external as well as personal causes of dependency: ignorance, idleness, intemperance, profligate spending of money, premature marriage, gambling, pawnbrokers, prostitution, and last but not least, the charitable organizations in the city, which contributed to the problem by allowing themselves to be exploited (Leiby, 44). But by the 1850s the tone had become more accusatory than analytical. For example, in its *Twenty-Fourth Annual Report* (1855), the Union Benevolent Association in Philadelphia urges its volunteers "to discriminate between the deserving and undeserving of their charge" and goes on to congratulate them for making sure very little of their resources "was wasted upon unworthy objects" (5, 7). Poverty was, in short, viewed as a moral problem, one of character, and in this censorial tone we hear echoes not only of the Puritans but of Franklin, with his equation of virtue and right conduct with prosperity and success.

In the *Annual Report of the State Board of Charities* (1824), Secretary of State J.V.N. Yates criticizes the current system: "The poor laws tend to encourage the sturdy beggar and profligate vagrant, to become pensioners upon the public funds. The facilities afforded them, in being placed upon the pauper list, operate as so many invitations to become beggars" (952). As a remedy, he calls for stricter enforcement of settlement laws and the establishment of "houses of employment," or workhouses, that would require all paupers to work and "put an end the practice of street beggary" (956).

Twenty years later, in view of the failure of workhouses to eliminate pauperism, the *Visitor's Manual of the New York Association for Improving the Condition of the Poor* takes an even stronger stand on "the misapplication of charity" by dividing the poor into three categories: "*First*, those who have been reduced to indigence by infirmity, sickness, old age, and unavoidable misfortune; *Second*, those who have brought themselves to want and suffering by their improvidence and vices; and, *Third*, persons who are able but unwilling to labour, and are beggars and vagrants by profession" (Appendix, *First Annual Report*, 27). The manual then goes on to advise its volunteers to give alms "with great delicacy and caution" to those in the first category; to withhold them completely from the drunkard and give as little as possible and only when essential to those in the second so that they will not be more comfortable receiving alms than working; and as for those ne'er-do-wells in the third category, "the Scriptural rule applies without qualification: 'This we command you, that if any will not work, neither should he eat'" (28). Clearly the point of these restrictions was to elevate the poor in morality, to inculcate Puritan values and the Protestant ethic, and to transform them into productive members of society.

As a means of social control, benevolence was a reaction to capitalism that sought to obscure the realities of economic competition and class conflict and preserve the status quo. It was also a form of self-deception by the privileged classes who wished to protect their own interests *and* their responsibility by hiding the need for reform behind sentimentality. The opposite of sentimentalism is the desire for reform that seeks not merely to alleviate social suffering but to eliminate its causes. As God-fearing Christians, the privileged classes obviously felt guilty not only about the reality of the poor but about their hostility to the poor. Moreover, their motives of self-interest were mixed with genuine compassion. But the one thing they were not prepared to do was change the system that served their interests and produced the poor. In order to mask these embarrassing conflicts and maintain a façade of moral concern, the privileged classes needed to place blame for the problem of poverty on a source other than the system or the poor themselves. In short, they needed scapegoats; hence, the rise of nativism that created an unprecedented climate of intolerance and drew social, economic, and even legal distinctions between the children of the republic and its orphans.[4]

The social and economic upheaval of the Jacksonian period constituted for the middle class the kind of crisis that generates, in Girardian terms, the need for scapegoats. It was unacceptable for a self-conscious, self-righteous Christian society to revile the poor openly, and the inevitable tendency was to look for someone to blame, some scapegoat who could unite the privileged classes against a common enemy, just as the Puritans had manipulated deviance to create unity within their own community. A scapegoat would provide them with not only an excuse for the uncomfortable problem of poverty but a target for displacement for inter- and intraclass rivalry. Thus, following the 1840 election that marked the ascendancy of the middle class with the victory of the Whigs, the middle class adroitly shifted the public focus away from class politics to sectional, racial, ethnic, and religious conflict (Sellers, 363).

Within the context of the upsurge in immigration and the emancipation of the northern Negro that took place during the Jacksonian period, it was inevitable that the role of scapegoat should gradually shift in the eastern United States from the Indians to other groups of outsiders. The Indians were now too far removed from the mainstream of the culture to be considered a significant social presence, and by the 1840s efforts to disguise the reason for the animus against them as anything other than pure greed proved increasingly ludicrous. It was obvious, for example, that the revived image of the Indian as an ignoble rather than a noble "savage" who must be removed from white civilization derived primarily from imperialist considerations, namely the expansion into the western territories. Philip Borden sums up the rationalizations and their consequences: "White Americans reasoned that for the welfare of the Indian, to say nothing of the safety of white frontiersmen, it was necessary to keep the Indian removed from civilized men.... Removal came to mean the piecemeal penning of the Indians. The basic picture of the savage Indian established in the seventeenth century was reinvoked until his culture was crushed" (72).

The "piecemeal penning of the Indians" was a consequence of the fact that the so-called "permanent" frontier of 1840, which had extended to the lines of the Louisiana Purchase, moved to include a million and a quarter more square miles by 1848. Within that area the Indians were pressured into giving up their lands and moving to dramatically smaller territories. For example, the Indians surrendered almost nine-tenths of their land in Kansas in the 1850s, and in California 119 tribes lost half their lands through "extortionate" treaties (Borden, 86). The fact that the Indians still clung to what must have seemed to the white setters a naive belief in the land as a "common wealth" that belonged only to God invited their further victimization and exploitation by the white man, who did not acknowledge their rights to either citizenship or ownership of property. Totally excluded from political representation in the republic, they were the original orphans in the family trope that represented the republic. Priscilla Wald, in her insightful essay "Terms of Assimilation," even connects the abrogation of legal rights to loss of humanity or "personhood" as well as familial identity (63).[5]

Although immigrants and Negroes did not suffer the dispossession the Indians did, nativism also subjected them to insidious forms of exclusion, removal, and "penning" that recapitulate the Puritans' treatment of outsiders. Excluded to varying degrees from the political process, restricted in their social and economic opportunities, and often persecuted for their religious beliefs, these cultural orphans inhabited, if not reservations, both real institutions such as asylums and symbolic institutions bounded by walls of prohibitions and prejudices intended less to help them than to protect the republic from their influence.

Nativism grew out of the enormous increase in the rate of immigration between 1820 and 1850, which resulted in America's shift from a relatively homogeneous to a distinctly heterogeneous society. For example, in 1820 about 10,000 immigrants landed on American shores; by 1830 the number had doubled, and by the early 1840s it had risen to about 100,000. The most staggering increase occurred between 1845 and 1854, when annual figures for five consecutive years were in the vicinity of 400,000. During this brief period, approximately 2,900,000 immigrants arrived in America, more than in the preceding seventy years put together (Anbinder, 3–4). The quantity alone was enough to alarm the "native" population, but there were other factors as well that induced those who came to be called "nativists" to regard the influx of the foreign-born as something akin to a barbarian invasion.

As Tyler Anbinder points out in *Nativism and Slavery,* the immigrants' background and reasons for emigration varied considerably from the beginning of the century to the peak period. Primarily from Ireland and Germany, the immigrants who arrived during the early stage tended to be hard-working, skilled, middle-class, and Protestant, and despite the outbreaks of xenophobia during the 1790s, post-Revolutionary Americans at first welcomed immigrants as laborers and settlers who would help build up the nation. But by the mid-1830s, the demographics of immigration had changed dramatically. Unskilled, impoverished Catholics now constituted the bulk of Irish immigrants, and following the potato famines of the 1840s their numbers grew alarmingly to about one and a half million. Similarly, poverty and mass unemployment drove more and more Germans to American shores, and like the Irish they tended to be Catholic, unskilled, and poor (Anbinder, 4–5, 7–8). Many were also political revolutionaries considered dangerous by the indigenous population.

An indication of the depth of animosity toward immigrants is the fact that it warped the attitudes even of women, the standard-bearers of the benevolent movement, and cast a shadow of sectarianism over their activities.[6] For example, *The American Woman*, a newspaper of female nativists in Philadelphia, equated nativism with both republicanism and Protestantism. Catholic foreigners, who made up the bulk of the immigrant population, were reviled not only for their poverty but for their religion, which in the eyes of nativists divided their loyalties between the church and the state. The ultimate evil was foreign political influence: "what will be the condition of this country twenty years hence; when by the constant influx of foreigners, men of the lowest grade, grossly ignorant, and steeped in crimes, will have so materially increased the population; and who by the very short term of naturalization laws, will have obtained an influence in the political affairs of the country which cannot but be subversive, both of our *civil* and *religious* liberty?" (quoted in Hunter, 15; italics in original).

Republican nativists in the Whig party so feared the power of naturalized immigrants in the Democratic party (and rightly so, since their naturalization and influence were often bought by party leaders) that they tried to legislate political orphanhood in the form of a twenty-one-year waiting period for naturalization, to correspond with the child's passage into adulthood, and to restrict political office-holding to native-born Americans. Most states had abrogated the property requirement for suffrage by 1820, and the tax-paying requirement was also gradually abandoned in the early part of the century. As a result, naturalization laws had become considerably less strict. The law stipulated only a five-year period of residency for naturalization, which meant that foreigners of any origin, class, or political persuasion could become naturalized citizens and vote. In other words, immigrants were now considered "adoptable" children of the republic with the rights of citizenship. Needless to say, this change in the law represented a significant liberalization of attitudes and the increasingly democratic spirit of the republic, and its significance should not be discounted. Nevertheless, because of nativist influence, their status as "adopted" was perceived to be less than that of a "natural" child.

Not surprisingly, naturalized citizens were subjected to various forms of discrimination and harassment by nativists and nativist sympathizers who complained that the requirements for naturalization were too lenient. (A candidate had only to renounce all hereditary titles and "all allegiance and fidelity to any foreign prince, potentate, state or sovereignty... whereof he was before a citizen or subject" and prove to the satisfaction of the court that "he has behaved as a man of good moral character, attached to the Constitution of the United States, and well disposed to the good order of the same" (*Immigration and Nationality Laws*, 454–455). The desire of nativists to make naturalization more difficult led anti-Catholic extremists to recommend a change in the naturalization law stating that "no foreigners who come into the country after the law was passed shall ever be allowed the right of suffrage" (An American, 28).

Even more alarming to nativists than the Catholicism and political radicalism of the immigrants was their poverty. The fact that the majority of the six million foreigners who emigrated to America between 1800 and 1860 were destitute did little to endear them to native inhabitants. The beneficial effects of immigration on industry and transportation were quickly forgotten as it became apparent from statistics that immigrants were more of a burden than a benefit to society. Typical statistics target immigrants as the largest source of pauperism in 1820, and as more than half the almshouse population in New York, Philadelphia, and Boston in 1835. By mid-century the situation had worsened, with half to two thirds of Boston's paupers consisting of immigrants; in New York immigrants accounted for 86 percent of those on relief by 1860 (M. Jones, 114).

Ignoring the effects of prejudice, nativists placed the blame for immigrants' poverty and lack of social mobility on the immigrants themselves. Immigrants were arbitrarily classified as the "undeserving poor," and while the pressure on them to lift themselves out of pauperism was intense, their ability to do so was far less than that of a native-born person. For example, in documenting the lack of upward social mobility of common laborers in Newburyport during the nineteenth century, Stephan Thernstrom concludes that the working class was the highest level to which the poor could aspire. Within the working class, immigrants, particularly the Irish, were at a significant disadvantage, and during the 1850–1880 period "disproportionately high numbers of the foreign-born remained concentrated at the bottom of the occupational scale" (100–101).

The excessive number of impoverished immigrants placed pressure on institutions to care for them and created enormous resentment even among those who were involved in charitable enterprises designed to help them. While it seems ironic that some of the most vitriolic expressions of nativist sentiment come from leaders of benevolent societies, one must bear in mind that the immigrant invasion had made their job that much more difficult. One of the most surprising exponents of this negative view is none other than Charles Loring Brace, the New York missionary who founded the Children's Aid Society (CAS) in 1853 with the goal of helping orphans, whom he viewed as poverty's most unfortunate victims. Brace wrote the society's annual reports and used them as a forum to express his ignoble as well as his noble sentiments about the "dangerous classes," i.e. the poor. (His autobiography, *The Dangerous Classes of New York and Twenty Years Work Among Them* [1872], elaborates on his decidedly ambivalent views about the poor, whom he largely identified with immigrants.) The following is a sampler on "the scum of poverty" culled from his first and second annual reports in 1854 and 1855.

In the first, he notes the "tide of... alien passengers" landing in New York at a rate of nearly one thousand a day, with the highest proportions from Ireland and Germany, and comments:

> A portion of this immigration has been good—sober, hard-working people have spread over the country and become mingled with our population. Another part has been bad, almost the worst—the off-scouring of the poorest districts and most degraded cities of the Old World. The pauperism and poverty of England and Ireland has been drained into New-York.... in the main it has settled and stagnated in the city.... Our poorest streets began to be filled up with a thriftless, beggared, dissolute population. As is always the case in such circumstances, vice and laziness stimulated each other. (*First Annual Report*, 3–4)

Conflating the political and the economic in the *Second Annual Report*, Brace moves into high gear and near hysteria, suggesting in his first paragraph that the poverty of the immigrants poses a revolutionary threat not only to the cities but to the entire country: "The greatest danger that can threaten a country like ours, is from the existence of an ignorant, debased, permanently poor class, in the great cities. It is still more threatening if this class be of foreign birth, and different in habits from those of our own people." He goes on to warn that this degraded class not only corrupts "the honesty of working poor who are around them," but poses a political threat because it can turn the balance of an election and a revolutionary threat because it has a propensity for violence: "If their numbers be large, times of great want or excitement may call them out in ungoverned license, to seize upon the luxuries which surround them, but which they are never allowed to taste. The Indulgence, which has so long been chained down by poverty, can easily burst forth into Rapine. Neither liberty nor property would be safe in such hands" (*Second Annual Report*, 3).

As a result of the proliferation of the poor, the demands on private charities increased and relief rolls grew, especially in cities. Inevitably, "native" Americans resented their rising taxes, which they felt were supporting "the host of worthless foreigners, disgorged upon our shores," as the Philadelphia Board of

Governors grumbled in 1827 (quoted in Katz, 17). Almost thirty years later, the Boston Society for the Prevention of Pauperism protested, "A vast influx of foreign pauperism ready made and hatched abroad, combined of the worst and most intractable elements constituting such a social pest... has been thrown upon us; and difficulties and embarrassments unknown to the men of an earlier day... have multiplied apace" (quoted in Billington, 324).

The virulence of anti-immigration sentiment led to legislation specifically geared toward controlling the influx of paupers and codifying their cultural orphanhood, much as the Puritans had done with their legislation against strangers and outsiders. For example, a significant conflict took place between the federal government and the state governments over the head tax. According to state statutes, of which the Massachusetts statute of 1830 is representative, "masters of vessels are required to give bonds to indemnify the towns where they may land alien passengers against liability for their support as paupers, unless excused from so doing by the overseers of the poor" (Abbott, 148). In other words, the head tax served as a kind of insurance policy against incurring the financial burden of immigrant paupers and also as a means of preventing those who could not afford to pay the tax from entering the country.

A U.S. Supreme Court decision rendered in 1849 (*Smith v. Turner, Health Commissioner of the Port of New York* and *Norris v. City of Boston*, or the so-called "Passenger Cases") declared the head tax unconstitutional. Following hard on the heels of the Preemption Law of 1841 that offered one hundred and sixty acres to settlers in the west and acted as a lure to immigrants, this decision further enraged the nativists. In the 1856 "Report of the Committee on Foreign Affairs of the House of Representatives on 'Foreign Criminals and Paupers,'" the committee protested "the influx of vicious foreigners... a large number of [whom] are paupers and convicts, whose passage across the Atlantic is paid for them, and who come here without character, morality, religion, industry, or anything else to commend them to our favor." The report continues, "So emboldened have foreign powers become in making our country the receptacle for the dregs and off-scourings of their population, and thus relieving themselves of the burden of pauperism and crime, that some of them even now have the audacity to deny our right to prevent them from so doing" (Abbott, 157).

The committee implicitly defied the Supreme Court, arguing in favor of "the internal power of the States being sufficiently extensive to enable them, *if they deem it necessary* to exercise it, to exclude entire classes of persons" (italics in original). Responding to their own question, "Who shall remedy the evil?", they assert, "Both the general and State governments can do much to stay the tide of immigration of this undesirable population, and to protect society against its pernicious influences, and the injuries it threatens, not only to the prosperity and welfare of the country, but the perpetuity of our republican institutions" (Abbott, 159). Among the "measures" they ominously advise the states to take are "safeguards around the community, and such obstacles in the way of disembarking foreign imbeciles and desperadoes, as will soon put an end to their transportation hither." They also recommend "measures of reform... to restrain and suppress those evil influences, now everywhere felt, and which, if they be not checked will evidently undermine public and private virtue and public and private liberty" (Abbott, 160).

Nativism was hardly confined to the middle and upper classes, for working-class Americans also saw immigrants as a threat to their economic well-being and social status, blaming foreign competition for low wages, rising prices, and unemployment (Leonard and Parmet, 51). Working-class nativism fed on racism as well as xenophobia and set immigrants and northern Negroes against each other. Negroes were construed as competitors for white jobs at a time when jobs were scarce, but since most of them qualified only for low-paying, unskilled jobs, the only constituency with which they regularly came into genuine competition were immigrants, especially the Irish, at the bottom of the socioeconomic ladder.[7] This competition became a problem during the huge wave of immigration from 1830 to 1860 when impoverished Irish immigrants began to take jobs away from the Negroes.

The Negroes, of course, reciprocated the hostility, deprecating Irishmen as "white niggers" and "white Buckra" who were steadily displacing them from their menial jobs—even as servants—and depressing wages. By the time of the Civil War, unskilled Irish laborers had effectively taken over the service occupations, as well as canal and railroad construction (Litwack, 164–166). For the Irish, economic competition was inextricably linked to racial and political issues. Despite the large antislavery movement in Ireland, Irish Americans resented enormously the degradation of competing with Negroes and sharing the status of pariahs. The result was a virulent racism and doctrine of white supremacy (Litwack, 163). They also adopted an anti-abolitionist stance because they wanted to disassociate their identity completely from that of Negroes, a goal best accomplished if Negroes remained slaves.

This reaction was shared by other immigrants and native-born Americans who were also leery of any connection between wage or "white" slavery and black servitude. In this connection, white workers attached great importance to the label "freeman" during the Age of Jackson, regarding it as an emblem of economic and political independence that even the freed Negro could not enjoy. In other words, even though white workers complained about wage slavery, they still considered themselves politically and economically "freemen" superior in status to the Negro and even to the common people of Europe (Roediger, 140).

As a measure of their inferiority, freed Negroes were effectively noncitizens and shared with impoverished immigrants the status of cultural orphans in relation to the children of the republic. By 1860 approximately one black male in fourteen was eligible to vote, and various technicalities were employed to prevent even these few from exercising their right to suffrage. Obviously the Negroes' socioeconomic resentments were exacerbated by the fact that immigrants, even the Irish, could become naturalized citizens and obtain the franchise. Negroes were actually considered "anticitizens" by white freemen because their dependency and powerlessness made them "pawns of the rich and powerful" (Roediger, 56–57).

The tendency of the working class to treat Negroes as social inferiors played into the hands of the middle class by deflecting working-class resentment away from them and onto Negroes. Paranoia that the top and bottom levels of society would unite against the middle class resulted in "a simple pushing down on the vulnerable bottom strata of society [the Negroes], even when there was little to be gained from such a push" other than "the advantage of reassuring whites in a society in which downward social mobility was a constant fear — one might lose everything but not whiteness" (Roediger, 56–57, 60). In other words, the scapegoating of the Negro, like that of the immigrant, had the desired effect of displacing class tensions and preserving social stability.

Antebellum racism expressed itself most dramatically in the form of riots. Most of the riots that took place during the 1830s were directed primarily against abolitionists. In 1837, for example, urban rioters, who tended to be from working-class and immigrant backgrounds, launched one of their most vicious attacks on Pennsylvania Hall, the headquarters of the Pennsylvania Abolitionist Society, and the following day laid siege to the Friends Shelter for Colored Orphans, which they attempted to burn.

By the 1840s and 1850s, in the wake of the Panic of 1837, the target of collective violence shifted from abolitionists to ethnic and racial groups, particularly the Irish and the Negroes. The Philadelphia riots of 1844 and other riots against Irish Catholics in northern cities during the 1830s and 1840s were surpassed in number by riots against Negroes. In fact, most of the collective violence in northern cities was directed against freed Negroes. Between 1832 and 1849, Philadelphia alone experienced five interracial battles in which the Irish and other white laborers played a significant role because they resented the hiring of Negroes during periods of depression and unemployment (Litwack, 101). Outside of Philadelphia, clashes occurred between Irish coal miners and their Negro competitors in 1842, and in 1853 armed Negroes replaced striking Irishmen on the Erie Railroad. Confrontations similar to those in Philadelphia took place in other cities, such as New York, where Irish and Negroes fought on the docks, a foreshadowing of the New York Draft Riots of 1863.

In analyzing the outbreaks of violence during the Jacksonian period, Michael Feldberg emphasizes the obvious racial component—that northern rioters were white and intent on sending a message to blacks to "'stay in their place.' Northern whites might not have owned slaves, but they could use rioting to prove to themselves that northern blacks were as powerless as their slave brothers" (43). But another explanation for racial rioting is that its goal, like that of the religious and ethnic riots of the Jacksonian period, was "preservatist" of class interests. The privileged classes who held economic, social, and political power used the riots to maintain their position in the social hierarchy by setting groups lower on the scale against each other (Feldberg, 34). The socioeconomic basis for these riots also reflects the degree to which Negroes served as scapegoats for class tensions between the oppressed working class (the "wage slaves") and the privileged classes who oppressed them.

In short, the scapegoating of immigrants and Negroes represented a diversion from class tensions. Sellers sums it up neatly: "Capitalism disarmed opposition by setting the most exploited at each other's throats. Phobic contempt for failure both energized effort and turned the shame of proletarianized whites against even more vulnerable blacks and immigrants. Establishment preachers and politicians, stirring plebeian racism and nativism to virulence during the Jackson years, diverted cresting plebeian anger from a frightened bourgeoisie" (386). It also masked hostility toward the poor, manifest in the treatment of its most pathetic representatives: orphans.

Just as the children of the middle class were idolized as the great white hope of the new republic, impoverished orphans were demonized as its nemesis. A pervasive and disturbing presence in American cities during the mid-nineteenth century, orphans represented the most abject form of poverty and destitution. In the popular imagination the homeless, parentless child also signified the capriciousness of fate that could catapult anyone, even a member of the upper or middle class, from prosperity into destitution. In this sense, the orphan was a powerful symbol that cut across class lines and epitomized the frightening reality of social vulnerability. Although few could rise to the rank of riches, anyone could become poor, or even an orphan. Nicholas Biddle, in his address on the laying of the cornerstone for the Girard College for Orphans in Philadelphia in 1833, posed the uncomfortable question: "what child is there who may not be a poor orphan? Who is there indeed among us whose children may not yet need the blessings of this institution? Let none of us, in the confidence of prosperity, deem his own offspring secure. Yes, fellow citizens, this college is our own; the property of us all. It is intended to remedy misfortunes to which all are equally liable" (15).

Helpless, dependent, and potentially dangerous, orphans incarnated the fears of the privileged classes, and their treatment serves as a yardstick by which to measure social attitudes toward the poor and the groups that made up their ranks. Orphans who existed literally outside the family were positioned figuratively outside it as well, as the benevolent movement played itself out in dynamics of inclusion and exclusion. A major reason orphanhood became such a troublesome issue during the first half of the nineteenth century was the marked increase in the number of orphans caused by the epidemics, depressions, vice, and other social ills that afflicted the expanding urban population. Orphans were already a problem even in the eighteenth century, when there was more poverty than ever before as a result of population growth, unemployment, and the effects of the French and Indian War. Families were no longer able to assume the responsibility of caring for orphans, even those who belonged to the community, and it fell to the government to subsidize custodial care and find alternatives to outdoor relief, apprenticeship, and contractual arrangements. The major innovation was the almshouse, which became the dominant form of poor relief in Massachusetts in the late eighteenth century.

The almshouse represented the beginning of institutionalized welfare and also of institutionalized ostracism of the poor. During the nineteenth century, the fate of orphans, first in almshouses and subsequently in orphanages intended specifically to meet their needs, illustrates this exclusionary trend. In the late eighteenth century, the options of placing children with relatives or indenturing them as servants were no longer as feasible because families preferred to hire cheap immigrant servants rather than assume the financial responsibility of raising an orphan. Thus, during the early part of the nineteenth century, children in need of public assistance were increasingly placed in almshouses where, despite efforts to keep them separate, they came in contact with the ill, the insane, and paupers (Bremner, *Children and Youth in America*, 262).

It soon became apparent that the almshouse was far from beneficial for children. Dorothea Dix, after visiting almshouses in New York in 1844, complained in a report, "They do not guard against the indiscriminate association of the children with the adult poor. The education of these children, with rare exceptions, is conducted on a very defective plan." In a similar vein, a New York Senate committee in 1856 declared it an outrage that children be incarcerated in poorhouses, which they compared to "the worst possible nurseries" (quoted in Folks, 27).

As a result of such criticism, orphanages, which were virtually nonexistent in the eighteenth century, began to proliferate. Between 1800 and 1830 fifteen orphan asylums opened under the auspices of private charities, Catholics, and Protestants. In the 1830s orphanages, as well as reformatories for disobedient children, showed a significant increase, numbering twenty-three; during the 1840s thirty more were founded. By 1850 there were twenty-seven private and public child-care institutions in New York State alone that had become viable alternatives to apprenticeship rather than mere dumping grounds (Rothman, 207).

A related development was that private orphanages gradually came to replace public, as the government became increasingly reluctant to fund separate institutions, particularly in view of unstable economic conditions. For example, the Philadelphia Children's Asylum, which opened in 1820, was closed in 1835, and a limited number of orphans were returned to the almshouse, a trend evident in other cities as well. It was left to private charities and benevolent societies to leap into the breach. The result was that sectarian, ethnic, and occupation-related benevolent societies expanded their efforts to include orphans to the extent that by the middle of the century in the four major cities (Boston, Philadelphia, New York, and Baltimore) private charities had become the major source of assistance for indigent youth (Clement, *Welfare and the Poor*, 137).

The reason for the increase in the number of orphan asylums was not as altruistic as one might surmise and is inseparable from the rise of nativism in the early years of the republic. Because the poor were considered such a deleterious moral influence on society, it was deemed prudent to prevent orphans from contributing to the corruption. Thus, along with their professed intention of inculcating values that would enable orphans to survive and become self-supporting members of society, orphanages, like other custodial institutions, were also an instrument of social control intended to protect the republic and its future heirs, the children of the privileged classes.

Benevolent societies focused on destitute children not only out of a desire to help them but to isolate them. Young rag-pickers, street Arabs, beggars, and thieves infested city streets, committed crimes, and created consternation among nativists, who were particularly alarmed about the baneful influence of immigrant orphans with alien religious, cultural, and political values. The purpose of institutionalization was not only to rehabilitate but to prevent these children from corrupting their native-born peers, and in this sense, institutionalization was a form not only of confinement but of quarantine.

The failure of public institutions—prisons, insane asylums, and almshouses—to rehabilitate adults also influenced the shift in focus to children, who were more amenable to instruction and influence. In both public and private orphanages discipline was rigorous, and children received religious and moral instruction in the traditional Protestant values of industry, thrift, honesty, and respect for authority that would presumably enable them to become useful, law-abiding members of society.

But during the 1850s removal of orphans from cities as well as from families was considered even more desirable than institutionalization, not only for reasons of rehabilitation. In the midst of a request for financial support, Brace makes the following appeal to the self-interest of CAS's benefactors, in the form of their property, their pocketbooks, and even the survival of the republic:

> It should be remembered, that there are no dangers to the value of property or to the permanency of our institutions, so great as those from the existence of such a class of vagabond, ignorant, ungoverned children. This "dangerous class" has not begun to show itself, as it will be in either eight or ten years, when these boys and girls are matured. Those who were too negligent and selfish to notice them as children, will be fully aware of them as men. They will vote. They will have the same rights as ourselves, though they have grown up ignorant of moral principle, as any savage or Indian. They will poison society. They will be perhaps be embittered at the wealth, and luxuries, they can never share. Then let Society beware, when the outcast, vicious, reckless multitude of New York boys, swarming now in every foul alley and low street, come to know their power and *use it*! (*First Annual Report*, 13–14; italics in original)

A more explicit statement of this nightmarish vision of class-based, European style revolution spearheaded by children is found in an 1854 address delivered on the occasion of the incorporation of the American Female Guardian Society (AFGS), which was founded in 1834 as the American Female Moral Reform Society and which published the influential periodical, *The Advocate of Moral Reform and Family Guardian,* in which the address appears. In urging intervention on behalf of destitute young "heathen," the address warns: "Let it be neglected, and the number of paupers and vagrants continue to multiply in the same ratio as at present, and the time may not be distant when the division of classes — the poor arrayed against the rich — may give us a revised edition of such scenes as have been once and again enacted in the streets of Paris" (*Twentieth Annual Report,* 82).

Brace's solution was to remove the orphans from the cities, which he blamed for the corruption of immigrants. Brace actually concedes, "These miserable creatures of Europe, the scum and refuse of ill-formed civilizations, or the victims of oppression and public neglect, have been scattered over our land, and have done a useful part" by performing manual labor and even improving in character, *except in cities,* where "the most idle and unenterprising, the most needy and dependent of these emigrants, the unprincipled and those who have been the lowest degraded by the inequalities of European society, have settled themselves" (*Third Annual Report,* 4). Following this logic, Brace concludes that the social and religious salvation of orphans, whom he compares to "savages or Indians," lies in their placement with families in the country, comparable to the removal of Indians to reservations, the "penning" that Borden describes.

CAS used volunteers, whom they called "visitors," to seek out neglected and orphaned children in the city and place them in institutions. CAS's ultimate goal was "to get these children of unhappy fortune utterly out of their surroundings, and to send them away to kind Christian *homes in the country.* No influence, we believe, is like the influence of a *Home* [of] a friendly religious family, where neatness, order and faithfulness are taught him" (*Third Annual Report,* 8; italics in original).

"Placing out" was in the tradition of indenture and apprenticeship and foreshadowed foster care, which became popular at the turn of this century. In New York, precedent for placing out was set by the American Female Moral Reform Society in the late 1830s. Founded to save young women from prostitution, the society began placing indigent women and children in homes where they could receive shelter and employment. Because supply exceeded demand, the society opened a "Home for the Friendless and House of Industry" in 1848 to accommodate women and children until they could be placed in homes, preferably rural and Protestant. Other New York benevolent societies, such as the American Female Guardian Society, the Asylum for Friendless Boys, and the Five Points House of Industry, also advocated and practiced it as a method for dealing with dependent children less expensive and more effective than institutionalization.

CAS achieved special notoriety because it concentrated on placing orphans and destitute children with families on farms in upstate New York, the Midwest, and the West, a policy that offered the advantage of getting rid of them, like the Indians. It was highly successful, with more than 100,000 children put on orphan trains and placed "in kind Christian homes in the country" before 1859.[8] (The children could only hope they were kind, as there was little opportunity to follow up.) The obligation of their new families was to raise and educate them, in return for which the children were to work as apprentices or hired hands. In other words, families were under no obligation to adopt them and thereby give them their name and the right to inherit, and in the majority of cases most orphans were not adopted.[9] Thus, orphans remained marginalized, on the socioeconomic and legal periphery of the family.

Advocates of placing out believed that it was essential to remove neglected and corrupted children from their own families and raise them in upstanding (i.e., Christian) families rather than institutionalize them. Brace writes: "children cannot all be shut up in Asylums, and indeed, it may be doubted, whether they are, even in the best Institutions, improved, by the crowding of numbers together. We have wished to make every kind of religious family, who desired the responsibility, an Asylum or a Reformatory Institution, for the vagrant children" (*Second Annual Report*, 5).

In according the family the status of an "asylum or reformatory institution," Brace is heaping upon it a high form of praise that is consistent with the idealization of the family as the ultimate source of Christian (i.e., Protestant) virtue. It is not "the family" in general that is so valued, however, but specifically the native-born, white, middle-class, Protestant family. So narrow was the definition of "family values" during this period and so tied to the welfare of the republic that it was even deemed acceptable to *remove* children from their families and subject them to a coerced form of orphanhood. For example, landmark legislation initiated by the American Female Guardian Society and enacted in New York in 1853 gave the state the right to act *in loco parentis* for the benefit of the "worse than orphan" children by removing them from their unfit parents or parent (*Twentieth Annual Report*, 81). "An Act to provide for the care and instruction of idle and truant children" reads: "By assuming the place of a parent to its helpless children, and undertaking their training, it [our state] raises them from the degradation of their previous condition to one of equality with the other pupils of our public schools, while it saves such pupils from the dread of debasement by intercourse with them" (New York Association for Improving the Condition of the Poor, *Tenth Annual Report*, 71)

The passage of this act clearly was a watershed in children's rights legislation and was motivated by genuine outrage at the treatment and suffering of neglected children. For example, in an article protesting the "Legal and Moral Claims of Dissolute Parents" (1854), the AFGS declares: "A self-abandoned parent, who leaves his offspring to suffer hunger, cold and nakedness, and the greater moral wrong of ignorance of all that is good and lovely and desirable in the paths of knowledge, who loves to indulge his appetite for strong drink, more than he loves the bodies or souls of his children, forfeits his legal and moral claim to retain them in his possession" (21). Thus, parents now could be forced to give up their children and to sign documents surrendering their rights. (CAS actually called these documents "surrender books.")

The new law reflected a desire for social control based on self-interest as well as altruism and was deeply implicated in nativist ideology. The fact that the Society sent "home missionaries" to save the "heathen" children by placing them in "Christian" homes with "Christian" families totally discounts the fact that virtually all the "heathen" children were Christian, albeit Catholic, an affiliation that placed them in the eyes of most reformers in the "dangerous" category that derived from the association of Catholic immigrants with political radicalism. Between 1848 and the Civil War, AFGS refused to accept any child for admission unless the parents agreed to place the child in a rural, Protestant home, a policy that naturally aroused the ire of Catholics. Furthermore, the AFGS went so far as to insist in "Claims of Orphan and Destitute Children" (1854) that good Christian (Protestant) families had a moral responsibility to adopt these children and serve as their foster parents, and tried to manipulate them with a neo-Puritanical argument that conflated good works with evidence of election: "those who have no children of their own... ought, *if they possess the spirit of the Gospel*, to manifest it by caring for some of the many who will perhaps otherwise be cast out to die; or, brought up in ignorance of physical and moral laws, perhaps prove a curse to themselves and community" (71; italics added).

It is noteworthy that the vast majority of private institutions founded prior to 1850 for the care of orphaned and neglected children were religiously affiliated, reflecting the competition between Protestants and Catholics both to "save" children from each other's influence and to increase their own ranks. Like the Puritans, Protestants continued to view themselves as a spiritual elite whose obligation was to keep the faith in order to preserve the republic. An example of the theocratic conflation of church and state is the following quotation from an article called "The Bible in Public Schools" that appeared in *The Quarterly Review of the American Protestant Association* in 1845: "We must never forget that this is a Protestant land, that the spirit of Protestant faith pervades the very genius of its institutions, and that its rights and privileges have been steeped in Protestant blood" (quoted in Hunter 30).

In keeping with that tradition, Brace was a Protestant missionary, the society was supported by Protestants of different denominations, and CAS placed its children with rural Protestant families. In Philadelphia fifteen new private charities, four of them for children, were established between 1840 and 1854, and most of them were under the auspices of reform-minded, evangelical Protestants anxious to convert Irish Catholic immigrants and save them from intemperance as well as poverty.

Overriding their goal of saving immigrant souls from Catholicism and their bodies from intemperance and poverty was the desire to save themselves from the various social and political evils they claimed Catholicism produced. In this respect, Protestant missionary organizations used Americanization as a form of social control (Bremner, *Children and Youth in America*, 400).

The sectarianism and evangelism of these Protestant benevolent institutions did little to encourage assimilation of immigrants and may even have subverted it. In Philadelphia, for example, it fed the tensions between Irish immigrants and native Philadelphians that led to the riots of 1844. It also resulted in the formation of more Catholic charities, including orphanages, following the riots. In contrast with Protestants, Catholics tended to prefer institutional care for dependent children because it presented more opportunity for structure and discipline than a home setting. Catholic resentment was understandable, particularly in light of such commentary as the following on the part of one of CAS's visitors, published in the *New York Daily Times*: "It is a fact worth noticing, that of all the many children who come under our operations, very seldom, indeed, is ever one an American or a Protestant. The Irish emigrants are generally more degraded, even than the German. They rise more slowly, and are cursed with that scourge of their race—Intemperance" (quoted in Bremner, *Children and Youth in America*, 416).

The practice of "placing out" coincided with the policy of segregation in public education. Since public education was based on residential patterns, immigrant children whose parents had settled in urban ghettos were educated separately from native children and effectively excluded from the social mainstream (Clement, "The City and the Child," 239). Moreover, these children generally attended institutional or industrial schools intended for the poor that kept them separate from middle-class WASP children on whom they might have a negative influence. The fact that CAS established its schools in local neighborhoods, which were ethnically distinct, further ensured the segregation.

The other effect of educational segregation was that it constrained the social and economic mobility of immigrant children. The education of orphans was intended not to elevate them to the level of their betters but to fit them for a life of genteel poverty as farmers, manual laborers, or factory workers. At CAS's industrial schools for girls, for example, the only skill taught was sewing, and the Industrial Home for the Instruction of Girls in the Arts of Housewifery and Sewing, founded in 1857, explicitly states that its goal is to make the girls fit to be "competent servants" (*First Annual Report*, 3). For orphans and destitute children, the glass ceiling was preferable to the black pit, and benevolent societies did their best to generate enthusiasm for their limited options. For example, the following is the first verse from a song, to be sung to the tune of Yankee Doodle Dandy, taken from the *Home Song Book* of the AFGS's Home for the Friendless:

> *A farmer's life is the life for me,*
>   *I own I love it dearly,*
> *And every season, full of glee,*
>   *I take its labor cheerily.*
> *To plough or sow, to reap or mow,*
>   *Or in the barn to thresh, sir,*
> *All's one to me, I plainly see,*
>   *'Twill give me health and cash, sir. (41)*

Negro and Indian children also attended their own schools as part of an unwritten policy of segregation that permeated the entire fabric of American society. As one scholar writes: "There were schools for rich and for poor, for blacks and for whites, for boys and for girls, for Catholics and for Protestant groups... clusters of like-mindedness, shielded from strangers by walls of social, political and intellectual protection" (Finkelstein, 116). Evidence that private charities defined Americanization in similar terms is reflected in the fact that Indian and Negro children were not admitted to the same orphanages as white children. Statistics corroborate the high number of institutions for "special classes" of children, with Philadelphia, Providence, New York, and the Cincinnati area establishing orphanages for "colored" children prior to 1855 and an asylum for destitute and orphaned Indian children near Buffalo, New York in 1845 (Folks, 39).

Homer Folks credits Quaker influence with their establishment, as if it was a positive development, but a more realistic interpretation is that these orphanages came into being because Negro and Indian children were unwelcome in private white orphanages. It was, of course, a less pressing issue for Indian children, most of whom were segregated on reservations anyway and did not have access to institutional care elsewhere. Indian education, which was minimal, consisted of efforts by private, religious, missionary agencies to "civilize" them in schools established on the reservations. Around the middle of the century, interest developed in placing Indian children in boarding schools off the reservation where they would be removed from the influence of their parents and the tribe and presumably become assimilable (Bremner, *Children and Youth in America*, 439). Instead of an improvement, this policy represented yet another form of segregation and cultural dislocation directed at the most vulnerable members of Indian society.

Discrimination against Negro orphans was even more explicit. For example, Stephen Girard, the philanthropist who established Girard College in Philadelphia for the care and education of orphans, specified that it was for "poor male, *white* orphan children" (italics added), a policy that did not change until 1968 (quoted in Herrick, 1927). Moreover, in Philadelphia black children could receive aid only in the public almshouse, not the separate children's asylum; compounding the problem was the fact that Negro orphanages were as unpopular as Negro orphans. The preface to the first report (1836) of the Association for the Care of Coloured Orphans in Philadelphia documents the "aversion of some of their white neighbours to the scheme," which was so strong that "it was difficult to locate the Shelter within city bounds." The preface also expresses the tendency of benevolent societies to view Negro orphans as the lowest of the low: "The association was formed for the purpose of relieving the necessities of the poorest of the poor; for where do we find, even in populous cities, a class of the human family more abject, or more deserving of the fostering hand of benevolence, than the parentless children of the African race in this country" (vi).

Ironically enough, the black community resisted the shelter as well, for reasons that are not clearly explained but may well have had to do with the fear of "attracting the depredations of lawless kidnappers" who resented the presence of the black orphans in their neighborhoods. Another possibility is that white administration of a black orphanage may have reminded the Negroes all too painfully of the relationship of the master/mistress/overseer to slaves, as suggested by the stated goal in the constitution (1857) of The Home for Destitute Colored Children: to "afford a home, food, clothing and instruction in school learning, and household labor to indigent colored children, and at a suitable age to place them in families [white obviously] to learn some useful occupation or trade" (*Second Annual Report*, 10). In general, the attitude of these institutions reflected a combination of guilt, condescension, and genuine compassion, dominated by value judgments. For example, following its proclamation in 1855 of its commitment to accepting everyone ("except those condemned by civil law"), the Colored Home in New York acknowledges this discriminatory policy: "but, as much as is possible, we separate the comparatively pure from the unworthy" (*Fifteenth Annual Report*, 7).

The treatment of orphans and destitute children by benevolent societies at mid-century epitomizes attitudes toward the poor in general and toward their scapegoats, impoverished Catholic immigrants and freed northern Negroes. Prejudice toward immigrant, Negro, and Catholic orphans was a manifestation not only of xenophobia, racism, and sectarianism but of hostility toward the poor and of the general tendency to blame these groups of outsiders who represented difference for the problem of poverty. As children who had lost or been removed from their families, orphans represented Catholic immigrants and poor immigrants who circled outside the orbit of the republican family, i.e. outside the class system, and were adoptable into it legally but on a socially and economically limited basis. Orphans also represented the unadoptable: Indians, Negroes, and to a certain extent women who were variously marginalized socially, economically, and politically by being denied the vote, property rights, and citizenship. As such, these orphans were the direct descendants of the "strangers" the Puritans took such pains to ostracize from their communities and the ancestors of the homeless, legal as well as illegal immigrants, ghetto blacks, reservation Indians, and welfare mothers who exist on the margins of society today.

CHAPTER SIX

Sentimental Strategies in "Orphan Tales"

> Mamma never kept house, and I never saw any body do it.
> —THE WIDE, WIDE WORLD

Because orphans were such a ubiquitous and disturbing presence in mid-nineteenth-century American cities, it is hardly surprising that they figure so prominently in sentimental fiction. What is surprising, however, is that fictional orphans are so unrepresentative of society's real orphans, who were stationary, as opposed to upwardly mobile, members of the underclass. From a cultural standpoint, a literary work can be as important for those aspects of social reality it does not portray as for those it does. Insofar as one can reasonably analyze a novel in terms of a poetics of absence (what is left out) as well as a poetics of presence (what is put in), then this criterion becomes, beyond a standard of realism, a measure of ideology. Fiction that professes sympathy for "poor" orphans but does not depict genuine representatives of the category validates the charges of hypocrisy typically leveled at the sentimental genre. But the irony is that precisely because sentimental novels failed to depict the reality of orphanhood, they are a "realistic" mirror of the middle-class ideology that ordained the factual as well as the fictional exclusion of the poor from the family of the republic.

It is not only in the sentimental novel that the poor received so little attention during this period. Robert Bremner surmises that the reason for the neglect of the poor in the canonical literature is not that they were unknown but that they were considered unworthy of notice. He maintains that the popular ethic of democratic individualism fostered a greater interest in moral than in economic issues, in psychology and character than in material circumstances (*From the Depths*, 87). Certainly poverty is not a major, or at least not an obvious, theme in the novels of mid-century American Renaissance authors.[1] However, popular male novelists of the 1840s and 1850s, such as Ned Buntline and George Lippard, wrote serialized thrillers that depicted poverty in a lurid and sensational manner. Melodramas, some based on novels by Lippard and Buntline and others on European plays, copied this approach by showcasing crime, vice, and disaster, as Daniel C. Gerould notes in *American Melodrama*. Both genres also tended to rely on a "rags to riches" fantasy in which it was revealed that the impoverished protagonists were really gentlemen and ladies who had lost their wealthy parents and their substantial inheritances (Bremner, *From the Depths*, 91).

The sentimental novel duplicates this formula by treating poverty as a temporary obstacle rather than an ineluctable condition, and through the archetypal orphan protagonist enacts the capitalist ideology that underlies sentimental fiction, specifically the orphan tale that was its most popular subgenre during the 1850s. The ideology encoded in the formula of loss and recovery establishes the orphan tale as an allegory of middle-class survival. The trajectory these novels follow is a brief downward and long upward curve as the orphaned protagonist, almost invariably a young female, falls from the middle class and regains her position in the social hierarchy by the end of the novel. This fantasy of recuperation contrasts with the fate of the typical orphan, whose parents were poor and who inherited a class identity that drastically curtailed her potential to ascend the socioeconomic ladder.

The values these novels implicitly endorse are not those of upward mobility but those of Social Darwinism. In this sense, the fictional orphan can be viewed as a reaction to middle-class anxiety about change, loss, and poverty; in short, about the precariousness of social identity in a rapidly changing world. Within this context, the formula of loss and recovery represents a symbolic effort to allay anxiety, and the orphan serves as a representative of the status quo insofar as the novels, in repeating the same formula, reiterate the fantasy of middle-class stability.

The fact that sentimental novels so frequently feature female orphans as their protagonists is not simply a reflection of the domestic ideal or the Cult of True Womanhood but of capitalist ideology. Despite the obvious complicity of the sentimental novel with middle-class values, most recent criticism has tended to focus on the gender issues that underlie their function as entertainment for a middle-class female audience. Certainly it is significant that the most popular novels from 1820 to 1870 were by, for, and about women, and in *Woman's Fiction* Nina Baym correctly interprets them in terms of female empowerment: "In essence, it is the story of a young girl who is faced with the necessity of winning her own way in the world.... The happy marriages with which most... of this fiction concludes are symbols of successful accomplishment of the required task and resolutions of the basic problems raised in the story, which is in the most primitive terms the story of the formation and assertion of a feminine ego" (11–12). This formation exemplifies, Baym believes, "a moderate, or limited, or pragmatic feminism" insofar as the heroine develops from a real or psychological child whose ego is damaged or nonexistent into a woman who has "developed a strong conviction of her own worth as a result of which she does ask much from herself" (18–19).

Although Baym acknowledges how industrialism and the rise of capitalism shaped gender roles during this period, she fails to address the class implications of the "overplots" in the two versions of the orphan tale: one who "begins as a poor and friendless child, most frequently an orphan" vs. the "pampered heiress who becomes poor and friendless in mid adolescence through the death or financial failure of legal protectors" (35). The point is that the two plots exemplify not only the fortitude of the heroine but the capacity of the middle class to survive and surmount *their* troubles.

To her credit, however, Baym does tie the orphan theme to economic events, particularly the Panic of 1837, and notes that many women began their careers as authors out of financial necessity. She infers that both the message in the novels that women should, and could, be prepared to support themselves and the formulaic nature of the orphan's tale derive from the justifiable anxiety middle-class women felt about their own financial security. Whereas they deplored (and envied?) the wealth and profligacy of the upper class, they also "abhorred and feared poverty" (35) and clung to a conviction that middle-class gentility represented the moral high ground on which merit assured one a place (46–47). But while Baym discerns in these women authors a judgmental attitude toward the poor that qualified their professions of sympathy, she, like most feminist critics, does not locate them within the larger context of class tensions.

Industrialization accentuated class divisions and had the effect of isolating middle- and upper-class women in the home. Whereas women in colonial times performed income-producing labor or otherwise contributed to the family livelihood, the Cult of True Womanhood attached a social stigma to "ladies" working outside the home and assigned that role to the lower classes. As Gerda

Lerner puts it, "Another result of industrialization was increasing differences in life styles between women of different classes. When female occupations, such as carding, spinning, and weaving, were transferred from home to factory, the poorer women followed their traditional work and became industrial workers. The women of the middle and upper classes could use their newly gained time for leisure pursuits: they became ladies" (190).

Yet some middle-class women were frustrated by their status, which provided them with education but prevented them using it. The only professions in which women could readily participate were nursing and teaching, and their basic exclusion from all others was one of the factors that inspired the woman's rights movement during the 1840s. This exclusion was part of the larger issue that incited women to take action against their degraded legal status, which denied them both the vote and legal rights apart from their husbands. Everything a woman owned became her husband's when she married, and she had no right to enter independently into any legal contract. Thus, from a purely political standpoint, women also numbered among the ranks of the republic's orphans, and compared with immigrants who could at least obtain political rights by becoming naturalized, they occupied an inferior position closer to that of a slave.

Of course, most middle-class women were untroubled by these distinctions and embraced their limited role in the home as if the domestic scene were a dominion instead of a prison. Leisure was a status symbol and work a stigma, a distinction reinforced by the ladies' mass-circulation magazines of the period, such as *Godey's Lady's Book* and *Peterson's*, which served as social gospel for middle-class women by indoctrinating them with standards of literary, moral, and domestic taste. Sarah Josepha Hale, editor of *Godey's*, even went so far as to connect the domestic ideal and the Cult of True Womanhood to the welfare of the republic, a republic that was not only middle-class but distinctly Anglo-Saxon in origin and composition.

As Hale writes in the preface to *Manners; or, Happy Homes and Good Society All the Year Round*, a book that summarizes her belief in the importance of power of the home: "When we study domestic life in its influence on national characteristics, it seems as if the two Anglo-Saxon Peoples were intrusted with the holy duty of keeping pure the home of woman and the altar of God" (5). She goes on to give examples from the nobility and even the monarchy of the purity of home life in England and suggests, "America has all needed means of making her history unparalleled in the reality of happy homes and good society through the Republic." She closes with a statement that sums up the purpose of her magazine, the dissemination of manners as a bulwark of the nation: "The Anglo-Saxon peoples have another bond of unity,—they represent home-life, in its highest characteristics among the nobility of England and in its best aspects of purity and happiness in America. These characteristics and virtues of the Princely and the Popular are united in the *Manners* that form the most perfect standard for social life and home happiness" (6; emphasis in original).

The point is that ladies' magazines were geared to an elite audience in terms of both class and ethnicity, and their content reflected the narrowness of their concerns. For example, the magazines published poetry and fiction, but these rarely pertained to the poor except as objects of pity or benevolence. But occasionally a story or poem appeared that directly critiqued the hardheartedness or hypocrisy of the privileged classes in relation to the poor. For example, a story that appeared in *Peterson's* in 1855, "Charity Begins at Home," is heavily didactic in its message. The protagonist, Mrs. Gray, who devotes herself to raising money for improving the appearance of the church and funding foreign missions, is thoroughly misguided in her zeal and understanding of charity. She neglects the needs of her own community and even her own family, namely her cousin who died leaving four orphaned children with whom she did not want to burden herself (Meany, 220–222). Similarly, "The Poor Man's Appeal," a poem that appeared in the same issue of *Peterson's*, chastises the privileged for their callousness and contempt. The first stanza reads:

> *Turn not away with scornful lips,*
> *From this our sad appeal,*
> *We only crave that sympathy*
> *Which all mankind should feel;*
> *And if you deem the iron chain*
> *Of poverty and woe,*
> *That weighs upon our care-worn frames*
> *Has made our mind as low;*
> *Remember that the tender bud,*
> *The blossom that you slight,*
> *Shoots upward from a fertile bed,*
> *And struggles for the light. (Anon., 281)*

The poem ends with the plea, "Show mercy to the poor."

In both the story and the poem, the focus is not really on the plight of the poor and the need for social reform but on the spiritual state of the privileged. The implication is that their attitude needs to change not only for the sake of the poor but *for their own sake* to demonstrate their state of grace and worthiness of salvation, just as the Puritans needed to prove to themselves and to others that they numbered among the elect.

In contrast with *Godey's* and *Peterson's* were the publications of the lower class, specifically of female mill workers who, under the aegis of the Lowell Female Labor Reform Association, called for labor reform through the *Voice of Industry*. The difference in not only the content but the fiery tone of the following excerpt, compared with the tepid didacticism of the preceding, speaks volumes about the ideological gap between women of the lower class and women of the privileged classes. The passage, signed "A Lowell Factory Girl," is from a letter written by "a peasant's daughter" who is now in the "City of Spindles" and "out of employment." The author begins on a bitter, resigned note: "It would be useless to attempt to portray the hardships and privations which are daily endured, for all that have toiled within the factory walls, must well be acquainted with the present system of labor, which can be properly termed slavery." The piece then builds to a tone of defiance: "Let the proud aristocrat who has tyrannized over your rights with oppressive severity, see that there is ambition and enterprise among the 'spindles,' and show a determination to have your plans fully executed. Use prudence and discretion in all your ways; act independently and no longer be a slave to petty tyrants, who, if they have an opportunity, will encroach upon your privileges" (A Lowell Factory Girl, 251).

What is so striking about this letter is its revolutionary rhetoric, which evokes not only the American Revolution but the class conflict underlying the French. Moreover, the target of the hostility is not only the tyranny of the aristocracy but its sentimental misprision of Christianity that favors benevolence over reform. Finally, the letter even includes an attack on the ideology that forms the foundation of the republic. The writer warns: "Some say that 'Capital will take good care of labor,' but don't believe it; don't trust them. Is it not plain, that they are trying to deceive the public, by telling them that your task is easy and pleasant, and that there is no need of reform? Too many are destitute of feeling and sympathy, and it is a great pity that they are not obliged to toil for one year" (251).

Clearly there was a gulf between privileged and lower-class women at mid-century. Just as the domestic ideal, and to a lesser extent the woman's rights movement, represented the interests of the middle and upper classes, labor reform represented the interests of the lower class. Their publications reflected these differences and the enormous tensions between them. There were, of course, no publications for the poor and no voice that spoke for the poor *in the voice of the poor*. The women's benevolent movement pretended to speak for the poor but did no more than throw its own voice, like a ventriloquist, and while documents such as the mill girl's letter articulated issues that pertained to the poor, working-class women had too many problems of their own to be directly concerned with them.

The absence of genuine advocacy for the poor is dramatically illustrated by the orphan tale that purports to be about the salvation of the poor but really is about the rehabilitation of middle-class women. If, as Mary Ryan states in *Empire of the Mother*, women were indeed the "agents of... the relations of social reproduction," women authors were the superagents (18). Because these authors were almost invariably middle-class, genteel women forced by economic circumstances to earn a living, they evinced a lively concern with the marketplace. In this regard, they showed a startling similarity to the lower-class mill girls, who were usually young, unmarried, and forced to work because they had neither father nor husband to support them. But this was clearly an identification to be shunned rather than embraced, as the message of their novels implies.

In their concern with their own economic survival, women authors served as spokeswomen for themselves and the middle class that constituted their eager readership. The middle class became a mass-reading audience during the antebellum period, due not only to the rise of literacy and the growth of the publishing industry but to the insecurity and instability of the times, which created a unique climate of receptivity for comforting and reassuring fiction (Ryan, 14). Ryan summarizes: "The urban middle class, too, craved literary companionship. Bemoaning crime-infested streets, and haunted by images of immigrants and paupers, its members felt isolated, cut off from society. The middle class was a very unstable and precarious social formation during the antebellum era, when men and women scrambled to find secure positions in a shifting occupational structure" (15).

As a representative of class as well as gender, the female orphan encodes the needs of a frightened middle class and enacts an allegory of social redemption. To exhume the ideological message buried in the orphan tale, I would like to examine in detail a selection of the most popular examples written at the beginning of the 1850s. Bearing in mind Baym's cautionary note about the difficulty of assessing accurately the popularity of the various authors during this period, I am focusing primarily on novels that qualify indisputably as "best sellers," such as *The Wide, Wide World* (1850) and *The Lamplighter* (1854) (Baym, 300–301). Although the novels evince differences in emphasis and perspective that would be of major significance in another study, the four I have selected share a rigid structure, a didactic intent, and an orphan protagonist who performs a similar ideological function in each novel.

Orphanhood as a class issue finds ample precedent in British literary tradition. The orphan is a common figure in nineteenth-century British fiction, and the popularity of Dickens's novels in this country, coupled with his reading tour in 1842 (following the serialization of *Oliver Twist* in 1837), helped insinuate the orphan into the American imagination. The children who figure so prominently in Dickens's novels serve as a vehicle for both social criticism and autobiographical expression. In his novels, children are victims of a cruel and harsh society that wreaks psychological and even physical violence upon them.

Dickens's use of the orphan figure to critique the callousness of the British middle class contrasts with the typically conservative role of the orphan in British children's literature. Asserting that the first important children's novel in English was *The History of Little Goody Two-Shoes*, written by an anonymous author and published in 1765, Isaac Kramnick notes that many of the characters in eighteenth-century children's literature are orphans and suggests that the reason is not only an all too justifiable anxiety about the loss or absence of parents but also bourgeois ideology: "Orphans allow a personalization of the basic bourgeois assumption that the individual is on his or her own, free from the weight of the past, from tradition, from family. It intensifies and dramatizes the individuals' responsibility for their own fate by dint of their own hard work, self-reliance, merit, and talent" (23). The message of *The History of Little Goody Two-Shoes* (1765), which appeared in America in 1787 and became just as popular as it had been in England, epitomizes the moral schizophrenia inherent in the Protestant ethic: one must accumulate wealth but also deny oneself (Kramnick, 25).

Goody Two-Shoes became the prototype of the orphan figure in nineteenth-century American children's fiction, with which the sentimental novel allied itself to promote middle-class values. Anne MacLeod, a children's literature scholar, discerns the following connection between the two genres: "Like other forms of popular literature, they mirrored the conventional thought of the dominant middle class in their time; indeed, their didactic reason for being ensured that they would promulgate accepted ideas almost exclusively and blur or obliterate controversy" (12–13).

Children's literature retained its didactic purpose during the Jacksonian period, while responding to the pressures of a rapidly changing society. Its purpose was not to entertain but to preserve and perpetuate middle-class values. Thus, the literary orphan in children's literature was a conservative rather than a revolutionary figure whose function was not to undermine the aristocracy but to represent a class system that positioned a predominantly white Anglo-Saxon Protestant middle class at the pinnacle of a precarious social hierarchy. This position of preeminence was linked not only to the preservation of the status quo but to the survival of the republic itself.

Children's literature was far from fanciful; rather, it was "realistic," to the extent that realism supported its didactic intent. For example, despite its professed commitment to portraying the American experience for American children, children's literature was notably deficient in American themes, such as the pioneers, the wilderness, and the Indians, and its patterns of inclusion and exclusion reveal a great deal about the prevailing ideology (MacLeod, 41–42). While children's stories seemed to purvey democratic social attitudes, the democracy was at best a highly qualified one, reflecting the growing concern after 1820 about the vulnerability of a democratic society to expanding urban centers, increasing poverty, and proliferating immigrants.

The 1850s witnessed significant changes in children's literature. The festering wound of urban poverty became impossible to ignore, and it inspired a juvenile literature that was on the one hand more direct and honest in its depiction of reality and on the other more unrealistic in its sentimental and melodramatic resolutions of social problems, a contradiction that reflected anxiety about living in an increasingly disordered world. MacLeod suggests: "Behind their sentimental solutions to problems, one senses a desperation, if not a despair, not common in earlier juvenile stories. Undoubtedly they thought they were presenting to children the same view of a morally ordered universe that the earlier fiction had always upheld; in fact, a modern reader discerns their doubts" (157).

The tendency to see poverty as a moral failing also became more explicit in children's literature during this period, with the appearance of the "vicious poor" who took advantage of the good Christians who tried to help them (MacLeod, 125). The alleged vices of the poor justified the alliance between capitalism and the Protestant ethic against them. Although excessive materialism and wealth were piously (and hypocritically) censured in the Jacksonian republic, a degree of prosperity was still regarded as a measure of virtue.

In other words, this was a society that continued, in the tradition of the Puritans and Franklin, to link moral character and Christian virtue with economic success and material rewards (MacLeod, 89).

In the 1850s an orphan, Little Rollo of the celebrated Rollo series, personifies this connection. Rollo and his sister eventually reunite with their parents, and "the great and constant lesson of the Rollo series is that merit lies in moral fitness and righteousness. Be good and all will be granted; be bad and you will lose both the world and heaven" (Wishy, 61). The unmistakable implication of this moral is that poverty is not a misfortune but a punishment, just as wealth is a reward.

In a particularly insightful essay, Daniel T. Rogers argues that the emphasis in children's literature on self-discipline, restraint, and hard work as guarantees of success represents a defense against destabilization and social breakdown. He also regards children's literature as a tool used by the Yankee bourgeoisie to "reproduce itself in its children" by reinforcing traditional values and isolating the children from the effects of change (120). The children's fiction of the 1850s, in which the hard-working child assumes nearly heroic stature, is evidence of this manipulative strategy (125).

The foregrounding of orphanhood allies sentimental fiction with children's fiction. Representing the quest for not only personal identity but social identity, the orphan tale is an allegory about the need for social control. Within this context, the orphan figure represents the hypocrisy of the middle class, which despite its professions of benevolence was distinctly nativist and hostile to the poor. The novels of the period are important because they encode the underlying anxiety that conditions the insularity of the middle class, circumscribes the family of the republic, and protects the status of its members.

The most elitist of the orphan tales is *The Wide, Wide World* by Susan Warner, which appeared in 1850 and caused "a sensation in the literary marketplace" (Tompkins, "Afterword," 584). Running through an unprecedented fourteen editions in two years, it became one of the best-selling novels of the nineteenth century in America and England. It recounts the simple, verbose, but engaging story of Ellen Montgomery, a ten-year-old girl from a well-to-do New York family whose beloved, ailing mother dies in Europe where, for business reasons, her father currently resides. While her parents are away, Ellen is sent to live with Aunt Fortune, her father's sister who lives in the country, and much of the novel chronicles Ellen's tribulations as she attempts to adjust to Aunt Fortune's querulous disposition and her demands that Ellen perform the unsavory domestic duties incumbent upon a rural life style.

The difficult adjustment prompts Ellen to weep copious tears and marshal all her religious resources to overcome her temper and instinct for rebellion. Needless to say, the theme of Christian submission and obedience to God's will figures prominently in the book. A large part of what Ellen needs to overcome is the snobbery that is a result of her social status. As the only child of a prosperous family, Ellen is somewhat spoiled. Accustomed to luxury and comfort, she is dismayed by the austerity of her accommodations at Aunt Fortune's (especially the *cotton* sheets and pillow case) and the expectation that she wash her own stockings and make her own bed (no *servants*?!). She confesses to her friend Alice, "Mamma never kept house, and I never saw any body do it" (168).

Ellen's aversion to housework reflects a larger philosophical difference between her and Aunt Fortune. Ellen is very concerned about her education and wants to go to school, whereas Aunt Fortune thinks it sufficient that she know how to read, write, and cipher. Ellen tells Aunt Fortune that she wants to study "French, and Italian, and Latin, and music, and arithmetic and chemistry, and all about animals and plants and insects"; Aunt Fortune responds that "it doesn't do for women to be bookworms" and dispatches her to do the dishes (140).

It is apparent from the first pages that Warner is as much concerned with class as with a feminine ideal of Christian conduct. A scene in the second chapter, after Ellen learns that her mother is going to Europe, epitomizes the ideological stance of the novel. Like a social voyeur, Ellen is looking out the window of her comfortable, bourgeois home "at an ugly city prospect of back walls of houses, with the yards belonging to them, and a bit of narrow street. But she had watched the people that showed themselves at the windows... and though they were for the most part dingy, dirty, and disagreeable,—women, children, houses, and all,—she certainly had taken a good deal of interest in their proceedings." But now that she is faced with the prospect of losing her mother, her perspective has changed, and "she could not bear to look at them" until her attention is captured by "a poor deformed child, whom she had often noticed before, and always with a sorrowful interest." What engages her now is not "his bodily infirmity," which was always present, but the fact that he had lost his mother: "Ellen's heart was easily touched this morning; she felt for him very much. 'Poor, poor little fellow!' she thought; 'he's a great deal worse off than I am. *His* mother is dead; mine is only going away for a few months—not forever; oh, what a difference! and then the joy of coming back again!'—poor Ellen was weeping already at the thought" (16; italics in original).

For Ellen the window is like a television screen; she looks at it, and the scene it frames entertains her. Although Ellen opens the window, a gesture that suggests interpenetration, a letting in as well as a looking out, it is apparent the reverse is the case. While usually it is her amusement, a kind of aesthetic detachment, that distances her from the "dingy, dirty, and disagreeable" scene, this time it is her own misery that makes her too self-involved to enjoy the show. She responds, however, to the "poor deformed child" who has lost his mother with an extra dollop of sympathy, not because she feels more deeply for him but because she is projecting upon him her own self-pity.

The point is that a distinction is clearly drawn between Ellen and the poor. She relates to them only as objects of curiosity, almost as if they were animals in a zoo, and the "gaze" here is one of depersonalization, like that of the male gaze upon the female Laura Mulvey describes in her landmark essay. Even though she seems to feel compassion for the orphaned boy, Ellen is only seeing him narcissistically, through the window of her own experience. While the scene is an obvious foreshadowing of her own orphanhood (her mother dies in Europe, followed by her father later in the novel), it also has the effect of establishing in no uncertain terms Ellen's *difference* from the world outside her window, the world of "poor" orphans. The reader knows that although Ellen may come to resemble the "poor, poor little fellow" through the fact of losing her mother, she will never be "poor" in the socioeconomic sense. The adjective "poor" has a double meaning Warner did not intend, one that reflects the novel's underlying preoccupation with class distinctions.

Ellen's gaze, her self-centered way of looking at the world, permeates the novel and creates an uneasy ambivalence in the reader. Her pose at the window defines her as the perpetual insider looking out. It is clear that although Ellen will become an orphan, she will never be a "poor" orphan. She will also never be a rural orphan like Nancy Vawse, who "ain't a good girl," according to Aunt Fortune (115). Nancy lives in the country with her Swiss grandmother and is the orphaned daughter of Mrs. Vawse's youngest son. Despite her grandmother's Old World virtues, Nancy is a common, wild creature who roams at will and plays mischievous, even malicious pranks. In the novel she functions as an evil twin who represents the rebellious side of Ellen's nature. It is significant that Ellen not only overcomes her own "wicked" impulses but also tames Nancy, a triumph of gentility over vulgarity as well as good over evil.

The female figure with whom Ellen identifies is Alice Humphreys, a cultivated, educated, refined paragon of Christian virtue. Parallels immediately establish Ellen's identification with Alice. Alice was born in England; Ellen's mother was born in Scotland. Both have also lost their mothers. But Ellen and Alice have more in common than their ethnic and personal circumstances. They share not only their religious values but their secular values as well — luxury, education, the arts, religion — and these secular values bear a significant cultural resemblance to those of the aristocracy as well as the middle class.

A seemingly unremarkable exchange between Alice and Ellen about laundry reflects how deeply embedded class distinctions are in this novel. Alice is as distressed by Ellen's Spartan quarters as Ellen is, and offers her some fabric to cover "those long legs" on her vanity. Ellen explains why Aunt Fortune would object:

> "Why the washing, Miss Alice — to have such a great thing to wash every now and then. You can't think what a fuss she makes if I have more than just so many white clothes in the wash every week."
>
> "That's too bad," said Alice. "Suppose you bring it up to me — it wouldn't be often — *and I'll have it washed for you* — if you care enough about it to take the trouble." (225; italics added)

The difference between Aunt Fortune and Alice in a socioeconomic nutshell is that the former does the wash and the latter has the wash done for her. At Aunt Fortune's house, where the atmosphere is one of domestic hubbub, Ellen sweeps the floor, churns the butter, and strings the apples. At Alice's house, where the atmosphere is one of "peace and purity," she takes drawing lessons, other lessons are begun, there are "fine long walks, and charming sleigh-rides... and what Ellen perhaps liked the best of all, the long evenings of conversation and reading aloud, and bright fire-lights, and brighter sympathy and intelligence and affection" (332–333).

In relation to the middle class, Aunt Fortune represents its peasant origins and Alice its evolution into a neo-aristocracy. The feudal analogy is apt in that it is not money that makes the difference, for it is intimated in the novel that Aunt Fortune, a frugal hoarder, is wealthy. The difference lies in breeding and upbringing, the traditional European criteria of class. Ellen is clearly a product of her mother's side of the family, not her father's, and Warner favorably contrasts her refined sensibility with Aunt Fortune's coarse avarice. Alice says to Ellen: "I thought your mother was a lady, from the honourable notions she had given you... I thought she must be a refined and cultivated person from the manner of your speech and behaviour; and I was sure she was a Christian, because she taught you the truth, and evidently had tried to lead you in it" (240).

Though Warner sets up a good mother/bad mother dichotomy between Ellen's mother and Aunt Fortune, her own attitude toward Ellen seems ambivalent. On the one hand, she appears to critique Ellen for her snobbery and disdain for menial tasks and couches Ellen's struggle to overcome her rebelliousness in Christian rhetoric. One almost suspects (and at times hopes) that the thrust of the novel will be the humbling of Ellen, but it becomes obvious as the novel unfolds that this is not Warner's intent. On a deeper level, Warner shares Ellen's values, and the moral is that Ellen must learn to submit to authority and obey God's will *despite* her social superiority. Warner is equally in the thrall of Alice, who is the spiritual (and social) kin of Ellen's mother, and the time Ellen spends living with Alice, her brother John, and her father is depicted in the glowing terms of paradise regained.

Warner plays even more coyly with the concept of class by sending Ellen off to Scotland to live with her mother's aristocratic family after her father dies. This experience brings to a head the identity issues woven throughout the novel. Whereas the Humphreys' "adoption" of Ellen restored her to her former social self, her Scottish relatives, the Lindsays, try to appropriate her identity as if it belongs to them by virtue of a blood tie. Ellen becomes "the plaything, pride, and delight of the whole family," and they marvel (with a stereotypical British snobbery that is an ironic echo of Ellen's attitude toward Aunt Fortune) that a product of the backwoods of America can read and "come out and speak pure English in a clear voice" (528, 505). Their arrogance, which evokes the former colonial relationship between England and America, makes Ellen long for independence.

In a crucial and chilling scene, Ellen's uncle, Mr. Lindsay, who has declared himself her father, kisses her and whispers: "you are my own child now,—you are my little daughter—do you know that, Ellen? I am your father henceforth;—you belong to me entirely, and I belong to you;—my own little daughter!" (504). It is a tyrannical pronouncement, charged with both conspiratorial and sexual innuendo, as if he were simultaneously seducing and violating her, which in a sense he is through his assertion of power. Later he even urges her: "Forget that you were American, Ellen,—you belong to me; your name is not Montgomery any more,—it is Lindsay;—and I will not have you call me 'uncle'—I am your father;—you are my own little daughter, and must do precisely what I tell you" (510).

Ellen ultimately rejects the Lindsays, and the tradition of European aristocracy they represent, in favor of her American, middle-class, republican origins. The radical and idealistic notion the novel *seems* to suggest is that social identity is determined not by natural law, in the form of biological kinship to Aunt Fortune or the Lindsays, but by a higher code of spiritual kinship. The irony of the novel is that Ellen's spirituality is clearly a function of the class into which she was born. Ellen returns to America, her "spiritual" home, where she marries her "spiritual" brother, John, a romantic and sentimental ending that not only idealizes marriage as a refuge and a reward for Christian virtue but affirms the bourgeois values with which she was raised. In other words, class, even more than biological kinship, is reified as the ultimate marker of identity. Thus, the underlying message of the novel is that while circumstances change, social identity is an immutable inheritance that survives all assaults upon it.

Baym and Jane Tompkins have both interpreted the ending as a projection of Warner's fantasies onto her heroine. Like Ellen, the Warner sisters lost their mother at any early age and also endured the trauma of their father's business failure, which catapulted them from a life of luxury and ease into one of penury and deprivation. Also like Ellen, Susan was an intellectual and social snob who looked askance at household drudgery, and the adjustment to social degradation was especially difficult for her. Ellen's reaction to the menial tasks she has to perform for Aunt Fortune is clearly a reflection of Warner's own disdain and dependence on servants, as is Ellen's predilection for the genteel aspects of life, whether they be servants or drawing lessons.

In this connection, it is important to keep in mind the connotation of servitude to a woman of privilege like Susan Warner. Just as leisure was considered the prerogative of middle- and upper-class women who had a man on whom to depend, work was considered the purview of the lower classes whose only opportunities were industrial labor in factories and servitude, the basest and lowest-paying form of labor. Gradually immigrants began taking over both occupations, and inevitably, many of the immigrants were orphans who learned their trade in the various industrial schools sponsored by benevolent societies. CAS's industrial schools, for example, instructed homeless and destitute girls in needlework to prepare them for work in the mills, whereas other societies, such as the Industrial Home for the Instruction of Girls in the Arts of Housewifery and Sewing in Philadelphia, concentrated on training young girls in housewifery and sewing and preparing them in general for servitude: "The girls are retained in the Home until their habits and dispositions are understood, and they are sufficiently instructed in household work to satisfy those who make application for them as domestics in their families" (*First Annual Report*, 4). Thus, to women like the Warner sisters, there was all the difference in the world between *having* a servant and *being* a servant. Servitude represented the worst fate that could befall an impoverished orphan and was regarded with a unique form of social dread.

Evidence of this fact is that a servant is rarely the protagonist in the orphan tale, an honor reserved almost exclusively for young women of genteel origins. A noteworthy exception is Catharine Sedgwick's *Live and Let Live* (1837), in which a young female orphan, Lucy Lee, is forced into servitude by poverty. Although her father is a lawyer, he is also a drunkard, and Lucy's mother, whose background consists of a "small fortune" and a "good education," prevails upon Lucy to go into service, arguing that "honest labour is never degrading" and can actually be advantageous: "In a well-ordered family, a girl is fitting herself for duties that belong to her sex. She is learning to fit honourably the stations of a wife, mistress, and mother of a family" (15, 17). Sure enough, Lucy does succeed in marrying and "moving up," but not far and certainly not beyond her original station. She marries her childhood sweetheart, a baker. Needless to say, Warner would hardly see Lucy's fate as a vindication of servitude.

Their marital prospects dashed by their straitened circumstances, the Warner sisters turned to writing and religious devotion. Writing, like teaching and nursing, was one of the few respectable professions in which an unmarried middle-class woman could engage without losing her status or respectability. Although writing was not labor, it was nevertheless work and resented as such. The novel's emphasis on Ellen's submission and self-sacrifice is surely a reflection of Warner's own struggle to overcome her frustrated desires for leisure and luxury. Tompkins writes in her Afterword: "In the final chapter, Warner gives her heroine everything that she herself wanted and couldn't get: city living, wealth and position, relief from household cares, people who adore her, and marriage to an all-powerful protector" (601). Ellen's love for "costly and precious objects," which Warner attempts to justify on the basis of their ability to elevate the mind to a higher spiritual plane, is clearly at odds with the Christian injunction against vanity and overvaluation of earthly possessions, and Tompkins suggests Warner is aware on some level "that the dream of wealth and comfort does not jibe with her hard-won resolve to accept the Lord's will. In turning the reward she had invented for Ellen into an elaborate rationalization of her own desire, a desire to which she had been socialized by her upbringing, Warner only makes more obvious the split she does not see and therefore cannot acknowledge within her culture and within herself" ("Afterword," 603).

The novel's ambivalent attitude toward materialism and affluence reflects the tension between capitalist and Christian values not only in Warner's consciousness but in middle-class women in general, who embraced on the one hand Christian ideals of charity and austerity and on the other the luxury and power that wealth afforded. In focusing on a mock heroic orphan like Ellen, whose task was not to find her identity but to refind the milieu that created her identity as a child of privilege, the novel creates sympathy for her, as if she were a "real" orphan, and thereby diverts attention from those "poor" orphans who were destined never to be adopted into a middle-class family except as servants.

Ellen is as important for who she is *not* as for who she is. Just as she is not "poor and deformed," she is neither illegitimate nor abandoned. She is also *not* an immigrant, a Negro, or an Indian, i.e. a social outcast whom the middle class certainly doesn't want to "adopt" as a member of its family. She is the child of genteel parents who happens to lose her parents, and beyond this fact she has about as much in common with those children who form the orphan population of New York as a noble with a serf. Ellen was *born* to her station in life, and nothing, not even orphanhood, can take that way from her. This is the world of hereditary privilege and hereditary want; it is a neo-aristocratic middle class in which class verges on caste and shifts in station are more apparent than real. The orphan who appears to rise above his or her circumstances is found to have already been there. In short, the purpose of this novel is no less polemical than that of children's fiction: to affirm the stability of the middle class. Not only does Ellen personify its values; her odyssey through orphanhood allegorizes its survival.

The orphan's role as an apologist for the status quo is evident in other novels of the period as well. Maria Stuart Cummins wrote *The Lamplighter* in 1854; it sold 40,000 copies during its first two months of publication and 70,000 in its first year (inspiring Hawthorne's peevish denunciation of the "d——-d mob of scribbling women"—Ticknor, 141). Cummins shared with Susan Warner not only phenomenal literary success but similar economic and personal circumstances. She was the daughter of a judge and accustomed to a genteel life style. Like Warner, Cummins lost her father as a means of support and did not marry.

Her literary aspirations were thus motivated by need as well as inclination, and it is obvious that she too projected her personal fantasies onto her heroine, an orphan named Gerty.

Gerty appears at first to be very different from Ellen. Orphaned at three under mysterious circumstances, Gerty is raised in Boston by an abusive Scots woman, Nan Grant, who beats her, locks her in the attic, and drowns her kitten. Nan is a demonized version of Aunt Fortune, and her cruelty leaves Gerty with a far greater legacy of anger and resentment than Ellen could even imagine. Because she knows nothing about her parents or her background, Gerty seems like raw material compared to Ellen's molded clay. She, and the reader, have no sense of who she is in relation to who she was, and the novel seems to adopt the proto-existentialist position that environment, not heredity, will form her.

A passage in the novel that epitomizes the apparent difference between the two orphans also involves a window. Gerty, who has been unofficially adopted by Trueman Flint (the eponymous lamplighter) after she runs away from Nan Grant, is out walking one evening with her newfound friend Willie Sullivan, the son of a widowed friend of Flint's. They are standing in front of a house in "a fine block of buildings" at dusk, as the lamps are being lit: "It was now quite dark, so that persons in a light room could not see any one out of doors; but Willie and Gerty had so much the better chance to look in. It was indeed a fine mansion, evidently the home of wealth.... There was an air of comfort, combined with all this elegance, which made it still more fascinating to a child of poverty and want... the children of the household, smiling and happy, were crowded together on a window-seat looking out" (55–56).

The children cannot see Gerty and Willie until Flint comes along with his torchlight; then "Gerty and Willie became, in their turn, the subjects of notice and conversation. Though Gerty does not know what they are saying, she does not like the idea of being stared at and talked about; and, hiding behind the post, she will not move or look up, though Willie laughs at her, and tells her it is now her *turn* to be looked at" (56; italics in original). Gerty runs away "to escape observation" and will not return to the window until the children have taken their places at the tea table.

The contrast is unmistakable. Unlike Ellen, the insider looking out, Gerty is the outsider looking in. Gerty's orphanhood seems to represent not a temporary hiatus in her social status but a permanent exclusion from genteel society. She is born an outsider and will presumably remain an outsider, but the novel's underlying message is that heredity is more important than environment. For example, Cummins makes clear that Gerty's propensity for self-improvement is not entirely learned: "Good taste is inborn, and Gerty had it in her" (58). Gerty is taken under the wing of Mr. Graham, an affluent businessman, and his blind daughter Emily, who becomes a spiritual mentor and surrogate sister for Gerty, much as Alice did for Ellen. Gerty quickly discovers that "the tie of kindred blood is not always needed to bind heart to heart in the closest bonds of sympathy and affection" (162). The Grahams experience a similar sense of affinity that is as much social as spiritual: "the child...though neither beautiful nor elegantly dressed, had a fairy lightness of step, a grace of movement and a dignity of bearing, which impressed them all with the conviction that she was no beggar in spirit, whatever might be her birth or fortune, — and all were in the invariable habit of addressing her as *Miss* Gertrude" (125; italics in original).

Gerty learns a degree of self-control and submission to the will of God from her mentor, Emily: "Those only, my child, who have learned submission; those who, in the severest afflictions, see the hand of a loving Father, and, obedient to his will, kiss the chastening rod" (121). But there is an elitist message underlying the novel in that Gerty's happy fate at the end derives more from her origins than from her Christian virtue. It turns out that Gerty is not a typical orphan, born of paupers "nine-tenths of [whom] will always be poor," as one character gloomily predicts (238). After a series of improbable disclosures, the reader learns that Gerty is the daughter of Philip Amory, who is not only Emily's long-lost stepbrother but the son of, according to Philip, "an honorable and high-minded man, whom it was ever my greatest pride to be told that I resembled" (415).

Gerty thus suddenly finds herself legitimized as a member of the Graham family, a family in relation to whom she has always felt, despite the kindness of Emily and Mr. Graham to her, like an outsider looking in. Now she has become an insider by virtue of her genteel origins, which validate earlier intuitions about her good breeding. Moreover, she has achieved the ultimate coup of winning Willie, now a successful businessman, and of winning his affections over her socially superior competitor, Isabel Clinton, who was one of the wealthy children upon whom Gerty once gazed wistfully from the street.

Thus, Gerty is hardly representative of the reality of orphanhood. Poverty, which pervades the early pages of the novel, is viewed narrowly, solely from Gerty's perspective, and it virtually disappears as a subject of concern as Gerty rises in station because she conforms to an ideal of feminine submission. This disappearance is consistent with the displacement of class onto gender issues that Amy Lang describes in her essay "Class and the Strategies of Sympathy": "*The Lamplighter* depends, in other words, on a strategy of displacement in which the language of class yields to the language of gender. The problem of poverty is not repressed but translated into a vocabulary that makes its redress inevitable: the distortions of poverty are answered by the naturalness of gender" (130).

Both *The Wide, Wide World* and *The Lamplighter* share similar strategies of displacement and evasion. Although Gerty appears to be quite a different kind of orphan from Ellen, a "poor," unadoptable orphan who does not know who her parents are, they are actually alike insofar as Gerty's task also consists of refinding her original identity rather than inventing one. Gerty's upward journey through adoption parallels this process. The child who was once described as "the city's property" (18) and who described the earth as "a good foster-mother to its orphaned child" (312) finds a surrogate parent briefly in the humble lamplighter (who was himself an orphan) and then progresses to Emily Graham, who plays the dual role of mother and sister. Their relationship implies that surrogate kinship is based not just on spiritual and moral affinities but on inherited values and prepares the way for the ending, in which Gerty and Willie do not accede to the middle class because they are virtuous but are virtuous because they were born to the middle class. The fact that Cummins takes such pains to prove that Gerty and Willie *deserve* good fortune is the key, and it conjures up the dark side of the Protestant ethic, the traditional Puritan connection between election and earthly gain, with class now serving as a substitute for grace. In making Gerty and Willie such paragons of Christian virtue, the novel insinuates the elitist notion that the predisposition to virtue is innate, bred in the bone of the better classes.

Although Ellen and Gerty have explicit ties to the middle class, not all orphans in the popular novels of the early 1850s represent it so clearly. But even in those instances where the protagonist's origins are more ambiguous, class is still destiny. For example, in Ann Stephens's *The Old Homestead* (the first half of which takes place in the slums of New York), the orphaned protagonist Mary Fuller has little to boast of in her parents. Her father is a sick pauper who, through no fault of his own, has fallen on hard times from a position in the lower reaches of the middle class. But despite his current humble circumstances, he continues to inhabit a high spiritual plane, whereas poverty has plunged Mary's mother into unredeemed degradation.

Flouting the Cult of True Womanhood, Stephens's novel establishes Mary's mother as a drunkard who physically and verbally abuses Mary, curses, and engages in all manner of vice. Obviously, Stephens is anxious to portray the dangers of intemperance, but she is also eager to make the point that the mother's former station in life was *better* than her current circumstances indicate. The following is the account of the policeman who arrests her: "The night before, he had entered one of those dismal houses, and had taken from thence a woman who, squalid and degraded as she was, had evidently once been in the higher walks of life.... The miserable destitution of her home, the glimpses of refinement that broke through her outbursts of passion, the state of revolting intoxication in which she was plunged — all arose vividly to his mind" (28).

The father and mother represent two extreme reactions to poverty, and Stephens is using an obvious sentimental ploy to elicit sympathy for those who fall from a higher station, even if it is only the lower middle class. But she is also making a covert class statement by connecting Mary to a better social and moral class than her abject origins suggest. The lessons she learns at her father's deathbed serve her well by enabling her to subsume her mother's behavior to her breeding, and Mary becomes a model of virtuous young womanhood. Thus, her marriage at the end of the novel to a wealthy young man seems as much an act of social as of moral justice.

The facile, contrived happy ending of this orphan's tale is harder to accept in Stephens's novel than in either Warner's or Cummins's because Stephens has presented herself as a reform-minded social realist. She states in her preface: "If the truth in this book serves to draw popular attention to the solemn trust imposed in these city charities, my first object will be accomplished; for the great popular heart of America is full of just such aspiration, and I would gladly turn it benevolently toward institutions where so much human misfortune and misery are concentrated" (147).

Nevertheless, Stephens reserves her greatest sympathy not for those who were born to poverty but for those who, like Mary's father, descended into it. For example, it is significant that in describing members of a "want-stricken crowd" of infirm elderly, destitute children, and starving immigrants, she comments: "*Most heartrending of all, persons of real refinement were mingled up with this rude mass*; poor wretches who had indeed seen better days, and their helpless, broken-hearted looks, the remnants of early sensitiveness, that still clung around them, was [sic] pitiful to behold" (147; italics added).

As the last sentence intimates, it would be a mistake to view Stephens as an unqualified champion of the poor. Stephens's sympathy with those who were not born low but brought low, "persons of real refinement" as opposed to the congenital poor, implies a social elitism, and even her explicit attacks on the abuses of capitalism resonate with class bias. For example, in a bitterly satiric passage in which she compares city government officials to fathers executing their children, she reserves her greatest compassion for members of the middle class who, like Mary's parents, have fallen into poverty:

> The Common Council was in session. Both marble wings of the City Hall were brilliantly illuminated, and crowds of eager spectators gathered around the two council chambers. Some fifty or sixty poor and efficient men were to be turned out of office, and the populace were eager to witness the jocose and delicate way in which the New York city fathers decapitated their children.... the heads of fifty or sixty families were thus playfully deprived of the means of an honest support. Efficient and experienced men were taken from almost all the city departments and cast without occupation upon the world. Men who had toiled in the city's service, for years, for a bare livelihood, were suddenly cast forth to want and penury. (112)

Stephens is depicting the middle-class nightmare of economic downfall, and Mary's rise, like her parents' fall, makes sense as an inscription of the fantasy of loss and recovery upon the orphan's tale. Her rise represents not only a return to but an improvement on her class origins, legitimized by her middle-class values. The implication is clear that Mary is not meant to be a member of the "rude mass" and belongs to the middle class by virtue of her origins. In short, Stephens's sentimentalization of the genteel poor reflects her greater sympathy for the middle class.

In contrast with Ellen, Gerty, and Mary, the class origins of the orphan protagonist in Elizabeth Oakes Smith's *The Newsboy* (1854) are totally unknown and remain unknown to the end. For this reason alone, the novel seems to be an exception to the formula of loss and recovery that characterizes the orphan tale, and the fact that the protagonist is male instead of female makes it appear even more atypical. But instead the novel is simply a variation on the formula because the androgynous character of the protagonist, the newsboy Bob, reflects Smith's desire to reconcile feminine and masculine values, Christianity and capitalism. As a feminized male, Bob personifies the inextricable relationship between class and gender in the orphan tale.

Smith, who did charity work with orphans in New York, discloses in the first chapter that she based this novel on an actual newsboy called Bob, who one day appeared outside her window. Her acquaintance with him seems to have had the impact of a conversion experience and inspired her to create a heroic mythology of orphanhood that synthesizes the story of Jesus with that of the self-made man: "Little by little, Bob... grew into my mind, not as a poor, forsaken, ignorant, neglected child, who ought to be taken up and sent to the Orphan Asylum or asylum for vagrants, but as a great soul'd boy, whose nobleness I dared not fathom, but which I could appreciate, the latchet of whose old, dilapidated shoes I was not worthy to unloose" (8).

Of his origins, the reader learns only that Bob grew up "amid creatures as forlorn as himself. He had known hunger, and cold, and misery, in every shape. He had been the companion of the outcast from the first dawning of his existence." He is abused, shunted from one cruel guardian to another, and finds himself on the streets after his last custodians die in a cholera epidemic. As a result Bob has learned to be "sturdy" and silent in his misery, self-reliant, and thrifty, virtues that entitle him to join that elite cadre of street urchins, the newsboys. Waxing rhapsodic, Smith extols this urban tribe: "As you look at the Newsboys, one thing will strike your attention. There is no appearance of vice amongst them. Nothing skulking, nothing mean, nothing vicious lurks in the aspect of the true Newsboy. No redness of eyes, no bloated face, no pallid debauchery" (33).

Obviously the newsboy is training to become a self-made man, a harbinger of Horatio Alger's heroes, and Bob does not disappoint the reader's expectations. Although he may not have been born to affluence, his character entitles him to it and enables him to ascend the socioeconomic ladder. Not only does Bob possess the traditional Franklinian virtues; his code of morals is "very old, very safe, and very respectable," summarized in the faint echo of his mother's voice telling him to "do right." Insofar as Bob's character reflects middle-class values, he *deserves* to succeed and belongs among the better classes: "There was something in that great heart of his that reached for the good, the beautiful; and this he sought" (161).

The question is why Bob is different from those "orphans and outcasts" who inhabit "dens of wickedness and sinks of corruption... and seem to hide themselves and their misery from human eye." Although Smith sentimentalizes the effects of poverty as opposed to wealth, the sheer fact of poverty alone is not enough to explain the difference because newsboys and non-newsboys alike share the same pernicious environment and absence of positive parental influence. The only possible variable, then, is heredity. His mother's voice and his memory of her as "an angel" suggest that character and values are a moral legacy absorbed through a kind of biological osmosis.

Smith also takes pains to suggest that because of his mother's influence, Bob embodies a feminine as well as a masculine ideal. He is both kind-hearted and compassionate, as illustrated by the fact that he cares for and raises two little orphaned girls as tenderly as would their own mothers. It is obvious that Bob's maternal dimension represents Smith's somewhat heavy-handed effort to offer an alternative image of masculinity and soften the heart of the hard-hearted capitalist (through the intervention of the reader, his wife). That is exactly the effect Bob has on Mr. Dinsmoor, a typical merchant who, under Bob's influence, gets religion; Bob, in turn, gets a job in Mr. Dinsmoor's firm — an exchange that neatly synthesizes Christianity and capitalism.

Although Mr. Dinsmoor changes by becoming more compassionate to the poor, Bob's character is unaffected by his newfound prosperity and status at Mr. Dinsmoor's firm. He now can "read and write and speak languages, and goes dressed like a gentlemen," but he keeps his old clothes to remind "him of his early life which he never means to forget, and for all he's so well to look at now, and knows so much, he's no more pride than an old shoe" (471). Not only does Bob retain the trappings of humility but his soul is uncorrupted by his good fortune, which he has the temerity to denounce to Mr. Dinsmoor along with all forms of "help" in what verges on an ideological attack: "you've been unfortunately born to wealth and station; you have learning and a high place in the world — partly made for you; and I'm bound to say, I think these things a misfortune, as it were, and hinderance [sic] to the manhood in us; and of course you cannot know the human heart, nor your own strength so well" (477).

Coming from an orphan who has received not only help but an identity from a wealthy capitalist, this speech sounds not only ungrateful but hypocritical. But Smith ignores these inconsistencies in order to drive home her redefinition of manhood, which yokes together in an uneasy balance the masculine and the feminine, the Christian and the capitalist, epitomized in Bob's manifesto, "It is work that makes the man after all...I would work not for riches but for manhood" (480).

Yet despite Smith's idealization of Bob, the ending of the novel suggests that she harbors feelings of ambivalence about the importance of breeding. Bob does not "get the girl" he loves, Mr. Dinsmoor's daughter, losing her to his polished, refined rival whose breeding is certain and upbringing impeccable. The mere possibility that Bob could be tainted with "bad blood" outweighs his moral aristocracy and erects a taboo against class miscegenation. The importance of blood as a marker of class has not only feudal but racial overtones and denotes an elitism that privileges blood over behavior, even when the amount of "bad blood" is minute, like Cora's in *The Prairie*. Thus, although Bob is entitled to join the middle class because of his virtue, he can never be fully adopted into it because of his unknown origins. He remains an orphan and retains his lonely purity, both morally superior and socially inferior to the new world he inhabits.

All four of these best sellers reveal the extent to which the orphan's quest for an identity encodes class issues. The explicit or implicit middle-class origin of these orphans reflects the rejecting attitude toward the poor that underlies both the benevolent movement and sentimental fiction. By enacting the adoption of these orphans into the higher strata of society, these novels simulate a social inclusiveness even as they belie it. The orphans who are fully "adopted" into the middle class were its children all along, through bonds of biological kinship that transmitted middle-class values and allied them with the socioeconomic interests of the republic. In professing sympathy for orphans who represent not the poor but their own class, the novelists successfully mask their ideological biases (even to themselves) and affirm bourgeois hegemony. It is not *real* orphans, born into poverty, who are adopted by the middle class in these orphan tales; rather, it is fallen orphans who need only to be rescued.

Even more noticeably absent from the orphan tale than the congenitally poor are the immigrants who made up such a high proportion of their numbers. Despite the number of immigrants pouring into America and the widespread concern over immigration, immigrants are left out of sentimental fiction, just as they were left out of the dominant culture. Their appearance tends to be limited to servitude, as in Catharine Sedgwick's *Live and Let Live* (1837), in which an incompetent French girl virtually causes the death of the master's son, illustrating Sedgwick's message that "the almost necessary dependance [*sic*] on foreign and uninstructed people [makes] it imperative upon American mothers to qualify their daughters to superintend their domestics" (v).

Even fewer novels from this period feature immigrants as orphan protagonists, and these few confirm rather than contradict the sentimental bias toward the middle class. One is Mary Jane Holmes's *The English Orphans* (1855), "a picaresque fiction of upward feminine mobility," according to Baym, that chronicles the social ascent of young orphan sisters of an English immigrant family. Ella is adopted by a wealthy widow, and Mary "begins at the lowest possible point, the poorhouse, and moves steadily up to wealth and high social position." Baym contends that "Holmes's special achievement here is to have made a heroine who has so few pretensions and is so apparently ordinary into someone clearly extraordinary. *Mary is a true democratic heroine*" (192; italics added). Hardly—the English orphans are the embodiment of neo-aristocracy, of white Anglo-Saxon Protestantism and the cultural superiority it denotes. (To drive home the point, a novel with the same plot entitled *The Irish Orphans* or *The Italian Orphans* is inconceivable during this period.) Thus, they *deserve* to rise to their former station.

Records of benevolent societies during this period provide a historical basis for the fictional tendency to place children of the same class in comparable homes. For example, the following case report from the AFGS's Home for the Friendless clearly reflects class bias: "The little girl is a fine child, and shows that she has had a watchful mother's training. The time has been when her father was worth a handsome property, and the family enjoyed many of the elegancies of life.... The little girl has a fine black eye, and an intelligent face. This dear child was adopted by an interesting Christian family and is tenderly cherished by them" (AFGS, *Fifteenth Annual Report*, 15).

One can reasonably assume that "interesting" means educated, affluent, and spiritually correct, whereas an account in the same annual report of Hannah, a "rude and uncultivated" child from an unknown family who is "placed" with "a good family" in the country and as a result much improves "in mind and manners," has a condescending tone, as if the child were an unruly pet in need of correction rather than a child worthy of admiration and reward (16). The most significant difference between the two descriptions is that the "fine child" is adopted, and will presumably enjoy all the legal and economic benefits of a natural child, whereas the "rude and uncultivated" child is merely "placed."

Immigrant orphans who appear in the fiction of the period are not only rare but anomalous in relation to the reality of the immigrant experience. For example, Louisa May Alcott's recently discovered, unpublished first novel, *The Inheritance*, written in 1849, tells the tale of Edith Adelon, an impoverished Italian orphan of unknown parentage who was brought to England by a British lord. Despite Edith's dubious origins, there are repeated suggestions throughout the novel that Edith is a girl of good breeding. Amy remarks, "She has told me that her mother was an Italian lady, poor indeed but of good family, and that you might know by Edith's grace and beauty." Arthur concurs: "Edith is of a good, perhaps a noble family, for there is a dignity and high-born look about her that would become any lady in the land" (23). Edith also possesses the virtues of kindness and self-sacrifice, which win the admiration of the well-born and highly eligible Lord Percy: "You are poor and humble, Miss Adelon, but rich in woman's truest virtues and rendered noble by a warm and sinless heart... I am one who finds his greatest happiness in simple things and cares little for the rank and riches of the world, for these are nothing to a noble human heart" (68–69).

But class-conscious Edith feels she cannot give her heart to one so far above her because she would cause him grief in the future. Describing a comparable situation, she explains: "He could not know how bitter a grief would be his when he should see her whom he loved so fondly sneered at for her poverty and looked coldly on because of humble birth.... To wed one so far beneath him in wealth and rank would be considered a stain upon his name and, with a woman's purest love, she has refused to win her own joy by the sacrifice of his hereafter" (109–110).

The not-so-surprising revelation at the end of the novel is that Edith's father is the elder brother of the Lord Hamilton who brought her to England and that Amy and Arthur are her cousins. Edith's father married her mother, "poor, indeed, but of noble birth," in Italy and subsequently died, leaving her a widow; shortly thereafter she died as well (130). Edith nobly decides to renounce her claim to the Hamilton fortune and her prospects of happiness with Percy. But the truth will out, and Edith tears up the will in which her father made her his heir and pleads to her adoptive family: "Can you love me for myself alone and forget that I have any right to the rank and wealth that are so worthless to one who only longs for tenderness and love?" (171). This supreme act of renunciation for her adopted family renders her "the poor orphan girl" again in means, but her breeding has been established and she is now worthy of Lord Percy, who approves her at the end: "And though I take you without earthly wealth, still in the tender reverence and fadeless gratitude of those you bless, surely, dearest, you have won a nobler Inheritance" (177).

The novel's unmistakable message is that heredity is destiny, and class conquers all. Edith is blessed with a father who is an English aristocrat and a mother who, although Italian, is at least of noble birth. Like class, character is also inherited from one's forebears, and this explains why some members of a class are good, like Edith, and some are bad, like Ida, her rival for Lord Percy's affections. The fact that a young *American* woman wrote this novel, which is set in England and pivots around class issues, reflects the extent to which class was a major factor in the assessment of immigrants in this country. After all, nativism as a form of prejudice was not directed at *all* immigrants, certainly not wealthy, well-born, Protestant immigrants, but rather at the poor and working-class Catholic immigrants. Thus, it is perfectly appropriate for an immigrant such as Edith to rise because her elevation represents a restoration.

The depiction of immigrant orphans and the immigrant poor in periodical literature also reinforces middle-class values. While they occasionally appear in *Peterson's* and *Godey's*, the focus is less on the condition of these characters than on their *effects* on the middle class. In this respect, their message is similar to that of general periodical fiction and poetry about orphans. For example, "The Orphan's Gratitude," a short story that appeared in *Peterson's* in 1852, recounts the loyalty of an adopted French girl to her adoptive family when they fall on hard times. Significantly, both the girl and her dying mother "bear the stamp of gentle blood," and the implication is that this "stamp" is the source of her unusual virtue (Stark, 198). The underlying middle-class moral of the story is that acts of benevolence to orphans (to the *right* orphans, at least) are good because they are rewarded; in other words, kindness begets kindness in a form of commercial exchange. It should be remembered that Ann Stephens, author of *The Old Homestead*, was the editor of *Peterson's*, and the magazine, like the novel, sends a message of benevolence that is class-biased.

Other magazine fiction about immigrants also covertly focuses on the middle class by casting those who perform acts of benevolence as instruments of God's will. For example, in "The Emigrant Family; or, the Secret of Success," a mother persuades a baker to give her bread to feed her starving family, and she is praised by her husband for putting her trust in God. The woman replies, "Yes, I have strong faith in God, and *in man, too*.... It is because we do not expect to find goodness in our fellow-men and do not encourage its development that we no oftener find it" (Shindler, 18; italics in original).

Similarly, "The Orphan Family" chronicles in sympathetic terms the sad tale of an impoverished Irish immigrant family, "pious people [with] a degree of intellectual refinement peculiar to those who make the Holy Scriptures an habitual study" (a practice more common among Protestants than Catholics, one might add). The parents die, of course, and as a result of the mother's faith in God ("I intend leaving them entirely in the care of God...and I feel that I can fearlessly repose this trust in him"), the five homeless, destitute orphans are swiftly adopted and the moral unequivocally implied, that God takes care *of* his own *with* his own: "God did more for them than earthly parents could have done, and exemplified in them how confidently a Christian orphan's repose rested upon his assurance, 'When thy father and mother forsake thee, I will take thee up'" (Hayes, 236). Stories such as this are significant because they reflect the complex nature of benevolence during this period in which genuine sympathy and nativist prejudice vie for dominance and achieve an uneasy truce in rationalizations of heavenly reward.

In summary, the few immigrant orphans depicted in women's fiction tend to meet with a happy fate either because of intervention from middle-class women in the form of benevolence or because their values were consistent with those of the middle class, the republican reincarnation of the Puritan elect. One does not find fiction about immigrant orphans who fall into vice or crime and die in misery. One does not find fiction about immigrant orphans "placed out" with families in the West. In general, one does not find the reality of orphanhood but instead self-serving, reassuring middle-class fantasies about inclusion in the family of the republic. Class was a reason for and a means of keeping the insiders in and the outsiders out. The outsiders were Indians, immigrants, Catholics, and Negroes—cultural orphans reviled for their differences and used as scapegoats for the poor. Of all these groups, the Negroes were the most unadoptable of all, excluded from not only the family of the republic but the family of humankind.

CHAPTER SEVEN

The Negro as Ultimate Orphan

> You are the children of Abraham Lincoln. We are at best
> only his step-children; children by adoption,
> children by forces of circumstance and necessity.
> —FREDERICK DOUGLASS

Negroes, like immigrants, were left out of sentimental fiction just as they were left out of the family of the republic. At best, they appear briefly in novels as slaves or servants, and their function tends to be either decorative or comic. In general, they are portrayed as stereotypes rather than fully developed characters. There are, however, a few instances in which Negroes appear as orphans, and these illustrate how the separation of slaves not only from their own families but from the human family reflects the insidious relationship between race and class.

For example, Lydia Maria Child, who is even better known for her abolitionist efforts than for her appeals on behalf of the Indians, wrote short stories during the antebellum period that express in fictional form the ideas set forth in *An Appeal in Favor of That Class of Americans Called Africans* (1833). Two of these stories feature orphans as their protagonists. One, "The Quadroons" (1842), sends a clear anticapitalist as well as antislavery message about the sexual exploitation of slave women. It focuses on "a handsome and wealthy young Georgian" who falls deeply in love with a quadroon, Rosalie, and "marries" her in a token rather than a legal sense since marriage between the races is not recognized by the law (62). They have a beautiful daughter, Xarifa, whom Edward adores, but despite his personal happiness he falls prey to political ambition and legally marries a well-connected white woman to further his career. The rejected Rosalie dies of grief shortly thereafter, and Edward, filled with remorse, tries to provide for Xarifa, but he dies, and Xarifa, now an orphan, is sold into slavery. Her master, who at first woos her, eventually rapes her, and Xarifa succumbs to madness and dies.

The story very clearly reflects Child's understanding of power, its temptations and its inequities as they affect relations not only between the races but between the sexes. The quadroons are portrayed as undeserving victims of the slave system, and Edward, who represents the white male capitalist oppressor, is punished for his mercenary values. Orphanhood in this story is a symbol of the powerlessness that results from the objectification of slavery and capitalism.

In a children's story, "Jumbo and Zairee," that Child wrote for *The Juvenile Miscellany* in 1831, orphanhood is the central subject and serves as a metaphor for the dehumanizing effects of slavery. Child wrote the story, based on an actual case history, as an indictment of the slave trade. Jumbo and Zairee, the son and daughter of an African prince, are kidnapped by American slave traders and sold into slavery. The implication is that even though they are of royal blood, they are not immune to the degradation of slavery. Child uses this separation trauma to engage the sympathy and identification of her young readers and laces the story with didactic asides about the betrayal of Negroes' political rights, which in her view are inseparable from their human rights. Of the hard-hearted slave trader she writes: "You will ask me if this man was an American? One of our own countrymen, who make it their boast that men are born free and equal? I am sorry to say that he was an American. Let us hope there are but few such" (291). Later, when Zairee is threatened with a whipping if she doesn't eat, Child exclaims, "This was in the United States of America, which boasts of being the only true republic in the world! the asylum of the distressed! the only land of perfect freedom and equality! 'Shame on my country—ever lasting shame.' History blushes as she writes the page of American slavery, and Europe points her finger at it in derision" (294–295). The children are miraculously reunited with their father, and all of them are rescued from slavery by "a good white man," an Englishman they helped in Africa many years before. The irony is bitter and unmistakable: America has failed to live up to the promise of the Revolution, and it takes an *Englishman* to restore the slave children to freedom and their family.

The most striking example of a fictional narrative in which Negroes figure as fully developed characters is Harriet Beecher Stowe's *Uncle Tom's Cabin* (1851–

1852), which also features an orphan. The drama of the central characters—Tom, Eliza, and George—revolves around the brutality with which slavery shatters families and separates parents from children, husbands from wives. The character who best exemplifies the dehumanizing effects of slavery is Topsy, who also raises unsettling questions about Stowe's attitudes toward race. Stowe's portrayal of Topsy, basically a white fantasy of Negro emancipation that has unmistakably racist overtones, is inseparable from the context of the slave narratives that provided much of her inspiration, such as those of Henry Bibb and Josiah Henson (Hedrick, 211). Frederick Douglass's narratives had the profoundest effect on Stowe's moral imagination, and she appropriated his imagery of orphanhood to dramatize slavery's worst sin, the break-up of families.

Despite the fact that Stowe and Douglass had their differences, notably in their attitudes toward colonization and the role of the church in abetting slavery, one issue on which they agreed was the devastating effect of slavery on the family and the individual. Douglass's autobiographical accounts begin by linking the separation from his family to various forms of dehumanization. Slavery not only made Douglass an orphan but robbed him of a personal and historical identity. His traumatic experience and the strategies of identity formation he developed in reaction to it are representative of the struggle undergone by all slaves, whose ancestors were snatched from their families in Africa and shipped like human cargo to America. Those who descended from them were unable to trace their heritage past its origins in captivity. Certainly a major reason for the success of slavery was its dissolution of family structure and bonds. As Charles Sellers points out, one in three slave families were broken up by sale between 1820 and 1860, and the separation of children from their parents was particularly common (397).

By prohibiting slaves from marrying, indiscriminately selling members of families, and forcing themselves sexually on their female slaves, white masters "fathered" a race of cultural orphans who were bereft of recognized family ties. Slave society was matrilineal, with the child's status determined by the mother, which protected masters who fathered children by slaves from obligations of paternity and ensured that slave children would have no legal rights. There were deeper implications as well. In a nation that predicated its identity on a patriarchal model of family government and passed power, property, and citizenship from father to son, slaves were conveniently left out of the family equation, as Russ Castronovo explains in *Fathering the Nation*.

The very first paragraph of his earliest autobiography, *The Narrative of the Life of Frederick Douglass, An American Slave* (1845), establishes both the void into which Douglass was born and his need for an identity, which is a very different proposition for a slave orphan than for a free white child. Although he knows where he was born, he does not know when: "I do not remember to have ever met a slave who could tell of his birthday. They seldom come nearer to it than planting-time, harvest-time, cherry-time, spring-time, or fall-time. A want of information concerning my own was a source of unhappiness to me even during childhood. The white children could tell their ages. I could not tell why I ought be deprived of the same privilege" (47).

Although he knew his mother's name, he was separated from her as an infant, "before I knew her as my mother":

> It is a common custom, in the part of Maryland from which I ran away, to part children from their mothers at a very early age. Frequently, before the child has reached its twelfth month, its mother is taken from it, and hired out on some farm a considerable distance off, and the child is placed under the care of an old woman, too old for field labor. For what this separation is done, I do not know, unless it be to hinder the development of the child's affection toward its mother, and to blunt and destroy the natural affection of the mother for the child. This is the inevitable result. (48)

Douglass saw his mother only four or five times in his life. She died when he was seven, and "never having enjoyed, to any considerable extent her soothing presence, her tender and watchful care, I received the tidings of her death with much the same emotions I should have probably felt at the death of a stranger" (49). She also died without telling him the identity of his father, whom he suspects is his master, and Douglass bitterly denounces the law that requires slave children to follow the condition of their mothers: "this is done too obviously to administer to their own lusts, and make a gratification of their wicked desires profitable as well as pleasurable; for by this cunning arrangement, the slaveholder, in cases not a few, sustains to his slaves the double relation of master and father" (49). In his second autobiography, *My Bondage and My Freedom* (1855), Douglass expands the account of his childhood to dramatize the harmful effects of slavery on Negro families and argues that one of the primary strategies of subjugation is to break down the institution of the family.

The trauma of separation pervades Douglass's autobiographical narratives, to the extent that orphanhood is the definitive experience of his early life (Reising, 256–272). Deprived of natural familial bonds and a sense of personal history, he is denied the fundamental human experience that shapes identity. As a result, he struggles to compensate by bonding with other slaves. The passionate intensity of his attachment is apparent in a passage that describes the year he spent serving a benevolent master and teaching his fellow slaves to read: "For the ease with which I passed the year, I was, however, somewhat indebted to the society of my fellow slaves. They were noble souls; they not only possessed loving hearts, but brave ones. We were linked and interlinked with each other. I loved them with a love stronger than any thing I have experienced since." Douglass attributes this intense attachment, which is evocative of that between a mother and child, not only to the affinity of their "tempers and dispositions" but to "the mutual hardships to which we were necessarily subjected by our condition as slaves" (121–122).

When Douglass and his fellow slaves are caught following an attempted escape, he confesses, "Our greatest concern was about separation. We dreaded that more than anything this side of death" (128). When his friends are taken home and he is left alone in jail, he falls into despair: "I regarded this separation as a final one. It caused me more pain than anything else in the whole transaction. I was ready for anything rather than separation" (129–130). On the verge of finally making his escape, Douglass ruminates about his state of mind and implies a connection between submission to slavery and attachment to one's friends: "It is my opinion that thousands would escape from slavery, who now remain, but for the strong cords of affection that bind them to their friends. The thought of leaving my friends was decidedly the most painful thought with which I had to contend. The love of them was my tender point, and shook my decision more than all things else" (142).[1]

After Douglass arrives in New York and the initial feeling of elation subsides, he re-experiences the sensations of orphanhood: "the loneliness overcame me. There I was in the midst of thousands, and yet a perfect stranger; without home and without friends, in the midst of thousands of my own brethren, children of a common Father, and yet I dared not to unfold to any one of them my sad condition" (143). The obvious reason for his mistrust is that as a fugitive slave Douglass was naturally terrified of capture, but the psychological message that emerges from his discourse is that he feels again like a lonely, bereft child without home or family who has now lost the "brethren" who made his life bearable. And while he may share a common spiritual father with his white "brethren," the implication is clearly that they are not his biological or emotional kin.

For Douglass and his fellow slaves, the struggle to achieve a sense of humanity depends on attachment to other slaves as a surrogate family. This communal bond serves as a transition to assuming an identity as a free man, but the narrative also suggests that the condition of orphanhood that supports slavery is conducive to such bonding. It is precisely the vacuum into which the slave is born that creates his vulnerability. As a nobody, something less than a human being, he can define himself only as a slave and belong only to the collective family of slavery.[2] The tragedy, as Douglass perceived, is that to be a slave means not to exist as a human being but to be orphaned from the human family as well as one's personal family.

Douglass makes reference throughout his narratives to the "dehumanizing" and "soul-killing" nature of slavery—a slave is not a person but an animal, a piece of property, with no rights to education, income, or legal protection—and his obsessive concern with achieving manhood has as much to do with humanity as with masculinity. His relationship with the brutal overseer, Mr. Covey, who savagely beats him, encapsulates his evolution from "a brute...broken in body, soul, and spirit" to a man (105): "You have seen how a man was made a slave; you shall see how a slave was made a man" (107). Douglass retaliates, and his attack on Covey is "the turning point in my career as a slave. It rekindled the few expiring embers of freedom, and revived within me a sense of my own manhood. It recalled the departed self-confidence, and inspired me again with a determination to be free.... It was a glorious resurrection, from the tomb of slavery, to the heaven of freedom" (113).

Here Douglass is struggling to convince himself that slavery is a state of mind as well as a political condition, and he gradually comes to the realization that slavery and freedom are also socioeconomic realities. The slave's assumption is that freedom alone confers identity upon the slave. But in order to achieve a social sense of self, the freed slave has to translate freedom into action and enter the marketplace. In other words, true emancipation lies in the ability to *work for wages* because money confers not only property and power but human identity. Just as Indians were commodified as land, Negroes were commodified as property, and both were victims of capitalist exploitation and oppression.[3] Thus, if the defining characteristic of a slave is that he is dehumanized as a piece of property, then the goal of liberation is to regain one's humanity, and with it identity as an American, by *owning* property rather than *being* property.

But the transition was not that simple. Few freed Negroes were able to rise above poverty level, and those who did were denied the rights of citizenship through various legal restrictions. One way freed Negroes were prevented from competing in the marketplace was by depriving them of an education. As Winthrop Jordan observes in *White over Black*: "Omission of Negroes from the American educational program rested on a mountain of practical difficulties, on fear of literacy among slaves, on the exclusion of Negroes from occupations requiring much use of the head, on the general tendency to set Negroes apart, and on widespread reluctance to think out the problem of future status" (356). He adds that in the North this reluctance derived from an unwillingness to consider the possibility of Negro education.

Having ensured that Negroes could not rise above poverty or the lower class at best, the government, in a classic example of circular reasoning, used their alleged inferior status as an argument for additional forms of oppression. Treated as neither citizens nor even aliens who at least had the option of naturalization, freed Negroes in the North occupied a legislative limbo that in 1840 denied 93 percent of them the right to vote. There was, in fact, a devolution in the status of free blacks inversely related to the status of whites; as suffrage expanded for whites, it became more restricted for Negroes. They were also prohibited from serving on juries, and anti-immigration provisions even restricted their right to cross some state lines. Other restrictions effectively barred them from churches, social circles, and schools. They were even buried separately from whites. Their degradation culminated in the Dred Scott decision of 1857, which found Negro citizenship incompatible with the Constitution, and by 1860 the situation of northern Negroes had improved very little from the time they were freed.[4] Adding insult to injury, whites blamed the Negroes themselves for their lack of progress and recommended exile. As Leon Litwack bitterly pronounced, "having stripped him of his claims to citizenship and having deprived him of opportunities for political and economic advancement, whites concluded that the Negro had demonstrated an incapacity for improvement in this country and should be colonized in Africa" (279).

Douglass's self-emancipation exemplifies the crucial transition not only from slavery to freedom but from property to potential property-holder. His new identity, which stands in striking contrast to that of most emancipated slaves, traces its origin to his earliest experience of work. While a slave, his master places him as an apprentice to a shipbuilder in Baltimore to learn caulking. Douglass is so proficient that he eventually earns the highest wages, given only to the most experienced caulkers. Despite his achievement, Douglass is still required to turn over all his wages to Master Hugh. Why? Outraged, Douglass responds to his own question: "Not because he earned it, — not because I owed it to him, — nor because he possessed the slightest shadow of a right to it; but solely because he had the power to compel me to give it up. The right of the grim-visaged pirate upon the high seas is exactly the same" (135).

Douglass subsequently finds employment "stowing a sloop with a load of oil" three days after his flight to the North, and the difference in his reaction is unmistakable: "It was new, dirty, and hard work for me; but I went at it with a glad heart and a willing hand. *I was now my own master.* It was a happy moment, the rapture of which can be understood only by those who have been slaves. It was the first work, the reward of which was to be entirely my own. There was no Master Hugh standing ready, the moment I earned the money, to rob me of it" (150; italics added).

Remunerated work thus represents the third stage of Douglass's liberation, beyond communal bonding and flight, and it reconstitutes his identity as an owner of capital rather than a piece of property. He also acquires a human identity, as if through the magic of the marketplace the "thing" were transformed into a man. Later in his career when Douglass is working as a writer and an orator, he develops an even more secure sense of identity. Describing the demands of his newspaper, *The North Star,* he writes: "it made it necessary for me to lean upon myself, and not upon the heads of our antislavery church — *to be a principal, and not an agent.* . . . There is nothing like the lash and sting of necessity to make a man work, and my paper furnished this motive and power" (*Life and Times,* 264; italics added). Despite the fact that he is denied the rights of citizenship, work has transformed Douglass from an orphan into an adopted child of the republic, at least in economic terms. But Douglass recognized only too well the constraints on adoption of the Negro. In a speech tinged with bitterness and disappointment delivered in 1876 to commemorate President Lincoln's death, Douglass reminded his white audience that their relationship with President Lincoln was different from that of his own race: "The race to which we belong were not the special objects of his consideration. . . . You are the children of Abraham Lincoln. We are at best only his stepchildren; children by adoption, children by forces of circumstances and necessity" (Foner, 312).

One of the more interesting interpretations of Douglass's spiritual journey is that it follows a path from orphanhood to self-fatherhood. For example, Eric Sundquist suggests that Douglass replaced both the absent antagonist, the father as slave master, and the Revolutionary "fathers" who betrayed the promise of benevolent parenthood, and became his own father, i.e. a self-made man like Benjamin Franklin (17). Along the same lines, in an essay called "Franklinian Douglass: The Afro-American as Representative Man," Rafia Zafar even proposes that Douglass is Franklin's alter ego or *Doppelgänger*, just as Franklin's autobiography can be viewed as a progenitor of slave narratives: "The great emphasis on personal freedom, espousal of hard work and industriousness, and announcement of lowly origins are hallmarks of both works" (99). Zafar borrows Orlando Patterson's description of the slave as a "genealogical isolate" in a state of "natal alienation" to explain how Douglass appropriates from Franklin the role of the self-made man, who rises from a state of orphanhood to one of identity (101). Zafar cites Douglass's "Self-Made Men," which describes his spiritual journey in similar terms: "Self-made men...are the men who owe little or nothing to birth, relationship, friendly surroundings; to wealth inherited or to early approved means of education; who are what they are, without the aid of any of the favoring conditions by which other men usually rise in the world and achieve great results" (quoted in Zafar, 113).

The question Zafar legitimately raises is to what extent Douglass's story is typical of that of other former slaves, and the unavoidable answer is that it is not. Not only is Douglass atypical of his impoverished peers; he is positively anomalous — an elite of virtually one who has risen by dint of the education he gave himself and gleaned from his oppressors, notably his mistress Mrs. Auld. The coincidence of education and his natural gifts enabled him to perform meaningful work and assume an identity in the white world by writing, an act of empowerment and humanization. Douglass was, after all, one of the few Negroes who could actually *write* his own autobiography (most slave narratives were narrated and recorded), an act of ontological significance. According to Charles T. Davis and Henry L. Gates, "The slave narrative represents the attempts of blacks to *write themselves into being*. What a curious idea: through the mastery of formal Western languages, the presupposition went, a black person could become a human being by an act of self-creation through the mastery of language" (xxiii).

Uncle Tom's Cabin recapitulates the central themes in Douglass's narratives, in particular the trauma of family separation and the dehumanization of slaves that it entails. But the consequences of orphanhood in Stowe's novel are far more representative of the freed Negro's experience than in Douglass's narrative. Stowe, like Douglass, was appalled by the break-up of slave families and recognized its impact on identity. Since the family is essential for conferring identity on an individual, separation from family, enacted through the exploitative institution of slavery, turns a man into a thing, to paraphrase Stowe's original subtitle about the "man that was a thing." In this respect, her novel reflects Douglass's perception of slavery as a negation of humanity. The most striking example in the novel of this ultimate form of degradation is the orphan Topsy who, even more than Tom, epitomizes the dehumanization that results from slavery. The contrast, however, between Topsy's journey from slavery to freedom and Douglass's suggests significant differences in Stowe's and Douglass's perceptions of what emancipation means.

In this regard, it is important to bear in mind, as Hedrick observes, that Stowe was singularly unprepared for her role as "the single most powerful voice on behalf of the slave. Her preparation for this political role had been virtually nil. She had never been a member of an antislavery society, much less an officer in one" (234). Moreover, she refused to align herself with any abolitionist society and instead scrupulously maintained her loyalty to "her natural power base: the women" (238). Constrained by the inability of women to speak in public, "Stowe's attack on the patriarchal institution [of slavery] radically undermined the ideology of separate spheres, yet her public behavior supported the fiction of woman's separation from the world" (241). In keeping with her primary allegiance, Stowe directed the emotional appeal of her novel to white, middle-class Christian women, specifically to mothers, with the result that racial issues were distorted by sentimental ideology to suit the biases of that power base.

For example, in Stowe's depiction of Topsy, she expresses the deep-seated fear of innate African heathenism and primitivism shared by Christian women imbued with missionary zeal and lofty notions of benevolence. Whereas Stowe flatteringly depicts mulattos such as Eliza and George Harris, her portrayal of full-blooded Negroes is derogatory, even in the case of Tom who, despite his dignity and spirituality, is debased by his passive, childlike qualities, to say nothing of his diction. Extreme to the point of offensiveness is her characterization of Topsy as virtually a different species not only from whites but even from mulattos. When Topsy, an eight or nine-year-old Negro girl, first appears in the St. Clare household in New Orleans, Stowe's description is so racist that it verges on parody:

> She was one of the blackest of her race; and her round, shining eyes, glittering as glass beads, moved with quick and restless glances over everything in the room. Her mouth, half open with astonishment at the wonders of the new Mas'r's parlor, displayed a white and brilliant set of teeth. Her woolly hair was braided in sundry little tails, which stuck out in every direction. The expression on her face was an odd mixture of shrewdness and cunning, over which was oddly drawn, like a kind of veil, an expression of the most doleful gravity and solemnity. She was dressed in a single, filthy, ragged garment made of bagging, and stood with her hands demurely folded. Altogether, there was something odd and goblin-like about her appearance,—something, as Miss Ophelia afterwards said, "so heathenish," as to inspire that good lady with utter dismay. (236–237)

Equally disturbing is Stowe's language of objectification and dehumanization. Miss Ophelia proceeds to ask St. Clare, Eva's father, what he has brought "that thing" here for. St. Clare replies that he thought her "a funny specimen in the Jim Crow line" and whistles, "as a man would call the attention of a dog," to get her to sing and dance. Topsy then gives an extraordinarily primitive performance ("the thing struck up, in a clear shrill voice, an odd negro melody... knocking her knees together in a wild, fantastic sort of time, and producing in her throat all those odd guttural sounds which distinguish the music of her race" [237]). One would like to think that Stowe paints this cruel and savage portrait to parody Southern stereotypes, but the fact that she is capable not only of making such observations but of conveying them with such relish suggests she shares to at least some degree the racist assumption that the Negro is subhuman, a dangerous "thing," until Christianized and "civilized." As Richard Yarborough puts it, "of paramount importance is the emphasis Stowe places on the grotesque freakishness of Topsy's strange performance, for she identifies this darkly magical and faintly sinister quality of the 'sooty gnome' with her unredeemed African nature.... Topsy is the imp child whose undisciplined devilish spirit must be controlled" (49).

Whatever the inconsistencies in Stowe's attitude, the value of her portrayal of Topsy lies in her perception that Topsy has internalized the racist image of the Negro in the form of self-hatred. It becomes apparent that Topsy is not only a neglected and abused child but one bereft of a personal as well as a human identity, as if connection to a family is essential to make a child part of the human race. When Miss Ophelia asks her personal questions, Topsy ("the creature") claims an anonymity even more extreme than Douglass's. She doesn't know her age, and "never was born... never had no father nor mother, nor nothin'" (240). Moreover, Topsy perceives herself as irredeemably wicked ("I spects I's the wickedest critter in the world") and attributes this condition to her blackness (249). To mitigate her lack of being, Topsy continues to give desperate performances, like the one described above, which seem driven by nothing so simple as a need for attention and the desire for recognition of her existence.

The issue of Topsy's lovability encodes these dynamics. Miss Ophelia, the northern bigot who doesn't want another one of "these little plagues" around the house, at first rejects St. Clare's idea that she give Topsy "a good orthodox New England bringing up, and see what it'll make of her," but eventually accepts the challenge out of duty rather than love. It requires the mediation of Eva's love to start Topsy down the path to salvation. Eva finds herself mysteriously drawn to Topsy, like Ellen to Nancy in *The Wide, Wide World,* and tries to fathom the secret of her wickedness. With Christian intuition, Eva asks Topsy if she hasn't ever loved anyone, and Topsy replies that she never had anyone to love: "never had nothing nor nobody." Topsy sees no point in trying to be good because she is black: "Couldn't never be nothin' but a nigger, if I was ever so good.... If I could be skinned, and come white, I'd try then." Eva tries to convince her that she can be loved although she's black and that Miss Ophelia would love her if she was good, to which Topsy accurately retorts that Miss Ophelia can't even bear to be touched by her (280).

In a great gush of feeling Eva replies, "O Topsy, poor child, *I* love you!... I love you, because you haven't had any father, or mother, or friends; —because you've been a poor, abused child! I love you, and I want you to be good" (280–281). Touched at last, Topsy weeps: "Yes, in that moment, a ray of real belief, a ray of heavenly love, had penetrated the darkness of her heathen soul! She laid her head down between her knees, and wept and sobbed, —while the beautiful child, bending over her, looked like the picture of some bright angel stooping to reclaim a sinner" (281).

Stowe would have the reader believe that as a result of Eva's "heavenly love," Topsy undergoes a change of heart and is redeemed. But from an ideological standpoint, it is less important that Topsy is redeemable than that her agent of redemption is a white "Saxon" and Southern aristocrat. Whereas Topsy is perceived as an animal, a heathen, a "thing" —a subhuman creature —the blond blue-eyed Eva is regarded as a superhuman celestial being. To Tom, for example, "she seemed something almost divine; and whenever her golden head and deep blue eyes peered out upon him from behind some dusky cotton-bale, or looked down upon him over some ridge of packages, he half believed that she was one of the angels stepped out of his New Testament" (144).

That Stowe saw the racial difference between the two children in qualitative terms is evident in the following passage in which she characterizes them as "representatives of the two extremes of society": "The fair, high-bred child, with her golden head, her deep eyes, her spiritual, noble brow, and prince-like movements; and her black, keen, subtle, cringing yet acute neighbor. There stood the representatives of their races. The Saxon, born of ages of cultivation, command, education, physical and moral eminence; the Afric, born of ages of oppression, submission, ignorance, toil, and vice" (244). The implication is clearly that whites exist not only on a higher evolutionary plane but on a higher spiritual one as well and are singularly equipped to lift the Negro out of the primeval ooze of paganism and heathenism.

The fact that a form of divine intervention is necessary before Miss Ophelia can love Topsy is implicit confirmation of Topsy's unlovability (and also of Miss Ophelia's racism). When Topsy becomes hysterical with grief because there is no one left to love her, Miss Ophelia's heart softens and she exclaims, "Topsy, you poor child . . . don't give up! *I* can love you, though I am not like that dear little child. I hope I've learnt something of the love of Christ from her. I can love you; I do, and I'll try to help you to grow up a good Christian girl" (297; italics in original). Stowe comments triumphantly, "Miss Ophelia's voice was more than her words, and more than that were the honest tears that fell down her face. From that hour, she acquired an influence over the mind of the destitute child that she never lost" (297). But her words ring as hollow as Miss Ophelia's alleged transformation.

Miss Ophelia, as the representative of the North and emancipation, serves as the secular agent of Topsy's redemption, but there is little evidence that she is now motivated by love rather than a sense of Christian duty. To Miss Ophelia, Topsy's salvation is a practical as well as a spiritual affair, and she sets about freeing Topsy from slavery in order to remove her from her own culture and raise her in the uplifting traditions of New England gentility. Insisting to St. Clare that he give Topsy to her legally, Miss Ophelia argues, "I want her mine, that I may have a right to take her to the free States, and give her her liberty, that all I am trying to do be not undone. . . . There is no use in my trying to make this child a Christian child, unless I save her from all the chances and reverses of slavery" (307). In her fervor, Miss Ophelia sounds like Charles Loring Brace advocating "placing out" as the only remedy for the corrupting influence of the culture (and, as neither explicitly states, the best remedy for the corrupting influence of the orphan on the culture). In short, the relationship between Miss Ophelia and Topsy is basically neocolonial. Topsy is a passive, malleable creature incapable of making efforts on her own behalf to educate, free, or save herself, and like Tom, she is totally dependent on the mercy and ministrations of her white owners. In contrast with Douglass, who basically emancipates himself, Topsy lacks any sense of autonomy and requires the intervention of both Miss Eva and Miss Ophelia to liberate her, with the result that she is saved on their terms.

Miss Ophelia's efforts are not in vain, but they are curiously limited. She takes Topsy home to Vermont where the once unruly "thing" grows "in grace and in favor with the family and neighborhood." There is no mention of adoption or, curiously enough, education (432). This is all the more surprising in view of Stowe's advocacy of education for freed Negroes, and her acknowledgment that "the first desire of the emancipated slave, generally, is for *education*" (443). As a young woman, Topsy is baptized and becomes a member of the church, but at this crucial moment, Stowe abruptly terminates the process of Topsy's assimilation into white society. In a genuine abolitionist fantasy, Topsy would enter a profession, like teaching, and be paid like Douglass. (Of course, even that fantasy would fall short of marrying her off to a white middle-class merchant.) But Stowe ducks the uncomfortable issues raised by Topsy's emancipation by exiling her from the country. In short, she sends her, like George Harris, back to Africa: "[Topsy] showed so much intelligence, activity and zeal, and desire to do good in the world, that she was at last recommended, and approved, as a missionary to one of the stations in Africa; and we have heard that the same activity and ingenuity which, when a child, made her so multiform and restless in her developments, is now employed, in a safer and wholesome manner, in teaching children in her own country" (432–433).

Topsy's fate is consistent with Stowe's policy on Liberia, the location in Africa where the American Colonization Society settled free blacks who were willing to return to their "native" land. The American Colonization Society was formed by delegates from several states in 1816 to develop a plan for colonizing free Negroes in Africa or any other place designated by Congress. Under the plan, approximately 11,000 Negroes were transported by 1860. Abolitionists were violently opposed to the society because they felt that the removal of free Negroes had the effect of strengthening slavery. The policy was an obvious variation on the Indian removal policy and was motivated by a similar desire to exile—in this case, the educated members of the Negro race who might attain power and influence and even assimilate. In short, Stowe's alternative is to turn the colonized into colonizers:

> To fill up Liberia with an ignorant, inexperienced, half-barbarized race, just escaped from the chains of slavery, would be only to prolong, for ages, the period of struggle and conflict which attends the inception of new enterprises. Let the church of the north receive these poor sufferers in the spirit of Christ; receive them to the educating advantages of Christian republican society and schools, until they have attained to somewhat of a moral and intellectual maturity, and then assist them in their passage to those shores, where they may put in practice the lessons they learned in America. (443)

In other words, let some free blacks, like Topsy, acquire an education here that suits them for missionary work in Africa rather than work within the capitalist economy of this country. For George as well, this appears to be his only opportunity to find meaningful work: "I go to *Liberia*, not as to an Elysium of romance, but as *a field of work*. I expect to work with both hands,—to work hard; to work against all sorts of difficulties and discouragements; and to work till I die" (432; italics in original).

Thus, although Topsy acquires a human identity to the extent that she is emancipated, no longer a thing but a person, she nevertheless remains a cultural orphan because Stowe excludes her from the marketplace and exiles her from the country. The striking difference between Topsy and Douglass is that Douglass acquires at least a social and economic identity in the white world, which pays and values him for his work, i.e. his writings. Stowe denies Topsy this empowerment, and her fate as a missionary constitutes a sentimental solution to the racism that exists within her own class and culture.

One of the painful realities Stowe avoids confronting is the collusion of sentimentalism with capitalism, which she ostensibly holds up for critique in *Uncle Tom's Cabin*. Stowe uses domestic ideology in the novel not only to emphasize the importance of family but to condemn the abuses of capitalism and the role it plays in slavery. She regards capitalism as the link between feudalism and slavery and makes clear her anticapitalist sentiments in two major scenes in the novel. The first takes place between St. Clare and Miss Ophelia. St. Clare is reminiscing about his childhood and proceeds to describe his father as "a born aristocrat": "*Among his equals,* never was a man more just and generous; but he considered the negro through all possible gradations of color, as an intermediate link between man and animals, and graded all his ideas of justice or generosity on this hypothesis" (224; italics in original).

Later St. Clare describes his brother Alfred as "high and haughty," an aristocrat and a despot, who defends the right of the American planter to behave like the English aristocracy and capitalists to appropriate the lower classes "body and bone, soul and spirit, to their use and convenience": "He says there can be no high civilization without enslavement of the masses, either nominal or real. There must, he says, be a lower class, given up to physical toil and confined to an animal nature; and a higher one thereby acquires leisure and wealth for a more expanded intelligence and improvement and becomes the directing soul of the lower" (228).

In a dialogue that follows shortly thereafter, Alfred articulates to St. Clare his own elitist ideology. Alfred refutes St. Clare's assertion that all men are born free and equal, countering, "It is the educated, the intelligent, the wealthy, the refined, who ought to have equal rights, and not the canaille" (266). They then go on to argue about education, with Alfred insisting that "the lower class must not be educated" and St. Clare linking their current education in "barbarism and brutality" to the revolutions that are taking place in Europe: "if there is anything that is revealed with the strength of a divine law in our times, it is that the masses are to rise, and the under class become the upper one." Alfred finally invokes race as the ultimate justification for the status quo: "The Anglo-Saxon is the dominant race of the world and *is to be so*" (267; italics in original).

It is evident from these exchanges that Stowe sees slavery as an economic as well as a racial issue and recognizes how capitalism conspires in the dehumanization of the Negro. As property, slaves function as objects to be owned, traded, bought, and sold and are an integral part of the economy that supports the class structure. In her imagination, domestic ideology, especially the influence of mothers, serves as a correction to the injustice and immorality of capitalism and as a model for a society in which there are no slaves or "orphans," and everyone, even Topsy and those outsiders she represents, is adopted into the family of the republic.

But the irony that escapes Stowe is that her own sentimental ideology of feminized, Christianized self-sacrifice epitomized by Uncle Tom represents a complicity with the very system she opposes. Stowe drew on domestic ideology to advocate a revolution of sentiment that would overturn slavery, as represented by what Sundquist calls "the paternal ideal of the Revolutionary past," but she does not recognize that sentimentalism is also a tainted product of capitalist ideology (17). As Sundquist puts it, "The romance of sentimental domesticity that lends her novel its great emotional power might free the slaves and crucify them at the same time" (20).

Rooted in sentimentalism, the same ambivalence that circumscribes so narrowly the appropriate role of women as well as the appropriate form of revolution limits Topsy's options. In this respect, Stowe's attitudes toward gender and class reinforce her racial prejudices. As Douglass's example illustrates, it is through entering the marketplace as an owner of capital rather than a piece of property that Negroes achieve the status of humanity in white middle-class society; yet with regard to Topsy, Stowe balks at this hurdle by making her a missionary. A more realistic ending to a story like Topsy's would have her become a servant, a domestic like impoverished female immigrants. But Stowe wants a sentimental ending, not a realistic one, because she does not want to deal with either the reality of limited options for freed black women or the reality of inequitable class differences in which she is implicated.

After all, Stowe had servants and depended heavily on them. Hedrick points out, "The complicated relation in which Stowe stood to her domestic servants is reflected in her contradictory consciousness. While she overidentified with them as women, she distanced herself from their race and class" (209). In other words, if Stowe had allowed Topsy to be representative, to stay and work as a servant rather than leave and become a missionary, she would have had to recognize Topsy's socioeconomic identity and acknowledge the system that kept her oppressed both as a woman and as a Negro. A captive of her "white-mistress consciousness," which appropriated the voices of the oppressed, Stowe was unable to confront the full extent of racial and class bias in herself and her society. Hedrick explains, "Stowe drew a highly colored portrait of the slave's humanity, inflected by a sense of 'otherness' not unlike the exotic image of woman created by man, through a similar hierarchical perception of a social inferior" (210).

Perhaps the most telling evidence of Stowe's racism is the colonizationist policy she endorses at the end of the novel as an alternative to social revolution. In sending George and Topsy back to Africa, she is symbolically killing them off as surely as she does Tom under the guise of Christian martyrdom. Exile replaces actual slavery with a displaced form of colonial oppression and recapitulates the exclusionary impulse that underlies nativist rhetoric and the Indian removal policy. It also reflects an important difference between sentimental white orphans and Topsy. Whereas white orphans lost the social status they once possessed or to which they were entitled by birth, Topsy irrevocably lost the human status she never possessed in the first place. Unlike Douglass, she could not earn it through working and acquiring power as an independent economic and social being. Despite her emancipation and the intercession of Miss Ophelia, Topsy was born and remained an orphan to the end, an unadoptable child in the family of the republic.

Topsy's story stands in illuminating contrast to that of another fictional missionary, Vara, and the difference between the two also epitomizes the dichotomy between the children of the republic and its cultural orphans. Vara Granger, in Jane Elizabeth Hornblower's *Vara; or, The Child of Adoption* (1852), is the daughter of American missionaries living on Hawaii, and her parents, both orphans themselves, impose upon her a form of exile, adoption by a family in America. As Patricia Grimshaw explains in her book *Paths of Duty*, the Sandwich Islands represented the first "independent endeavor" undertaken abroad by the American Board of Commissioners for Foreign Missions (ABCFM). Begun in 1819, the mission expanded through the 1820s and 1830s and consisted of 153 inhabitants by 1850 (xv).

Having lost their fortune mysteriously, Vara's parents have no money with which to educate her abroad, and there is no question in their minds but that she must leave the island: "They could not educate her there. They dreaded the effect on her character of the evil influences of that half-civilized island" (17). Among the evil influences are Vara's native friend Rutea, who is variously described as "heathen" and "stupid," and who "hates white men who destroy our race" (35). In a clearly racist passage reminiscent of Stowe's comparison of Eva and Topsy, Hornblower connects the physical differences between the two children to mental traits: "Her [Rutea's] dark complexion, black hair, large black, dreamy though somewhat stupid eyes, and rounded form, were in perfect contrast to the fragile, pale spiritual little Vara" (12–13).

Hornblower grounds the Grangers' fears in the reality of the missionary experience in Hawaii. Patricia Grimshaw reports, "The realization that young children could acquire so readily a culture quite different from their parents' was a shock to successive missionaries as it had been to the pioneers" (131). Included among the fears were religious and sexual corruption, with the result that missionary children were kept as separate as possible from "heathen" children. One is inevitably reminded of the Puritans' reaction to the susceptibility of their children to Indian influences while in captivity. Within this context, the fact that Vara was named after the first heathen her father converted can be viewed as almost talismanic.

In this connection, one of the important issues concerning foreign missions at that time was the education of missionary children. Their education was entirely segregated, against the wishes of the ABCFM, which believed the children should be involved in the missionary effort. But even segregation was not enough to allay the fears of some missionary parents, who, like the Grangers, insisted on sending their children home to be educated. Given the middle-class idealization of the family as essential for the proper religious and moral upbringing of the child, this variation on Brace's "placing out" was quite an extraordinary step to take. But on closer examination, it proves consistent with the philosophy of the period that privileged middle-class "family values" over family unity. In other words, parental rights were deemed less important than the "right" family environment, one that could indoctrinate children with republican ideology.

Vara reluctantly leaves her wild, lush island for a "busy, brick-built town" (ironically called Liberty) in New York, where she undergoes a difficult adjustment as an immigrant who, like Edith Adelon, is actually *superior* to her new adoptive family—in Vara's case, a coarse dry goods merchant, his common wife, and their vulgar son (52). Like Ellen in *The Wide, Wide World*, Vara is clearly used to an upper-class version of wealth, which in her case verges on the neocolonial—a beautiful tropical home and plenty of servants to do the housework (" 'My mother scrub?' cried Vara, half amused—half angry")—and her "fastidious taste" has developed accordingly (90). As a result, she scorns the "dreadfully ugly" fabrics in her new home, such as calicos and linens, and feels herself far more comfortable in the home of a wealthy acquaintance "amidst all this elegance, than in the stiff little parlor of Mrs. Stephens' where, in spite of the pervading order and neatness, no one article of furniture seemed to be where it ought to be or to adorn the apartment" (96). Also like Ellen, she resents "the treadmill of drudgery" (225) and feels herself superior to her adoptive mother: "The loftier aspirations and deeper sensibilities of Vara's nature, are beyond the reach of her plain thinking, right-minded, practical and energetic mother" (188).

The question is where Vara acquired her fancy taste, and the predictable answer is that she inherited it. Her mother was "a beautiful, elegant, accomplished heiress" whose guardian embezzled all her money because he disapproved of her marrying a missionary. But despite opportunities to improve her social and material status by marrying well, Vara spurns such temptations because she aspires "to be a worthy assistant in the evangelization of the poor inhabitants of her native isle" and vows that she can never marry anyone but a missionary (188). At the end of the novel, she returns to Hawaii with a wealthy, well-born missionary husband and the noble intention of converting the heathen by becoming "one of them" rather than forcing conversion on them and acting superior to them like her father, who basically subscribed to the professed goal of the American Board of Commissioners for Foreign Missions: "the speedy establishment of protestant puritan institutions in the North Pacific" (*Forty-First Annual Report*, 173).

There is a great deal of tension in this novel surrounding the subject of missionary work. On the one hand, Hornblower shows an appreciation of and even respect for the natives, whom she depicts in romantic, primitivist terms, and she acknowledges that their influence on Vara, the "child of nature," has been at least somewhat benign. But superseding this appreciation is the assumption of religious and cultural superiority that necessitated Vara's removal from the island *to* America in an ironic reversal of the usual practice of removing immigrants, Negroes, and Indians *from* America, whether socially, economically, legally, or even physically. Vara is clearly the exceptional immigrant who leaves her "native" land in an act of self-removal because it is alien. In reality, Vara is not an immigrant, even though she emigrates to America, but a native returning home protected by a legacy of privilege. She is also not a real orphan. Real nineteenth-century orphans lived on reservations, in urban slums, in exile out West, on southern plantations, or in Africa. Missionary Hawaii was, in fact, a New England enclave, and Vara's emigration to America thus represents a symbolic return to her homeland and a restoration to her elite origins. The fact that she eventually goes back to Hawaii as a missionary is an affirmation rather than a negation of her superiority under the guise of benevolence, a clear example of noblesse oblige. As an insider, a child of the republic, bringing the sacred and secular word to the heathen, Vara is the antithesis of Topsy, the outsider and the orphan who goes to Africa because she is still identified with the heathen.

The missionary context of this novel also reflects the ideological posture of the "family of the republic" toward its "orphans" at home and abroad. The claim of the dominant culture was that it wanted to convert, protect, and elevate the "unfortunate" — Indians, Negroes, immigrants, the poor — but in reality the goal was to ostracize them as much as possible from mainstream society; in effect, to colonize them. In the mid-nineteenth century the obvious imperialist motives behind expansionism and the foreign mission movement were merely an extension of these domestic policies of colonization, pursued ever since the Puritans. Foreign missions abounded all over the world by the 1850s and fell under criticism from members of benevolent societies who urged concentration on home missions.[5] But the foreign mission movement was thoroughly implicated in the wave of expansionism that was sweeping the country during this period and that was a major factor in the Mexican war of 1848.

The complicity of missionary activity and imperialism is apparent in President Zachary Taylor's message to Congress in 1850 about the Sandwich Islands, in which he unabashedly conflates missionary goals and American economic interests: "the success of our persevering and benevolent citizens who have repaired to that remote quarter, in Christianizing the natives and inducing them to adopt a system of laws suited to their capacities and wants; and the use made by our numerous whale ships of the harbors of the Islands, as places of resort for obtaining refreshment and repairs, all combines to render their destiny peculiarly interesting to us." He continues portentously, "We desire that the Islands maintain their Independence, and that other nations should concur with us in this sentiment. We could in no event be indifferent to their passing under the dominion of any other power" (ABCFM, *Forty-First Annual Report*, 180).

The intimation of future possession and aggression against those who would thwart the republic's interests suggests a new attitude toward adoption — that foreigners, even those of other races, could become part of the republic as long as the acquisition of property and economic power warranted the assimilation. Precedent was already set for this in Hawaii, which missionaries called "the child of our adoption, through rights given the missionaries to purchase land cheaply and set up capitalist enterprises" (Grimshaw, 180). These inducements were designed not only to encourage them to stay there but to further American economic interests. The work of missionaries thus served an imperialist purpose as well as a religious one by rendering natives more "adoptable."

The fictional orphan tale of the early nineteenth century expresses the desire for social control found in the factual orphan tale. In their departure from the social reality of orphanhood, these novels and stories about orphans encode in their formula of loss and recovery policies of cultural inclusion and exclusion. The repetitive nature of this formula is suggestive of a neurotic symptom—and I use the word symptom advisedly, with a nod to Jacques Lacan, who, with his famous statement "in the unconscious is the whole structure of language," established grounds for connecting the literary metaphor and the symptom as forms of symbolization (147). The essence of a neurotic symptom, according to Freud in *Beyond the Pleasure Principle*, is its uncontrollable repetition, and he connects the "compulsion to repeat" not only to the repression of a painful or traumatic experience in the unconscious but to the need to *master* that experience through symbolic behavior (609). Applying his theory to the cultural arena, one can speculate that a recurrent literary theme, motif, or figure functions like a neurosis, expressing the repressed material through symbolization and trying to master it through repetition.

Looked at from this perspective, the orphan tale becomes comprehensible as a ritualistic effort to master the threat to the identity of the dominant culture as white, privileged, Protestant, and predominantly Anglo-Saxon. The formula also represents codification in novelistic form of the "family values" that have shaped American culture since its beginnings. The Puritans, confronted with the loss of their political parents and their spiritual Father, reacted to the trauma of the Great Migration by scapegoating those who represented religious difference and displacing onto them their orphanhood. Cultural reasons for exclusion from the "family" became mixed with economic reasons and led the Puritans to view Indian land as both a commodity and an emblem of cultural identity. This mixture of cultural and economic reasons also influenced the exclusionary laws of the colonial period, which clearly reflect a desire to exclude the poor not only because they were burdensome but also because they were potentially dangerous to established values. Thus, using the official injunction against helping indigent outsiders partly as a pretext, God's "children" were able to ostracize from their covenanted family outsiders whom they did not want to adopt and to consign them to perpetual orphanhood. They thereby established the connection between poverty and difference that was to shape social policy in subsequent centuries.

During the Revolution, the family became the symbol of the republic and reflected the necessity of binding together the newly formed nation into a union. In the aftermath of the Revolution, the discrepancy between republican ideals and the self-interest of the "natural aristocracy" intensified the identity crisis created by the rupture with England and induced the Founding Fathers to find scapegoats onto whom they could project blame for internal dissension and conflict. Again, economics played a pivotal role, for these scapegoats were Indians exploited for their land, immigrants exploited as a source of cheap labor, and Negroes exploited for their servitude. Prevented by various forms of oppression from holding property or even the rights of citizenship, they were unadoptable victims of poverty and of political as well as cultural orphanhood.

In the nineteenth century, the middle-class family became the model for the republic. In a period of social upheaval and class conflict, the middle class found itself increasingly troubled and menaced by the presence of the poor and displaced its hostility onto those immigrants, Catholics, and Negroes who constituted its ranks. Despite the fact that the liberalization of naturalization requirements and the increasing number of freed Negroes suggested a broadened definition of adoptability, nativism cast a pall over the enlightened spirit of the republic and subjected these groups to subtle and not-so-subtle forms of social and economic orphanhood. As a result, familial lines began to be drawn along class lines, and poverty became the defining characteristic of cultural orphanhood.

These three periods — the Great Migration, the Revolution, and the rise of the republic — share certain obvious features: a crisis that threatens identity; an identification with orphanhood in response to that crisis; a need for denial; the scapegoating of outsiders; and the projection of orphanhood onto scapegoats. What is striking is how the actual treatment of orphans during these times of crisis parallels and reflects these underlying ideological dynamics. What is less clear is the economic framework in which these patterns unfold. Obviously, the dispossession of the Indians and the enslavement of the Negroes were economically as well as racially motivated. In addition, the Puritans' ostracism of the poor, the Founding Fathers' property requirement for citizenship, and the middle class's incarceration of the poor in asylums and actual removal of the poor through the "placing out" of orphans describe an arc of cultural oppression accomplished through economic means. The familial context in which the orphan trope is embedded supports the theory that class divisions in America did not suddenly spring into being in the nineteenth century but resulted from a slow process of evolution that dates back to colonial times. It also suggests that "family values" are far more economic in origin than leaders at any period of American history, past or present, would care to admit.

A subject for future study is the orphan's cultural function in later nineteenth-century and modern American fiction. A harbinger of transformation is Herman Melville's *Moby Dick*, in which the ideology of orphanhood signifies implicit rebellion against rather than complicity with the dominant culture. In his oppositional role, the protagonist, Ishmael, is an orphan whose victimization represents Melville's critique of a dehumanized, capitalist society of which Ahab, also an orphan, is its supreme and most monstrous example.

With *Moby Dick*, the orphan is no longer an overt or even covert advocate of the dominant culture but has become instead its adversary. Whereas Edgar, Natty, and sentimental heroines ultimately encode the interests of a capitalist, racist, xenophobic society, Ishmael remains profoundly alienated from that society and from all sense of belonging. In the last sentences of the novel, the marooned Ishmael describes his fate, as he clings to the "coffin life-buoy," following the devastation of the *Pequod*: "On the second day, a sail drew near, nearer, and picked me up at last. It was the devious-cruising *Rachel*, that in her retracing search after her missing children, only found another orphan" (470).

The provocative question for future scholarship is to what extent Huck Finn, Isabel Archer, Maisie Farange, Milly Theale, Lily Bart, Jay Gatsby, Joe Christmas, and Janie in *Their Eyes Were Watching God*, to name but a few memorable orphans whose individual quest for an identity is inseparable from cultural critique, partake of Ishmael's legacy of victimization, alienation, and finally subversion.

Notes

Introduction

1. I am referring here to largely discredited theories of exceptionalism espoused by cultural theorists of the 1950s and 1960s who advanced the idea that certain aspects of the literary tradition were unique to American culture.
2. While the middle class did not exist in identifiable form until the nineteenth century, its socioeconomic origins are traceable to the Revolutionary period, and its ideology finds its roots in Puritanism.
3. For the purpose of this study, I rely primarily on the intersubjective theory of the scapegoat, which the contemporary French literary critic René Girard derives from the psychoanalytic tradition and expounds in his book, *The Scapegoat*.
4. I have deliberately elected to use the terms Indians and Negroes in this study because of their historical accuracy. I trust that most readers recognize the ideological connotations of these obsolete terms and of the contemporaneous terms "Native American" and "African American."

Chapter 1

1. In my discussion of Puritan and colonial texts, I have whenever possible deliberately cited those that modernize spelling and syntax. Otherwise, I have made such alterations myself to avoid confusing or frustrating the reader.
2. Although *Patriarcha* was not published until 1680, Filmer wrote it in the 1630s or 1640s to describe an ideological construct that shaped British attitudes toward power and hierarchy in the seventeenth century, as well as those of Britain's colonies.

3. The Pilgrims, like the settlers of the Massachusetts Bay Colony, were also Puritans who left England in a similar spirit of protest against the government and the Anglican Church, but they were not imbued with the same sense of mission and were thus under less pressure to disguise their misery, as Bradford's more candid entries reveal. The denominational difference between the two groups, according to Perry Miller, is reflected in their attitude toward the Church of England. Whereas the Puritans who came to Massachusetts Bay were Congregationalists who saw themselves less as separating from the Church of England than as improving upon it and the Reformation by their example, the Pilgrims were Separatists, "reluctant voyagers; they had never wanted to leave England, but had been obliged to depart because the authorities made life impossible for Separatists" (*Errand into the Wilderness*, 3). While there were many similarities between the sects, two of the most significant differences were dispersion of the Plymouth colony and more liberal standards for church membership among the Pilgrims.

4. Other settlements besides Plymouth, such as Virginia, shared a sense of religious purpose similar to that of the Massachusetts Bay colony. Miller writes, "For the men of 1600 to 1625, the new land was redemption even as it was also riches; the working out of society and institutions cannot be understood (and it has not been understood), except as an effort toward salvation. Religion, in short, was the really energizing propulsion in this settlement, as in others" (101). But the crucial difference between Massachusetts Bay and the other colonies was the typological belief in a holy covenant.

CHAPTER 2

1. I rely for much of this summary on Christopher Marsh's *The Family of Love in English Society, 1550–1630*, the most recent and comprehensive treatment of the Familists to date. Other useful sources on which I have drawn and that I would recommend to those wishing to pursue an inquiry into the connection between the Familists and the Puritans are Alastair Hamilton's *The Family of Love* and Jean Dietz Moss's *"Godded with God": Henrik Niclaes and His Family of Love*.

2. Because "the Other" has been so widely bandied about in academic and even lay discourse that it has virtually lost its meaning, I would like to clarify my use of the term. The Other, like the Self, obviously does not designate a specific person or group but functions instead like a heuristic that describes the dynamics of identity formation. In this book, I am using "the Other" to invoke this process and apply it to the interaction between social groups.

3. The extraordinary persistence of Puritan hysteria over "the heathen" is illustrated by the role it played as late as the end of the century in the Salem witchcraft crisis of 1692. The slave Tituba, a composite Negro and Indian, was blamed for the possession of several young white girls, and in his account of Mercy Short's possession, "A

Brand Pluck'd Out of the Burning," Cotton Mather connects it to her captivity "by our cruel and bloody Indians in the East, who at the same time horribly butchered her father, her mother, her brother, her sister, and other of her kindred and then carried her... unto Canada" (Burr, *Narratives of the Witchcraft Cases*, 259).

4. Annette Kolodny in *The Lay of the Land* explores the gender connotations of settlement in the New World, which played the role of both mother and virgin in the Puritan imagination, and relates the emigration to the need for a new symbolic family. She writes: "just as the impulse for emigration was an impulse to begin again... so, too, the place of that new beginning was in a sense, the New Mother, her adopted children having cast off the bonds of Europe" (9).

5. Ira M. Leonard and Robert D. Parmet in *American Nativism, 1830-1860* trace the roots of nineteenth-century American nativism back to the colonial period when the belief in America as a New Eden, or chosen nation, was generated by Protestantism: "It was widely believed that God had chosen America to be a Protestant land, to be settled, worked, and enjoyed by followers of the Protestant faith" (3). Of course, the Puritans defined Protestant in their own narrow, sectarian terms.

CHAPTER 3

1. Lynn Hunt, in her provocative psychoanalytic study of the French Revolution, *The Family Romance of the French Revolution*, invokes the Freudian model of the family romance in which the child fantasizes about acquiring parents of a higher social standing to explain why "most Europeans in the eighteenth century thought of their rulers as fathers and of their nations as families writ large. This familial grid operated on both the conscious and unconscious level of experience" (xiii–xiv). The grid also operated on both sides of the Atlantic.

2. This is not as much of a departure from the Puritan concept of the child as one might imagine. One can also argue, as does Joseph E. Illick in "Anglo-American Child-Rearing," that the Puritans, with their penchant for rebellion and differentiation, also bore a startling resemblance to adolescents (323–324).

3. Wesley Frank Craven coined the term "national covenant" in his book, *The Founding Fathers*.

4. The origin of the designation "Founding Fathers" is uncertain and appears not to derive from the period to which it is applied. Craven is of the opinion that "the common use of the term... seems to be a relatively recent development... and a surprisingly modern one. Lincoln's 'our fathers' and such other descriptions as 'the fathers of the Republic' are certainly more representative of the common usage through most of our history" (2).

5. In *Totem and Taboo* (1913), Freud expounds the myth of the primal horde to explain the origin of the incest taboo. According to the myth, the sons, impelled by an Oedipal desire to possess the mother, kill the father. The overthrow of the father

leads in turn to the replacement of the primal horde with the fraternal clan, bound together by a taboo against committing incest with the mother. The formation of a sanctified blood tie prevents the brothers from killing each other as they killed the father.

6. Women were excluded as well, and one has to study Jefferson's drafts of the Declaration to appreciate how carefully crafted the document was to ignore certain categories of persons. Of particular significance is his omission of the adjective "inherent" before "inalienable rights" (Jefferson, *Autobiography*, 960).

7. Women, who could not vote or hold property in their own name, fell into a unique category because they enjoyed a kind of citizenship by proxy through their association with a male (husband or father) who qualified.

8. Sharing Washington's opinion of the Indians' bestiality, John Adams similarly warned in 1775 about the dangers of engaging them in battle: "To let loose these blood Hounds to scalp Men and to butcher Women and Children is horrid" (quoted in Drinnon, 70).

9. Winthrop Jordan suggests in his previously cited essay on Thomas Paine that a similar conflict with his father made Paine "a person who delighted in the destruction of tyrants" (304). It is interesting to speculate to what extent the filial relationships of the Founding Fathers shaped their revolutionary zeal.

10. In this connection, Stephen Fender, in his essay "Franklin and Emigration: The Trajectory of Use," attributes what appears to be Franklin's contradictory attitude to the "rhetorical distance" between "emigrants" and "immigrants." Whereas the latter category connotes "an alien, disorderly mass," the former conjures up the image of brave voyagers settling in the new world. Fender suggests, "The discourse of American emigration and settlement is quite distinct from the litany of complaints against the immigrants—so distinct that the same person could ringingly proclaim both sides of the argument, without any visible sign of embarrassment at the contradiction. One of these persons was Benjamin Franklin himself" (335–336).

11. Myra Jehlen argues in "J. Hector St. John Crèvecoeur: A Monarcho-Anarchist in Revolutionary America" that Crèvecoeur's commitment to social equality was so profound that it formed the basis for his misplaced loyalty to the king during the Revolution: "Crèvecoeur was...a supporter of the King because monarchy was for him the corollary of social equality. His opposition to the American Revolution was grounded in the principal that all men are created equal—and that so they should remain" (221).

Chapter 4

1. Jared Gardner's article, "Alien Nation: Edgar Huntly's Savage Awakening," provides an excellent summary of the first political pamphlet Brown wrote after he gave up novels, *An Address to the Government on the Cession of Louisiana to the French*

(1803), which Gardner interprets as a reformulation of "the lessons of *Edgar Huntly*'s engagement with the Alien and Sedition Acts: constructing and exorcising the alien is the precondition of a national identity. Without the alien, there is no American" (432).

2. Richard Slotkin argues persuasively in *Regeneration Through Violence* that this episode in the novel is based on the Abraham Panther captivity narrative (256).

3. See for example Ronald Hagenbüchle's essay, "American Literature and the Nineteenth-Century Crisis in Epistemology: The Example of Charles Brockden Brown": "The very impossibility of achieving dependable knowledge stands in ironic contrast to the characters' desire for knowledge that is as vehement as the corresponding epistemological despair" (127). Similarly, Beverly Voloshin, in "*Edgar Huntly* and the Coherence of the Self," interprets the novel as questioning "the coherence of the external world and, more pointedly, the coherence of the perceiving self" (262).

4. Carroll Smith-Rosenberg, in her essay "Subject Female: Authorizing American Identity," interprets the novel as a projection of tensions between "his colonizing and postcolonial selves" (494). Edgar is a colonist in relation to both the Indians, whose land he needs in order to claim an identity, and Clithero, with whom he identifies as a colonial subject. She concludes, "Euro-Americans... can never completely abandon their connection with the colonized, for to do so would be to refuse their identity as Euro-Americans.... *Edgar Huntly*'s refusal of rational and cohesive subjectivity suggests that the Euro-American is always a divided self" (493). I agree with Smith-Rosenberg's reading and her emphasis on the "negative others" as necessary for identity formation, but I think she overlooks the full destructive implications of the divided "Euro-American" self for Indians and immigrants (485).

5. Robert Montgomery Bird's *Nick of the Woods* (1837) is a revenge novel about an Indian killer whose family was slaughtered by the Indians. In contrast with Cooper, Bird portrays Indians in an entirely unsympathetic and racist light.

6. An influential work that dealt with the adoption of whites by Indians was the captivity narrative of Daniel Boone (written by John Filson in 1784), who served as an obvious model for Leatherstocking.

7. A number of stimulating articles have recently appeared that interpret these novels, particularly *Hope Leslie*, not only in protofeminist terms but as revisionist in relation to the patriarchal, neo-imperialist view of Indian culture that extends from Puritan texts to Cooper's novels.

CHAPTER 5

1. For reasons of consistency and clarity, I will use the generic term "middle class" unless there is a reason for calling attention to its heterogeneous composition.

2. Mary Ryan, in *Cradle of the Middle Class: The Family in Oneida County, New York, 1790–1865*, perceptively explains how "the making of the middle class in the indus-

trial age was conditioned by family changes dating from the canal era" and maintains that "the family itself became the cradle of middle-class individuals" who sustained the industrial system (239).
3. In fairness, it should be noted that there were exceptions, such as Lydia Maria Child who, in her *Letters from New York,* is outspoken in her compassion for the poor, orphans, and immigrants and in her outrage against the social injustice that brought misery upon them. See in particular Letters XIV and XIX and Carolyn L. Karcher's commentary in her comprehensive biography of Child, *The First Woman in the Republic: A Cultural Biography of Lydia Maria Child.* Karcher writes: "While seeking to awaken sympathy for a class of people commonly viewed with disgust and fear, if seen at all, Child also takes her genteel readers on a tour of the institutions designed to segregate the poor from the rich and to punish any transgression of boundaries: prisons, insane asylums, almshouses, and orphanages" (303).
4. According to Leonard and Parmet, historians and sociologists define nativism as "*a deep-seated American antipathy towards internal 'foreign' groups of various kinds—cultural, national, religious, racial—which has erupted periodically into intensive efforts to safeguard America from such perceived 'threats'*" (6; italics in original).
5. It is also relevant that the political orphanhood of the Indians persisted until the twentieth century. They were not allowed to become citizens until 1924.
6. There are a number of misconceptions surrounding the benevolent movement. While there is a tendency to think of benevolence as the province of women, it is important to remember that while women performed the work of benevolence, men provided the money and the influence, as the perusal of most lists of administrators and financial supporters will readily confirm. Moreover, their acts of charity, which were neither universal nor uncomplicated, make it easy to forget that women could be just as harsh and judgmental as men in their attitudes toward the poor and immigrants.
7. Other immigrant groups were more secure than the Irish and had less to fear from Negro competition. In general, they were more tolerant of Negroes, although there were exceptions, as evidenced by the item in the New York German-language newspaper that called Negroes the "apes of the white race" and urged that they be sent back to Africa (quoted in Litwack, 167).
8. Institutions in other cities also tried to place children, but with less success. As Priscilla Clement explains in *Welfare and the Poor in the Nineteenth-Century City,* "Philadelphia's system of public indenture grew increasingly less popular, with the result that fewer children were admitted to almshouses and economic strictures on releasing children to their birth parents were loosened." She concludes, "By midcentury, thrift in public child-welfare administration was of preeminent importance" (139).

9. Unfortunately, exact figures for the percentage actually adopted are not yet available. (The Children's Aid Society is currently compiling them in New York.) In the opinion of a spokesperson for the Orphan Train Heritage Society in Arkansas, "I would say that the majority of the children probably were not legally adopted because most farm people would not take the extra step of getting an attorney involved. They would not go to that much trouble."

CHAPTER 6

1. This does not belie the fact, however, that economic issues figure prominently in the works of such major American Renaissance novelists as Nathaniel Hawthorne and Herman Melville, and that these writers were highly ambivalent about the effects of industrialization and capitalism, as seen, for example, in Hawthorne's *The House of the Seven Gables* and Melville's *Moby Dick*. The latter has frequently been interpreted as a critique of capitalism, as has Melville's novella *Bartleby the Scrivener* and several of his short stories, notably "Poor Man's Pudding and Rich Man's Crumbs." Michael T. Gilmore argues in the introduction to *American Romanticism and the Marketplace* that this ambivalence was played out in the authors' relationship to the marketplace: "The marketplace, then, was a contested issue for the American romantics, a source not of simple opposition but of complex and often contradictory attitudes. Their major works are deeply marked by their divided feelings about the changes transforming their roles as writers and revolutionizing their society" (11).

CHAPTER 7

1. Several scholars have noted the importance of kinship ties among slaves who formed a community that compensated for the loss of family. A particularly memorable example is the slave response to the singing of a Negro spiritual about orphanhood, "Room in There," which Sterling Stuckey describes in *Slave Culture*: "The repetition of stanzas as the dancers circled around and around with ever greater acceleration reinforced and deepened the spirit of familial attachment, drawing within the ancestral orbit slaves who may not have known either a father or mother, their involvement being an extension of that of others, the circle symbolizing the unbroken unity of the community" (29).
2. The use of the male pronoun is a function of the fact that I am analyzing Douglass's texts. Obviously, female slaves experienced a similar sense of dehumanization and objectification, which was compounded by their doubly degraded status as women and victims of sexual abuse by their masters.
3. Priscilla Wald, in her essay "Terms of Assimilation," neatly summarizes the relationship between citizenship and property as it relates to both Indians and slaves:

"Where citizenship is defined through the natural right to own property, and, following Locke, the most basic expression of this concept rests in the citizen's *self-ownership*, members of tribes and slaves... constitute two ways of not owning the self: the former in the tribal absences of an 'American' concept of private property, and the latter in their being owned by someone else" (65). Like Castronovo, Wald also sees citizenship as genealogical and patriarchal, passed like a legacy from generation to generation, father to son.

4. In comparing the two infamous Supreme Court cases, *Cherokee Nation v. Georgia* (1831) and *Scott v. Sanford* (or Dred Scott), Wald notes that within the context of the family trope that "commonly represents the Union," the rhetoric in the decisions effectively excludes both groups from the "family of nations" (63–64). But there is a crucial difference. Because of their removal, the Indians no longer pose a distinct threat, "and their lack of proximity to the white family permits suggestions of assimilability" (76). The Dred Scott decision, on the other hand, consigns the Negro to a political limbo. Wald writes, "Whereas Indian removal makes it possible to emblematize (and thus Americanize) tribal culture, however, the slave remains with United States culture a visible symbol of nonpersonhood, neither *potential* citizen nor alien" (77; italics in original).

5. It is noteworthy that among the foreign missions were missions to the Indians, who were treated as if they were foreigners. Another parallel is that one of the major thrusts at home and abroad was education in boarding schools, which were intended to remove Indian children from the influence of their parents and the community.

Bibliography

Abbott, Edith, ed. *Immigration: Select Documents and Case Records.* Chicago: University of Illinois Press, 1968.
Alcott, Louisa May. *The Inheritance.* New York: Dutton, 1997.
Allen, W. B., ed. *George Washington: A Collection.* Indianapolis: Library Classics, 1988.
An American. *Imminent Dangers to the Free Institutions of the United States through Foreign Immigration.* Ed. Samuel B. Morse. New York: Arno, 1969.
American Board of Commissioners for Foreign Missions. *Forty-First Annual Report.* Boston, 1850.
American Female Guardian Society. *Fifteenth Annual Report.* New York, 1849.
———. *Home Song Book.* New York: AFGS, 1857.
———. *Twentieth Annual Report. The Advocate of Moral Reform and Family Guardian* 20 (1 June 1854):81–82.
Anbinder, Tyler. *Nativism and Slavery: The Northern Know Nothings and the Politics of the 1850s.* New York: Oxford University Press, 1992.
Association for the Care of Coloured Orphans. *First Report.* Philadelphia, 1836.
Axtell, James. *The Invasion from Within.* New York: Oxford University Press, 1985.
Bailyn, Bernard. *The Ideological Origins of the American Revolution.* Enlarged ed. Cambridge: Belknap-Harvard University Press, 1992.
Banner, Lois W. "Religious Benevolence as Social Control: A Critique of an Interpretation." *Journal of American History* 60 (1973):23–41.
Baym, Nina. *Woman's Fiction: A Guide to Novels by and about Women in America, 1820–1870.* Ithaca, N.Y.: Cornell University Press, 1978.

Beales Jr., Ross W. "The Child in Seventeenth-Century America." Hawes and Hiner. 15–56.

Beecher, Catharine. *A Treatise on Domestic Economy.* Woloch. 210–213.

Bercovitch, Sacvan. *The Puritan Origins of the American Self.* New Haven, Conn.: Yale University Press, 1975.

Berkhofer Jr., Robert F. *The White Man's Indian: Image of the American Indian from Columbus to the Present.* New York: Knopf, 1978.

Bettelheim, Bruno. *The Uses of Enchantment.* New York: Knopf, 1976.

Biddle, Nicholas. "Address." *Account of the Proceedings on Laying the Corner Stone of Girard College for Orphans.* Philadelphia: printed by Lydia R. Bailey, 1833. 8–23.

Billington, Ray A. *The Protestant Crusade, 1800–1860.* 2nd ed. Chicago: Quadrangle, 1964.

Bird, Robert Montgomery. *Nick of the Woods.* New York: W. J. Widdleton, 1837.

Blumin, Stuart M. *The Emergence of the Middle Class: Social Experience in the American City, 1760–1900.* Cambridge: Cambridge University Press, 1989.

Borden, Philip. "Found Cumbering the Soil: Manifest Destiny and the Indian in the Nineteenth Century." *The Great Fear: Race in the Mind of America.* Eds. Gary B. Nash and Richard Weiss. New York: Holt, 1970. 71–97.

Bradford, William. *Of Plymouth Plantation, 1620–1647.* New York: Modern Library, 1981.

Brady, Marilyn Dell. "The New Model Middle-Class Family (1815–1930)." *American Families: A Research Guide and Handbook.* Eds. Joseph M. Hawes and Elizabeth I. Nybakken. New York: Greenwood, 1991. 83–123.

Bremner, Robert H., ed. *Children and Youth in America.* Vol. 1. Cambridge: Harvard University Press, 1970. 3 vols. 1970–1974.

———. *From the Depths: The Discovery of Poverty in the United States.* New York: New York University Press, 1972.

Brookhiser, Richard. *Founding Father: Rediscovering George Washington.* New York: Free Press, 1996.

Brown, Charles Brockden. *Edgar Huntly; or, Memoirs of a Sleepwalker.* Ed. David Stinebeck. Albany, N.Y.: New College and University Press, 1973.

———. "Walstein's School of History." *The Rhapsodist and Other Collected Writings.* Ed. Harry Warfel. New York: Scholars' Facsimiles and Reprints, 1943. 145–156.

Brumm, Ursula. "Transfer and Arrival in the Narratives of the First Immigrants to New England." *The Transit of Civilization from Europe to America.* Eds. Winifred Herget and Karl Ortsifen. Tübingen: Gunter Narr, 1986. 29–36.

Bulkeley, Peter. "The Gospel Covenant." *The Annals of America.* Ed. Mortimer J. Adler. Vol. 1. Chicago: Encyclopedia Britannica, Inc., 1976. 21 vols. 1976–1987. 211–212.

Burr, George Lincoln, ed. *Narratives of the Witchcraft Cases, 1648–1706.* New York: Scribner's, 1914.

Burrows, Edwin G., and Michael Wallace. "The American Revolution: The Ideology and Psychology of National Liberation." *Perspectives in American History.* Vol. 6.

Eds. Donald Fleming and Bernard Bailyn. Cambridge: Charles Warren Center for Studies in American History and Harvard University Press, 1972. 167–335.

Bushman, Richard L. *King and People in Provincial Massachusetts*. Chapel Hill: University of North Carolina Press, 1985.

Cagidemetrio, Alice. "A Plea for Fictional Histories and Old-Time 'Jewesses'." *The Invention of Ethnicity*. Ed. Werner Sollors. New York: Oxford University Press, 1989. 14–43.

Caldwell, Patricia. *The Puritan Conversion Narrative: The Beginnings of American Expression*. Cambridge: Cambridge University Press, 1985.

Canny, Nicholas. "The Marginal Kingdom: Ireland as a Problem in the First British Empire." *Strangers Within the Realm: Cultural Margins of the First British Empire*. Eds. Bernard Bailyn and Philip D. Morgan. Chapel Hill: University of North Carolina Press, 1991. 35–66.

Canup, John. *Out of the Wilderness: The Emergence of an American Identity in Colonial New England*. Middletown, Conn.: Wesleyan University Press, 1990.

Castronovo, Russ. *Fathering the Nation*. Berkeley: University of California Press, 1995.

Chandler, Thomas Bradbury. *The American Querist: or, Some Questions Proposed Relative to the Present Disputes between Great Britain, and Her American Colonies*. New York: James Rivington, 1774.

Cheyfetz, Eric. "Savage Law." Kaplan and Pease. 109–128.

Child, Lydia Maria. "An Appeal for the Indians." Karcher, *Hobomok*. 213–232.

———. "Jumbo and Zairee." *The Juvenile Miscellany III*. Boston: Putnam and Hunt, 1831. 285–299.

———. "History of the Condition of Women in Various Ages and Nations." Karcher, *Hobomok*. 170–180.

Children's Aid Society. *Annual Reports of the Children's Aid Society*. 1–10, 1854–1863. Ed. David J. Rothman. New York: Arno, 1971.

———. "The Quadroons." *The Children of Mount Ida*. New York: Charles S. Francis, 1872. 61–77.

"Claims of Orphan and Destitute Children." *The Advocate of Moral Reform and Family Guardian* 20 (1 May 1854):71.

Clement, Priscilla Ferguson. "The City and the Child, 1860–1885." Hawes and Hiner. 235–272.

———. *Welfare and the Poor in the Nineteenth-Century City: Philadelphia, 1800–1854*. Rutherford, N.J.: Fairleigh Dickinson University Press, 1985.

Coleman, Emma. *New England Captives Carried to Canada*. Vol. 1. Portland, Maine: Southworth Press, 1925. 2 vols.

Colonial Laws of Massachusetts. Ed. William H. Whitmore. Boston, 1887.

Colored Home. *Fifteenth Annual Report*. New York, 1855.

Cooper, James Fenimore. *The Last of the Mohicans*. New York: Viking Penguin, 1988.

———. *The Prairie*. New York: Signet-NAL, 1964.

Cott, Nancy F. *The Bonds of Womanhood*. New Haven, Conn.: Yale University Press, 1977.
Cotton, John. "God's Promise to His Plantations." *Old South Leaflets*. Vol. 3. Boston: Old South Work, 1833. 1–16.
———. "Spiritual Milk for Boston Babes in Either England." Boston, 1856. *Early American Imprints*, 1639–1800. Worcester, Mass.: American Antiquarian Society, 1963.
———. "The Way of Congregational Churches Cleared." London: printed by Matthew Simmons, 1648.
———. "The Way of Congregational Churches Cleared." Hall. 396–437.
Craven, Wesley Frank. *The Legend of the Founding Fathers*. New York: New York University Press, 1956.
Cressy, David. *Coming Over*. Cambridge: Cambridge University Press, 1987.
Crèvecoeur, J. Hector St. John de. *Letters from an American Farmer*. New York: Albert and Charles Boni, 1925.
Cummins, Maria S. *The Lamplighter*. New York: Thomas Y. Crowell, n.d.
Cushman, Robert. "Reasons and Considerations Touching the Lawfulness of Removing out of England into the Parts of America." Heimert and Delbanco. 41–44.
Davidson, Cathy N. *Revolution and the Word: The Rise of the Novel in America*. New York: Oxford University Press, 1986.
Davis, Charles T., and Henry Louis Gates Jr. Introduction. *The Slave's Narrative*. Eds. Davis and Gates. Oxford: Oxford University Press, 1984. xi–xxxiv.
Delbanco, Andrew. *The Puritan Ordeal*. Cambridge: Harvard University Press, 1989.
Demos, John. *A Little Commonwealth: Family Life in Plymouth Colony*. London: Oxford University Press, 1970.
———. *The Unredeemed Captive*. New York: Vintage, 1994.
Devereux, George. *Ethnopsychoanalysis*. Berkeley: University of California Press, 1978.
Dippie, Brian. *The Vanishing American: White Attitudes and U.S. Indian Policy*. Middletown, Conn.: Wesleyan University Press, 1982.
Douglas, Ann. *The Feminization of American Culture*. New York: Knopf, 1977.
Douglass, Frederick. *Life and Times of Frederick Douglass*. New York: Collier Books, 1962.
———. *Life and Writings of Frederick Douglass*. Vol. 4. Ed. Philip S. Foner. New York: International Universities Press, 1955. 5 vols. 1950–1975.
———. *Narrative of the Life of Frederick Douglass, An American Slave*. Ed. Houston A. Baker Jr. New York: Viking Penguin, 1982.
Drinnon, Richard. *Facing West: The Metaphysics of Indian-Hating and Empire-Building*. Minneapolis: University of Minnesota Press, 1980.
Dwight, Timothy. *The Conquest of Canaan*. Westport, Conn.: Greenwood, 1970.
Eliot, John. "The Day-Breaking of the Gospel with the Indians." *Old South Leaflets*. Vol. 6. Boston: Old South Work, 1833. 381–404.

Elliott, James P. Introduction. *The Prairie.* By James Fenimore Cooper. Albany: State University of New York Press, 1985. xv–xxxiii.

Erikson, Erik. *Childhood and Society.* New York: Norton, 1963.

Erikson, Kai. *Wayward Puritans: A Study in the Sociology of Deviance.* New York: Macmillan, 1966.

Feldberg, Michael. *The Turbulent Era: Riot and Disorder in Jacksonian America.* New York: Oxford University Press, 1980.

Fender, Stephen. "Franklin and Emigration: The Trajectory of Use." Lemay, *Reappraising.* 335–358.

Ferguson, Robert A. "'We Hold These Truths': Strategies in Control of the Literature of the Founders." *Reconstructing American History.* Ed. Sacvan Bercovitch. Cambridge: Harvard University Press, 1986. 1–28.

Fiedler, Leslie. *Love and Death in the American Novel.* New York: Dell, 1966.

Finkelstein, Barbara. "The Reconstruction of Childhood in the United States." Hawes and Hiner. 111–152.

Fisher, Philip. *Hard Facts: Setting and Form in the American Novel.* New York: Oxford University Press, 1987.

Flexner, James Thomas. *Washington: The Indispensable Man.* Boston: Little, 1974.

Fliegelman, Jay. *Prodigals and Pilgrims: The American Revolution Against Patriarchal Authority, 1750–1800.* Cambridge: Cambridge University Press, 1982.

Folks, Homer. *The Care of Destitute, Neglected, and Delinquent Children.* New York: Arno, 1971.

Foner, Eric. *Tom Paine and Revolutionary America.* London: Oxford University Press, 1976.

Franklin, Benjamin. *Autobiography.* In *Autobiography and Other Writings.* Ed. Kenneth Silverman. New York: Viking Penguin, 1987. 3–197.

———. "Information to Those Who Would Remove to America." Lemay, *Writings.* 975–983.

———. Letter to Peter Collinson. 9 May 1753. Lemay, *Writings.* 468–474.

———. "A Narrative of the Late Massacres." *The Heath Anthology of American Literature.* Vol. 1. Ed. Paul Lauter et al. 1st ed. Boston: Heath, 1990. 2 vols. 794–806.

———. "Observations Concerning the Increase of Mankind, Peopling of Countries, &c." Lemay, *Writings.* 367–374.

———. "On Claims to the Soil of America." 16 March 1973. Letter to the printer of the *Public Advertiser. Benjamin Franklin's Letters to the Press, 1758–1775.* Ed. Verner W. Crane. Chapel Hill: University of North Carolina Press, 1950. 226–229.

———. "Remarks Concerning the Savages of North America." Lemay, *Writings.* 969–974.

Freud, Sigmund. "Beyond the Pleasure Principle." Gay. 594–626.

———. "Civilization and Its Discontents." Gay. 722–772.

———. "Three Essays on the Theory of Sexuality." Gay. 239–293.

Friedenberg, Daniel M. *Life, Liberty, and the Pursuit of Land.* Buffalo, N.Y.: Prometheus, 1992.

Gardner, Jared. "Alien Nation: Edgar Huntly's Savage Awakening." *American Literature* 66 (1994):429–461.

Gay, Peter, ed. *The Freud Reader.* New York: Norton, 1989.

Gerould, Daniel C. Introduction. *American Melodrama.* Ed. Gerould. New York: Performing Arts Journal, 1983. 7–29.

Gilmore, Michael T. *American Romanticism and the Marketplace.* Chicago: University of Chicago Press, 1985.

Girard, René. *The Scapegoat.* Trans. Yvonne Freccero. Baltimore: Johns Hopkins University Press, 1986.

Gould, Philip. "Catharine Sedgwick's Recital of the Pequot War." *American Literature* 4 (1966):641–662.

Greven, Philip. *The Protestant Temperament: Patterns of Child-Rearing, Religious Experience, and the Self in Early America.* New York: Knopf, 1977.

Griffin, Clifford S. "Religious Benevolence as Social Control, 1815–1860." *Mississippi Valley Historical Review* 44 (1957):423–444.

Grimshaw, Patricia. *Paths of Duty.* Honolulu: University of Hawaii Press, 1989.

Hagenbüchle, Ronald. "American Literature and the Nineteenth-Century Literary Crisis in Epistemology: The Example of Charles Brockden Brown." *Early American Literature* 23 (1988):121–151.

Hale, Sarah J. *Manners; or, Happy Homes and Good Society All the Year Round.* 1852. New York: Arno, 1972.

Hall, David D., ed. *The Antinomian Controversy, 1636–1638.* Durham, N.C.: Duke University Press, 1990.

Halttunen, Karen. *Confidence Men and Painted Women: A Study of Middle-Class Culture in America, 1830–1870.* New Haven, Conn.: Yale University Press, 1982.

Handlin, Oscar. "The Significance of the Seventeenth Century." *Seventeenth Century America: Essays in Colonial History.* Ed. James Morton Smith. Chapel Hill: University of North Carolina Press, 1959. 3–12.

Hawes, Joseph M., and N. Ray Hiner, eds. *American Childhood: A Research Guide and Historical Handbook.* Westport, Conn.: Greenwood, 1985.

Hayes, Sarah Hepburn. "The Orphan Family." *Godey's Lady's Book* (March 1850):232–236.

Haynal, André. "Psychoanalytic Discourse on Orphans and Deprivation." *Parental Loss and Achievement.* Eds. Marvin Eisenstadt et al. Madison, Conn.: International Universities Press, 1989. 135–190.

Hedrick, Joan D. *Harriet Beecher Stowe: A Life.* New York: Oxford University Press, 1994.

Heimert, Alan, and Andrew Delbanco, eds. *The Puritans in America: A Narrative Anthology.* Cambridge: Harvard University Press, 1985.

Hensley, Jeannine. *The Works of Anne Bradstreet*. Cambridge: Belknap-Harvard University Press, 1967.
Henretta, James A. *The Origins of American Capitalism*. Boston: Northeastern University Press, 1991.
Herrick, Cheesman A. *History of Girard College*. Philadelphia: Girard College, 1927.
Hiner, N. Ray. "Adolescence in Eighteenth-Century America." *History of Childhood Quarterly* 3 (1975):253–280.
Holy Bible. Revised Standard Version. 2nd ed. Dallas: Melton, 1971.
Home for Destitute Colored Children. *Second Annual Report*. Philadelphia, 1857.
Hornblower, Jane Elizabeth. *Vara; or, the Child of Adoption*. New York: Robert Carter, 1854.
Hunt, Isaac. *The Political Family; or, A Discourse Pointing Out the Reciprocal Advantages Which Flow from an Uninterrupted Union Between Great-Britain and Her American Colonies*. Philadelphia: James Humphreys Jr., 1775.
Hunt, Lynn. *The Family Romance of the French Revolution*. Berkeley: University of California Press, 1992.
Hunter, Judith A. "Republicanism and Nativism: Inseparable Beliefs of the Native Americans and Their Followers in Mid-Century Philadelphia." Paper presented to the Philadelphia Center for Early American Studies, 16 October 1987.
Illick, Joseph E. "Anglo-American Child-Rearing." *The History of Childhood*. Ed. Lloyd deMause. New York: Psychohistory, 1974. 303–350.
Immigration and Nationality Laws and Regulations. Washington, D.C.: United States Government Printing Office, 1944.
Industrial Home for the Instruction of Girls. *First Report*. Philadelphia, 1859.
James I. *Basilicon Doron. Political Writings*. Ed. Johann P. Sommerville. Cambridge: Cambridge University Press, 1994. 1–61.
Jefferson, Thomas. *Autobiography of Thomas Jefferson*. Lauter. 960–964.
———. Letter to John Adams, 1813. Peterson. 1304–1310.
———. *Notes on the State of Virginia*. Peterson. 123–325.
Jehlen, Myra. "J. Hector St. John Crèvecoeur: A Monarcho-Anarchist in Revolutionary America." *American Quarterly* 31 (1979):204–222.
Johnson, Susanna Hastings. *A Narrative of the Captivity of Mrs. Johnson*. Walpole, N.H.: printed by David Carlisle, 1796.
Jones, Douglas Lamar. "The Transformation of the Law of Poverty in Eighteenth-Century Massachusetts." *Law in Colonial Massachusetts, 1630–1800*. Boston: The Colonial Society of Massachusetts, 1984.
Jones, Maldwyn Allen. *American Immigration*. 2nd ed. Chicago: University of Chicago Press, 1992.
Jordan, Winthrop D. "Thomas Paine and the Killing of the King, 1776." *Journal of American History* 50 (1973):294–308.

———. *White over Black: American Attitudes Toward the Negro, 1550–1812.* Chapel Hill: University of North Carolina Press, 1968.

Kaplan, Amy, and Donald E. Pease, eds. *Cultures of United States Imperialism.* Durham, N.C.: Duke University Press, 1993.

Karcher, Carolyn. *The First Woman in the Republic: A Cultural Biography of Lydia Maria Child.* Durham, N.C.: Duke University Press, 1994.

———, ed. *Hobomok and Other Writings on Indians.* New Brunswick, N.J.: Rutgers University Press, 1986.

———. Introduction. Karcher, *Hobomok.* ix–xxxviii.

Katz, Michael. *In the Shadow of the Poorhouse: A History of Social Welfare in America.* New York: Basic, 1986.

Kolodny, Annette. *The Lay of the Land.* Chapel Hill: University of North Carolina Press, 1975.

Kramnick, Isaac. "Children's Literature and Bourgeois Ideology: Observations on Culture and Industrial Capitalism in the Later Eighteenth Century." *Studies in Eighteenth Century Culture* 12 (1983):11–44.

Lacan, Jacques. "The Mirror Stage as Formative of the Function of the I." *Ecrits: A Selection.* Trans. Alan Sheridan. New York: Norton, 1977. 1–7.

Lang, Amy Schrager. "Class and Strategies of Sympathy." *The Culture of Sentiment: Race, Gender and Sentimentality in Nineteenth-Century America.* Ed. Shirley Samuels. New York: Oxford University Press, 1992. 128–142.

Lauter, Paul, et al., eds. *Heath Anthology of American Literature.* Vol. 1. Lexington, Mass.: Heath, 1990. 2 vols.

Leiby, James. *A History of Social Welfare and Social Work in the United States.* New York: Columbia University Press, 1978.

"Legal and Moral Claims of Dissolute Parents." *The Advocate of Moral Reform and Family Guardian* 20 (1 February 1854):21.

Lemay, J. A. Leo, ed. *Benjamin Franklin: Writings.* New York: Literary Classics-Viking, 1987.

———. "Franklin and Ethno-cultural Issues." Lemay, *Reappraising.* 332–334.

———, ed. *Reappraising Benjamin Franklin: A Bicentennial Perspective.* Newark: University of Delaware Press, 1993.

Leonard, Ira M., and Robert D. Parmet. *American Nativism, 1830–1860.* New York: Van Nostrand Reinhold, 1971.

Lerner, Gerda. "The Lady and the Mill Girl." *A Heritage of Her Own: Toward a New Social History of American Women.* Eds. and intro. Nancy F. Cott and Elizabeth H. Pleck. New York: Simon and Schuster, 1979.

Leverenz, David. *The Language of Puritan Feeling.* New Brunswick, N.J.: Rutgers University Press, 1980.

Litwack, Leon T. *North of Slavery.* Chicago: University of Chicago Press, 1961.

Longmore, Paul K. *The Invention of George Washington*. Berkeley: University of California Press, 1988.
A Lowell Factory Girl. "To the Female Labor Reform Association in Manchester." Woloch.
MacLeod, Anne. *A Moral Tale: Children's Fiction and American Culture, 1820–1860*. Hamden, Conn.: Archon, 1975.
Marsh, Christopher. *The Family of Love in English Society, 1550–1630*. Cambridge: Cambridge University Press, 1994.
Mather, Cotton. "A Brand Pluck'd Out of the Burning." *Narratives of the Witchcraft Cases, 1648–1706*. Ed. George Lincoln Burr. New York: Scribner's, 1914.
———. Decennium Luctuosom. *Magnalia Christi Americana; or, The Ecclesiastial History of New England*. 1852. Vol. 2. New York: Russell-Atheneum, 1967. 2 vols. 580–681.
———. *Good Fetch'd Out of Evil*. New York: Garland, 1977.
Mather, Richard. "To the Christian Reader." *Tears of Repentance*. By John Eliot and Thomas Mayhew. London: printed by Thomas Cole, 1653.
Meany, Mary L. "Charity Begins at Home." *Peterson's* (March 1855):220–222.
Melville, Herman. *Moby Dick*. Eds. Harrison Hayford and Hershel Parker. New York: Norton, 1967.
Miller, Perry. *Errand into the Wilderness*. Cambridge: Belknap-Harvard University Press, 1956.
Mintz, Steven, and Susan Kellogg. *Domestic Revolutions: A Social History of American Family Life*. New York: Free Press, 1988.
Mitchell, Stewart, ed. *Winthrop Papers*. Vol. 2. New York: Russell & Russell, 1968.
Morgan, Edmund S. *The Puritan Family: Religion & Domestic Relations in Seventeenth-Century New England*. Revised ed. New York: Torchbooks-Harper, 1966.
Mulford, Carla J. "*Caritas* and Capital: Franklin's *Narrative of the Late Massacres*." Lemay, *Reappraising*. 347–358.
Mulvey, Laura. "Visual Pleasure and Narrative Cinema." *Film Theory and Criticism*. Eds. Gerald Mast and Marshall Cohen. New York: Oxford University Press, 1984. 803–816.
Nash, Gary B. *Race, Class, and Politics: Essays on American Colonial and Revolutionary Society*. Urbana: University of Illinois Press, 1966.
"New England's First Fruits." *New England's History*. Sabin's Reprints, Quarto Series, no. 1. New York: Joseph L. Sabin, 1865. 1–47.
New York Association for Improving the Condition of the Poor. Appendix. *First Annual Report*. 1845. *Annual Reports of the New York Association for Improving the Condition of the Poor*. Ed. David J. Rothman. New York: Arno, 1971.
———. *Tenth Annual Report*. New York, 1853.
Norton Anthology of American Literature. Eds. Nina Baym et al. 3rd ed. Vol. 1. New York: Norton, 1989. 2 vols.
Paine, Thomas. "Common Sense." *Political Writings*. Ed. Bruce Kuklick. Cambridge: Cambridge University Press, 1989. 3–38.

———. Appendix. "Common Sense." *The Complete Works of Thomas Paine*. London: E. Truelove, 1875. 30–34.

Pearce, Roy Harvey, ed. "John Smith: From *A Desription of New England*." *Colonial American Writings*. New York: Rinehart, 1963.

Pessen, Edward. "The Egalitarian Myth and the American Social Reality: Wealth, Mobility, and Quality in the 'Era of the Common Man.'" Pessen, ed. 7–46.

———, ed. *The Many-Faceted Jacksonian Era*. Westport, Conn.: Greenwood, 1977.

———. "Who Governed the Nation's Cities in the 'Era of the Common Man'?" Pessen, ed. 242–260.

Peterson, Merrill, ed. *Thomas Jefferson: Writings*. New York: Library of America, 1984.

"The Poor Man's Appeal." *Peterson's* (March 1855):281.

Records of the Governor and Company of the Massachusetts Bay of New England. Young. 197–200.

Regis, Pamela. *Describing Early America: Bartram, Jefferson, Crèvecoeur, and the Rhetoric of Natural History*. Dekalb: Northern Illiniois University Press, 1992.

Reising, Russell. *The Unusable Past: Theory and the Study of American Literature*. New York: Methuen, 1986.

Rich, Adrienne. Foreword. Hensley. ix–xx.

Roediger, David R. *The Wages of Whiteness: Race and the Making of the American Working Class*. London: Verso, 1991.

Rogers, Daniel T. "Socializing Middle-Class Children: Institutions, Fables, and Work Values in Nineteenth-Century America." Hawes and Hiner. 119–134.

Rogin, Michael Paul. *Fathers and Children: Andrew Jackson and the Subjugation of the American Indian*. New York: Knopf, 1975.

Rothman, David J. *The Discovery of the Asylum: Social Order and Disorder in the New Republic*. New York: Little, 1971.

Ryan, Mary. *Cradle of the Middle Class: The Family in Oneida County, New York, 1790–1865*. Cambridge: Cambridge University Press, 1981.

———. *The Empire of the Mother: American Writing about Domesticity, 1830–1860*. New York: Haworth, 1982.

Salisbury, Neal. *Manitou and Providence: Indians, Europeans, and the Making of New England, 1500–1643*. New York: Oxford University Press, 1982.

Seattle. "Speech of Chief Seattle." Lauter et al., 1770–1771.

Sedgwick, Catharine Maria. *Hope Leslie; or, Early Times in Massachusetts*. Ed. and intro. Mary Kelley. New Brunswick, N.J.: Rutgers University Press, 1986.

———. *Live and Let Live; or, Domestic Service*. New York: Harper, 1837.

Selement, George, and Bruce C. Woolley. *Thomas Shepard's Confessions. Collections*. Vol. 58. Boston: Colonial Society of Massachusetts, 1981. 66 vols. 1895–1993.

Sellers, Charles. *The Market Revolution: Jacksonian America, 1815–1846*. New York: Oxford University Press, 1991.

Shepard, Thomas. "The Church Membership of Children, and Their Right to Baptism." Cambridge, 1663. *Early American Imprints, 1639–1800.* Worcester, Mass.: American Antiquarian Society, 1963.

Shindler, Mary S. B. "The Emigrant Family; or, The Secret of Success." *Godey's Lady's Book* (January 1852):16–18.

Simpson, Eileen. *Orphans: Real and Imaginary.* New York: Weidenfeld & Nicholson, 1987.

Slotkin, Richard. *The Fatal Environment.* New York: Atheneum, 1985.

———. *Regeneration Through Violence: The Mythology of the American Frontier.* Middletown, Conn.: Wesleyan University Press, 1973.

Smith, Abbot Emerson. *Colonists in Bondage: White Servitude and Convict Labor in America.* Gloucester, Mass.: Peter Smith, 1965.

Smith, Elizabeth Oakes. *The Newsboy.* New York: J. C. Derby, 1854.

Smith-Rosenberg, Carroll. *Disorderly Conduct: Visions of Gender in Victorian America.* New York: Knopf, 1985.

———. *Religion and the Rise of the American City: The New York City Mission Movement.* Ithaca, N.Y.: Cornell University Press, 1971.

———. "Subject Female: Authorizing American Identity." *American Literary History* 5 (1993):481–511.

Stark, Caroline. "The Orphan's Gratitude." *Peterson's* (October 1852):197–201.

Stephens, Ann S. *The Old Homestead.* New York: Bunce & Brother, 1855.

Stepto, Robert. "Sharing the Thunder: The Literary Exchanges of Harriet Beecher Stowe, Henry Bibb, and Frederick Douglass." *New Essays on Uncle Tom's Cabin.* Ed. Eric J. Sundquist. Cambridge: Cambridge University Press, 1986. 135–153.

Stoughton, William. "New Englands True Interest; Not To Lie." Cambridge, 1670. *Early American Imprints, 1639–1800.* Worcester, Mass.: American Antiquarian Society, 1963.

Stowe, Harriet Beecher. *Uncle Tom's Cabin.* Toronto: Bantam, 1981.

Stuckey, Sterling. *Slave Culture: Nationalist Theory and the Foundations of Black America.* New York: Oxford University Press, 1987.

Sundquist, Eric J. "Slavery, Revolution, and the American Renaissance." *The American Renaissance Reconsidered.* Eds. Walter Benn Michaels and Donald E. Pease. Baltimore, Md.: Johns Hopkins University Press, 1985. 1–33.

Thernstrom, Stephan. *Poverty and Progress: Social Mobility in a Nineteenth Century City.* Cambridge: Harvard University Press, 1964.

Ticknor, Caroline. *Hawthorne and His Publisher.* Boston: Houghton, 1913.

Tompkins, Jane. Afterword. *The Wide, Wide World.* By Susan Warner. New York: Feminist-CUNY, 1987. 584–608.

———. *Sensational Designs.* New York: Oxford University Press, 1985.

Trattner, Walter I. *From Poor Law to Welfare State: A History of Social Welfare in America.* New York: Free Press, 1979.

———. Introduction. *Social Welfare or Social Control?* Ed. Trattner. Knoxville: University of Tennessee Press, 1983. 3–14.

Twichell, John Hopkins, ed. *Some Old Puritan Love-Letters: John and Margaret Winthrop, 1618–1638.* "Governor Winthrop to His Wife," 16 July 1930. Letter XLVIII. New York: Dodd, 1894. 159–162.

Union Benevolent Association. *Twenty-Fourth Annual Report.* Philadelphia, 1855.

Vaughan, Alden T., and Edward W. Clark. Introduction. *Puritans among the Indians.* Eds. Vaughn and Clark. Cambridge: Harvard University Press, 1981. 1–18.

Vaughan, Alden T., and Daniel K. Richter. "Crossing the Cultural Divide: Indians and New Englanders, 1605–1763." Reprinted from *Proceedings of the American Antiquarian Society* 90 (1980):23–99.

Voloshin, Beverly. "*Edgar Huntly* and the Coherence of the Self." *Early American Literature* 23 (1988):262–280.

Wald, Priscilla. "Terms of Assimilation." Kaplan and Pease. 59–84.

Warner, Susan. *The Wide, Wide World.* New York: Feminist-CUNY, 1987.

Weber, Max. *The Protestant Ethic and the Spirit of Capitalism.* New York: Scribner's, 1930.

Wharton, Donald P. *In the Trough of the Sea: Selected American Sea-Deliverance Narratives, 1610–1766.* Westport, Conn.: Greenwood, 1979.

White, Elizabeth Wade. *Anne Bradstreet: The Tenth Muse.* New York: Oxford University Press, 1971.

White, John. *The Planter's Plea.* London: printed by William Jones, 1630.

Winthrop, John. "A Defense of an Order of Court." Heimert. 164–167.

———. "A Model of Christian Charity." Mitchell. 282–295.

———. "Reasons to Be Considered for Justifying the Undertaking of the Intended Plantation in New England and for Encouraging Such Whose Hearts God Shall Move to Join with Them in It." Heimert. 70–74.

———. "A Short Story of the Rise, reign and ruine of the Antinomians, Familists & Libertines." Hall. 199–310.

———. *Winthrop's Journal: "History of New England."* Ed. James Kendall Hosmer. 2 vols. New York: Barnes, 1959.

Winthrop, John, et al. "The Company's Humble Request." Young. 295–299.

Wishy, Bernard. *The Child and the Republic: The Dawn of Modern American Child Nurture.* Philadelphia: University of Pennsylvania Press, 1968.

Woloch, Nancy, ed. *Early American Women: A Documentary History, 1600–1900.* Belmont, Calif.: Wadsworth, 1992.

Wood, Gordon. Rev. of *Benjamin Franklin and His Enemies,* by Robert Middlekauff, and *The Devious Dr. Franklin, Colonial Agent: Benjamin Franklin's Years in London,* by David T. Morgan. *New York Review of Books* (6 June 1996):47–51.

Wright, Conrad Edick. *The Transformation of Charity in Postrevolutionary New England*. Boston: Northeastern University Press, 1992.

Yarborough, Richard. "Strategies of Black Characterization in *Uncle Tom's Cabin* and the Early Afro-American Novel." *New Essays on Uncle Tom's Cabin*. Ed. Eric J. Sundquist. Cambridge: Cambridge University Press, 1986. 45–84.

Yates, J.V.N. *Report of the Secretary of State in 1824 on the Relief and Settlement of the Poor*. In *The Almshouse Experience*. Ed. David J. Rothman. New York: Arno, 1971.

Young, Alexander, ed. *Chronicles of the First Planters of the Colony of Massachusetts Bay, 1623–1636*. Boston: Little, Brown, 1846.

Index

Abolitionists, 137, 178, 179, 187, 191–92
Account of an Expedition..., An (Lewis and Clark), 102
Account of the History, Manners, and Customs of the Indian..., An (Heckewelder), 116
Adams, John, 56, 60, 61, 82–83, 84, 103
Adams, John Quincy, 68
Adolescence, 58
Adoption, 4, 8, 26, 28, 39, 41–42, 59–60, 64–65, 77, 80, 84, 94–96, 106, 107, 109, 110, 111–12, 114, 116, 118, 132, 168, 173, 174, 185–86, 193, 198
Advocate of Moral Reform and Family Guardian, The, 142
Africa, 191–92
Aggression, 32, 33, 42–43, 65, 137–38
Agrarianism, 76, 78–79
Alcott, Louisa May, 174–76
Alien and Sedition Acts (1798), 83–84, 89, 91
Almshouses, 139–40, 147

American Board of Commissioners for Foreign Missions, 195, 196, 197
American Colonization Society, 191–92
American Crisis (Paine), 55–56
American Female Guardian Society, 141–42, 143, 144, 146, 174
American Female Moral Reform Society, 142
American Querist (Chandler), 52
American Revolution: agricultural imagery, 54, 55; exclusionism, 62, 63–65, 69–70, 79, 83; familial imagery, 51–57, 60, 61–64, 78; loyalists, 52–53; as rebirth, 59
American Woman, The, 132
Anabaptists, 29, 30
Anglicans, 10–11, 19, 43
Antagonistic acculturation, 110
Antinomians, 13, 43, 44–45
Appeal in Favor of That Class of Americans Called Africans, An (Child), 178

Arbella, 2, 6–7, 13, 18
Asians, 75
Association for the Care of Coloured Orphans, 147
Asylum for Friendless Boys, 143
Autobiography (Franklin), 70–71, 72

Baltimore, 140
Bank War, 120
Basilicon Doron, 30–31
Beecher, Catharine, 123
Beecher, Lyman, 123
Benevolent movement, 126–27, 128–29, 133–35, 139, 140–46, 147, 148, 155, 173, 174, 176, 187, 197, 198
Bibb, Henry, 180
Biddle, Nicholas, 139
Blackness, as emblem of heathenism, 34–35
Boston, 19, 133, 140
Boston Society for the Prevention of Pauperism, 135
Boucher, Jonathan, 52–53
Brace, Charles Loring, 133–34, 141, 142, 143, 145, 191, 196
Bradford, William, 12–13, 14
Bradstreet, Anne, 18–24; "A Dialogue between Old England and New; Concerning Their Present Troubles, Anno 1642," 19–20; "As a Weary Pilgrim," 23; "Here Follow Some Verses upon the Burning of Our House," 21; "In Memory of My Dear Grandchild Anne Bradstreet," 20–21; "Meditations Divine and Moral," 21, 22–23; "On My Dear Grandchild Simon Bradstreet," 21; "Quarternions," 19; "To My Dear Children," 18–19, 21–22
Brown, Charles Brockden, 86–99, 116, 117

Buffalo (N.Y.), 147
Bulkeley, Peter, 25, 49
Buntline, Ned, 150

California, 130
Cambridge, 17
Canada, 91, 92, 95
Candidus, 61
Cape Cod, 12
Capitalism, 64, 65, 73, 76, 119–20, 126, 127, 129, 138, 150, 165, 192–93
Captivity narratives, 92–93, 94, 95–96, 114, 115, 116
Catholics, 10–11, 19, 27, 40, 43–44, 60, 64, 82–83, 91, 131, 132, 137–38, 144–45, 148, 176
Chandler, Thomas Bradbury, 52
"Charity Begins at Home," 153
Charles I, 19
Charlestown, 18
Cherokee Nation v. the State of Georgia, The, 104
Cherokees, 68, 70, 104
Chickasaws, 68
Child, Lydia Maria, 112–14, 115–16, 178–79
Children's Aid Society, 133, 141, 142, 143, 144, 145, 146, 163
Children's literature, 156–58
Choctaw, 68
Church of England, 6
Cincinnati, 147
Civil War (England), 19, 45
Clark, William, 102, 116
Class conflict, 119–20, 122, 126–30, 134, 137, 138, 141–42, 154
Collins, Edward, 17
Collinson, Peter, 74
Colored Home, 148
Common Sense (Paine), 53–56, 62, 83
Concord, 49

Conquest of Canaan, The (Dwight), 63
Constitutional Convention, 73–74
Conversion narratives, 16–18
Cooper, James Fenimore, 99–112, 116, 117
Cotton, John, 6, 8, 36, 41, 44
Council of New England, 27
Crèvecoeur, J. Hector St. John de, 70, 76–80, 84–85, 94–95, 97
Cromwell, Oliver, 11–12
Cult of True Womanhood, 123–26, 150, 151, 152, 169
Cummins, Maria Stuart, 165–68
Cushman, Robert, 12
Cutter, Elizabeth, 17–18
Cutter, Richard, 16

Davenport, John, 14
Decennium Luctuousum (Mather), 93
Declaration of Independence, 56, 63
Deerslayer, The (Cooper), 100–01
Delaware Indians, 96–97
Democratic party, 132
Demos, John, 1
Dickens, Charles, 156
Dissertation on the Canon and Feudal Law (Adams), 56, 82
Dix, Dorothea, 140
Douglass, Frederick, 178, 180, 181–83, 184–87, 191, 194
Dred Scott decision, 184
Du Bartas, Guillaume, 19
Duane, James, 65
Dudley, Thomas, 13, 14, 18
Duwamish, 111
Dwight, Timothy, 63
Dyer, Mary and William, 45

Edgar Huntly; or, Memoirs of a Sleepwalker (Brown), 86–88, 89–92, 93, 94, 96–99, 109, 115

Educational segregation, 146–48, 196
Egalitarianism, 77, 79
Eliot, John, 40, 115
Elizabeth I, 31, 51–52
Endecott, John, 11
English Orphans, The (Holmes), 173–74
English Poor Laws, 47
Enlightenment, 87, 88
Ethnic diversity, 80
Expansionism, 67–69, 102, 130, 198

Familists, 29–31, 44–45
Family: in captivity narratives, 93–94; egalitarianism, 57–58; fathers, 5–6, 57, 71, 125; idealization of, 123, 143, 196; as metaphor for the commonwealth, 1–2, 5, 6, 9, 19–20, 51–57, 59–60, 61, 63, 68, 78, 79–80, 123, 197, 199–200; as metaphor for land, 77; as metaphor for relationship to God and church, 2–3, 6, 9, 20, 22, 23, 30, 44–45, 49, 59–60; middle-class, 122–26, 196, 200; mothers, 6, 123–25; nuclear, 1, 3, 28; Puritan, 1, 3–4, 5–6, 10, 25–29, 36, 58; slave, 180, 181, 187
Family of Love. *See* Familists
Federalists, 83–84, 91, 118
Filmer, Robert, 5, 52
Finney, Charles, 125
Five Points House of Industry, 143
Foster parents, 144
Founding Fathers, 62, 63–64, 65, 68, 69, 71, 74, 79–80, 81, 82, 84
Franklin, Benjamin, 70–76, 81, 82, 103, 128, 158, 186
French and Indian wars, 91, 92, 139
French and Spanish wars, 83
French Huguenots, 46, 80
French immigrants, 83, 176

Index

French Revolution, 83, 88, 89
Friends Shelter for Colored Orphans, 137
Frontier, 78, 87–88, 130

George III, 57, 60, 61, 62–63, 72, 80
Georgia, 70
German immigrants, 46, 74–75, 79, 80–81, 131, 134, 145
Girard College for Orphans, 139, 147
Girard, René, 32–33
Girard, Stephen, 147
Godey's Lady's Book, 124, 152, 176
Good Fetch'd out of Evil (Mather), 93
Great Awakening: First, 58; Second, 126
Great Migration, 6–8, 10, 11–12, 15–18, 19, 21, 22, 23–24, 25, 29, 32–33, 39, 47

Hale, Sarah Josepha, 124, 152–53
Hamilton, Alexander, 64
"Hansel and Gretel," 13
Harvard College, 14, 27
Hawaii, 195–97, 198
Heathenism, 34–36, 39–40, 44
Heckewelder, John, 116
Henson, Josiah, 180
History (Lewis and Clark), 102
History of Little Goody Two-Shoes, The, 156
Hobbes, Thomas, 5
Hobomok (Child), 112–14
Holmes, Mary Jane, 173–74
Home for Destitute Colored Children, 148
Home for the Friendless and House of Industry, 142–43, 146, 174
Home Song Book, 146
Hooker, Thomas, 6, 15
Hope Leslie (Sedgwick), 112, 114–17
Hornblower, Jane Elizabeth, 195–98

Howes, Edward, 27
Hunt, Isaac, 52
Hutchinson, Anne, 44, 45

Identity formation, 31–33, 42, 43, 72, 76–78, 79, 84–85, 86, 98, 110, 180, 184–85, 192, 200
Immigrants, 74–78, 79–81, 82, 83–84, 131–37, 141, 142, 145–46, 148, 163, 173–74, 176
Indian Removal Act, 70, 104, 192
Indians, 25, 34–36, 37, 38–43, 44, 46, 64, 65–70, 72–75, 76, 77–80, 86–87, 89, 92–93, 94–96, 99–102, 103–17, 130, 146–47
Industrial Home for the Instruction of Girls in the Arts of Housewifery and Sewing, 146, 163–64
Industrialization, 124, 151, 152
Inheritance, The (Alcott), 174–76
Irish immigrants, 46, 79, 80, 81, 83, 90–91, 131, 133, 134, 136, 137–38, 145–46, 176–78
Irish Rebellion (1798), 91
Italian immigrants, 174

Jackson, Andrew, 65, 70, 102, 104
James I, 30–31, 51–52
Jefferson, Thomas, 60, 61, 64, 65, 66–69, 75, 84, 89, 102, 103, 104, 110
Jemison, Mary, 114
Jews, 46, 80
Johnson, Edward, 14
Johnson, Susanna Hastings, 94
Johnson, Sylvanus, 94
Johnson and Graham's Lessee V. M'Intosh, 101
"Jumbo and Zairee" (Child), 179
Juvenile Miscellany, The, 179

Kansas, 130
Key into the Language of America, The (Williams), 115

King Philip's War, 92
King, Titus, 95

Labor reform, 154
Lake Superior, 70
Lamplighter, The (Cummins), 156, 165–68
Last of the Mohicans, The (Cooper), 99, 100, 105
Leatherstocking tales (Cooper), 99–112
Letters from an American Farmer, 76
Leviathan (Hobbes), 5
Lewis, Meriwether, 102, 116
Liberia, 191, 192
Liberty Tree, 62
Lincoln, Abraham, 185–86
Lippard, George, 150
Little Rollo series, 158
Live and Let Live (Sedgwick), 164
Locke, John, 56–57, 71
London, 26–27
Louisiana Purchase, 67–68, 102, 130
Lowell Female Labor Reform Association, 154

Manners; or, Happy Homes and Good Society All the Year Round (Hale), 152–53
Marshall, John, 101, 104
Massachusetts, 81, 82, 91, 135, 139
"Massachusetts Act Against Heresy and Error, The," 46
Massachusetts Bay colony, 6–7, 11, 12
Mather, Cotton, 8, 93, 100
Mather, Increase, 3, 14
Mather, Richard, 14, 42
Melville, Herman, 201
Middle class, 64, 119, 120–26, 129–30, 137, 149, 150–52, 155, 156, 157, 158, 161, 163, 165, 168, 170, 173, 176, 196, 200

Miscegenation, 100–01, 103–04, 111–14, 115, 116
Missionaries, 104, 133–35, 145, 147, 192, 195–96, 197–98
Moby Dick (Melville), 201
Monroe, James, 70, 102
My Bondage and My Freedom (Douglass), 181

Narrative of Captivity and Restoration (Rowlandson), 96
Narrative of the Life of Frederick Douglass, An American Slave (Douglass), 181
Nativism, 129, 131–36, 138, 140, 141, 158, 176, 195
Natural aristocracy, 60–61, 63, 64, 75, 86
Natural history, 67
Natural law, 57
Naturalization Act (1790), 83
Naturalization laws, 83, 118, 132–33
Negroes, 34, 35, 46, 63, 64, 66, 67, 68, 75, 80, 103, 131, 136–38, 146–48; citizenship of, 184; colonization of, 191–92, 194–95; education of, 184, 191, 192; legal restrictions on, 184; and work for wages, 185, 194. *See also* Slaves
New York, 71, 128, 133, 134, 138, 140, 142–43, 147, 170, 182
New York Daily Times, 145–46
New York Draft Day Riots, 138
Newsboy, The (Smith), 170–73
Norris v. City of Boston, 135
North Star, The, 185
Notes on the State of Virginia (Jefferson), 67
Niclaes, Henrik, 29, 30

Of Plymouth Plantation (Bradford), 12–13
Old Homestead, The (Stephens), 168–70
Oliver Twist (Dickens), 156

Index

"Orphan Family, The," 176–77
"Orphan's Gratitude, The," 176
Orphans: actual, 17, 26–28, 58–59, 104–05, 133–34, 138–43, 145–48, 163–64, 170–71, 181–82, 197, 200; cultural, 41, 68, 70, 77, 79, 104, 111, 135, 137, 192, 197, 200; economic, 64, 76, 138; elective, 71–72, 116; as emblematic of slavery, 179, 180, 182, 183, 186, 195; in fiction, 86–87, 88, 89, 90, 94, 97, 98–99, 105, 106–07, 109, 110–11, 114, 149–51, 153, 155–77, 178–79, 180, 188–90, 195–99, 200; political, 9, 10, 16, 61–62, 64, 65, 91, 130, 132, 152; removed from unfit parents, 143–44; spiritual, 4, 6, 8, 9–10, 12, 13, 16, 17, 18, 20, 21–22, 23–24, 34, 35, 49, 111
Orphanages, 139, 140–41, 145, 147–48
Otis, Harrison Gray, 91

Paine, Thomas, 51, 53–56, 59, 61, 62, 83
Panic of 1837, 120, 137, 151
Passenger Cases, 135
Patriarcha (Filmer), 5
Patriarchal authority, 52–53, 56, 57, 61, 116
Paul (apostle), 60
Pawnee, 99
Pennsylvania, 74, 75, 80, 81, 91
Pennsylvania Abolitionist Society, 137
Pequot War, 42, 114
Peterson's, 152, 153, 176
Philadelphia, 71, 128, 132, 133, 134–35, 137, 138, 139, 140, 145, 147
Philadelphia Children's Asylum, 140
Pilgrims, 6, 11, 12
Pioneers, The (Cooper), 99, 101–02
Placing out, 142–46, 174, 191, 196
Planter's Plea, 37
Plymouth plantation, 12
"Poor Man's Appeal, The," 153

Poverty, 47–49, 76, 81–82, 122, 126–29, 131, 132–35, 138–39, 140, 148, 149–50, 153–55, 157–58, 159–60, 167–68, 169–70
Prairie, The (Cooper), 99–100, 102–03, 105–11
Preemption Law of 1841, 135
Property, ownership of, 64–66, 67, 69, 72, 73–74, 76–78, 79, 82, 96–97, 101–04, 112, 183–84
Protestantism, 60, 82–83, 123, 129, 144–45, 168, 176, 199
Providence (R.I.), 147
Puritans: adoption, 26, 59–60; binding out, 28; defectors, 13–14, 15; divine order, 29; economic motives, 11–12, 36, 47; election, 2, 4–5, 24, 34, 45, 47–48, 59; exclusionism, 25–26, 29, 31, 33–34, 40, 42, 45–49, 58; families, 1, 3–4, 5–6, 10, 13, 25–29, 36, 56, 58; in fiction, 112, 114; and guilt, 6, 10–11, 12, 93; hardships, 14–15, 18, 22, 23; homesickness, 14, 16, 19; and Indians, 34–36, 37, 38–43; land ownership, 36–39, 41; and Negroes, 33–34; religious intolerance, 43–47; repressiveness, 13–14; and separation, 6, 8–9, 10; views of God, 4–5

"Quadroons, The" (Child), 178–79
Quakers, 13, 34, 43, 44, 147
Quarterly Review of the American Protestant Association, The, 145

Ramus, Petrus, 28–29
Reformation, 29
Reformatories, 140
Republican party, 84, 91, 132
Rich, Adrienne, 19
Riots, 137–38, 145
Robinson, John, 115
Rowlandson, Mary, 96, 116

Salem, 11, 14, 18, 45, 112
Sandwich Islands. *See* Hawaii
Santo Domingo, 83
Scapegoat, The (Girard), 32–33
Scapegoating, 32–34, 62, 129–30, 199–200; of Catholics, 148; of French Huguenots, 46; of Germans, 46; of immigrants, 85, 86, 98–99, 138, 148; of Indians, 25, 34–36, 42–43, 46, 65, 70, 79–80, 85, 86, 98–99; of the Irish and Scots-Irish, 46; of Negroes, 34, 46, 137, 138, 148; of the poor, 148; of religious outsiders, 31, 34, 43, 46
Scots, 46, 79, 80, 81
Seattle, Chief, 86, 111
Sedgwick, Catharine, 112, 114–15, 116, 164
Sentimentalism, 129, 149, 150, 156, 157, 158, 173, 178, 187, 192, 193–94
Settlement laws, 81–82, 128
Seven Years' War, 66, 91
Shawnee, 95
Shepard, Thomas, 4, 14, 15, 16, 26
Six Nations, 73
Slave narrative, 180, 186
Slave trade, 179, 180
Slaves, 35, 63; bonding of, 182–83; dehumanizing of, 183–84, 187, 188, 193; families, 180, 181, 187; in fiction, 178–80, 187–95; fugitives, 182; sexual exploitation of, 178–79, 180, 181; stereotypes of, 188. *See also* Negroes
Smith, Elizabeth Oakes, 170–73
Smith, John, 9, 116
Smith v. Turner, Health Commissioner of the Port of New York, 135
Social Darwinism, 150
Sons of liberty, 59, 60, 61–62
Stamp Act, 56, 71

Stephens, Ann, 168–70, 176
Stoughton, William, 4, 45
Stowe, Harriet Beecher, 179–80, 187–95
Stuarts (royal family), 51–52
Suquamish, 111

Talbot, 14
Taxation, 53, 135
Taylor, Zachary, 198
Tears of Repentance (Mather and Eliot), 42
Terra pacis (Niclaes), 30
Thomas Shepard's Confessions, 16
Trail of tears, 70
Treatise on Domestic Economy . . . , A (Beecher), 123

Uncle Tom's Cabin (Stowe), 179–80, 187–95
Union Benevolent Association, 128
Upper class, 121

Vara; or, The Child of Adoption (Hornblower), 195–98
Virginia, 27, 43
Voice of Industry, 154
Voting rights, 64, 73–74, 91, 132, 137, 184

War of 1812, 89
Warner, Susan, 158–63, 164–65
Washington, George, 60, 61, 63, 65–66, 103
Washington Territory, 111
Welfare, 126
Wept of Wish-Ton-Wish, The (Cooper), 111
Whig party, 120, 130, 132
Wide, Wide World, The (Warner), 156, 158–63, 164–65, 166, 167, 189, 196

Wieland; or, The Transformation (Brown), 87, 88, 89, 97
Williams, Eunice, 95–96, 111, 114, 116
Williams, John, 95
Williams, Roger, 42, 115
Williams, Stephen, 95–96
Winthrop, Henry, 14
Winthrop, John, Jr., 27
Winthrop, John, Sr., 1–2, 4, 6, 7, 8–9, 11, 12, 13, 14–15, 16, 18, 27, 29, 30, 36, 37–38, 41, 44–46, 47–48, 49, 59, 77, 123, 127
Woman's rights movement (1840s), 152, 154
Women: fiction for, 151, 155; magazines for, 152–54, 176; as source of moral stability, 123–26
Wonder-Working Providence of Sion's Savior in New England (Johnson), 14
Workhouses, 128
Working class, 133, 136–37, 138, 152–53, 154, 155, 163
Wyeth, Nicholas, 17

Xenophobia, 46–47, 72, 75, 81, 82, 86, 91, 118, 131, 136

Yates, J. V. N., 128

www.ingramcontent.com/pod-product-compliance
Lightning Source LLC
Chambersburg PA
CBHW030340240426
43661CB00052B/1698